Aesthetic Ecology of Communication Ethics

THE FAIRLEIGH DICKINSON UNIVERSITY PRESS SERIES IN COMMUNICATION STUDIES

General Editor: Gary Radford, Department of Communication Studies, Fairleigh Dickinson University, Madison, New Jersey.

The Fairleigh Dickinson University Press Series in Communication Studies publishes scholarly works in communication theory, practice, history, and culture.

On the Web at http://www.fdu.edu/fdupress

Recent Publications in Communication Studies

Özüm Üçok-Sayrak, *Aesthetic Ecology of Communication Ethics: Existential Rootedness* (2019)

Jennifer Biedendorf, *Cosmopolitanism and the Development of the International Criminal Court: Non-Governmental Organizations' Advocacy and Transnational Human Rights* (2019)

Kate Dunsmore, *Discourse of Reciprocity* (2019)

Paul Matthew St. Pierre, *Cinematography of Carl Theodor Dreyer: Performative Camerawork, Transgressing the Frame* (2018)

Michelle Scollo and Trudy Milburn (eds.), *Engaging and Transforming Global Communication through Cultural Discourse Analysis: A Tribute to Donal Carbaugh* (2018)

Isaac E. Catt, *Embodiment in the Semiotic Matrix: Communicology in Peirce, Dewey, Bateson, and Bourdieu* (2017)

Craig T. Maier, *Communicating Catholicism: Rhetoric, Ecclesial Leadership, and the Future of the American Roman Catholic Diocese* (2016)

Paul Matthew St. Pierre, *Cinematography in the Weimar Republic: Lola-Lola, Dirty Singles, and the Men Who Shot Them* (2016)

Anastacia Kurylo and Tatyana Dumov (eds.), *Social Networking: Redefining Communication in the Digital Age* (2016)

Phil Rose, *Radiohead and the Global Movement for Change: "Pragmatism Not Idealism"* (2015)

Brent C. Sleasman, *Creating Albert Camus: Foundations and Explorations in His Philosophy of Communication* (2015)

Michael Warren Tumolo, *Just Remembering, Rhetorics of Genocide Remembrance and Sociopolitical Judgment* (2015)

Phil Rose, *Roger Waters and Pink Floyd* (2015)

Ronald C. Arnett and Pat Arneson (eds.), *Philosophy of Communication Ethics: Alterity and the Other* (2014)

Pat Arneson, *Communicative Engagement and Social Liberation: Justice Will Be Made* (2014)

Aesthetic Ecology of Communication Ethics

Existential Rootedness

Özüm Üçok-Sayrak

FAIRLEIGH DICKINSON UNIVERSITY PRESS
Vancouver • Madison • Teaneck • Wroxton

Published by Fairleigh Dickinson University Press
Copublished by The Rowman & Littlefield Publishing Group, Inc.
4501 Forbes Boulevard, Suite 200, Lanham, Maryland 20706
www.rowman.com

6 Tinworth Street, London SE11 5AL, United Kingdom

Copyright © 2019 by Özüm Üçok-Sayrak

Excerpt from Rainer Maria Rilke (1918), Das Stundenbuch. Leipzig: Insel Verlag. Translated by Eva-Maria Simms and Michael Simms, 2019. Pittsburgh: Vox Populi, under open license.

Permission to excerpt Thomas P. Picket's Psalm of Days (2014) provided by *Listening: Journal of Communication Ethics, Religion, and Culture.*

All rights reserved. No part of this book may be reproduced in any form or by any electronic or mechanical means, including information storage and retrieval systems, without written permission from the publisher, except by a reviewer who may quote passages in a review.

Fairleigh Dickinson University Press gratefully acknowledges the support received for scholarly publishing from the Friends of FDU Press.

British Library Cataloguing in Publication Information Available

Library of Congress Cataloging-in-Publication Data Available

ISBN 978-1-68393-224-6 (cloth)
ISBN 978-1-68393-226-0 (pbk)
ISBN 978-1-68393-225-3 (electronic)

Contents

Acknowledgments	vii
Introduction: Being Reminded of Roots	1
1 The Poíētic Sense of Meaning	29
2 The "Weight" of Meaning	53
3 Signlessness	73
4 Learning to Be (in Con/tact)	93
5 Attending to the Breath (of the Other)	117
6 Silence, Solitude, Reverence	133
Closing	153
Index	157
About the Author	161

Acknowledgments

I offer my deepest gratitude to Duquesne University and my colleagues in the Department of Communication and Rhetorical Studies. I am particularly grateful for the leadership, support, and thoughtful comments of Ronald C. Arnett and Janie M. Harden Fritz—you cultivate a special academic home filled with intellectual richness and sense of care, and I am honored to be part of it. Special thanks to my colleague Pat Arneson whose scholarly work on communicative engagement informed this book. I wish to acknowledge the research assistance of Sophia Nagle, Johan Bodaski, William Aungst, Nicole Brazelton, Rachel Morrell, and Abbey McCann. Thank you for your valuable work! The warm and welcoming presence of Rita McCaffrey, our administrative assistant at the department, makes this place shine and becomes part of everything we do, thank you deeply!

Special thanks to Dr. James Swindal, dean of the McAnulty College and Graduate School of Liberal Arts, whose kind and encouraging presence has supported this work. I am grateful for the generous support of the Wimmer Family Foundation Fellowship and the Presidential Scholarship Award from Duquesne University.

The presence of the Spiritans on campus and Duquesne's Spiritan tradition create a special campus climate characterized by kindness, respect, and a sense of the sacred. I am grateful for working and serving as part of this community and culture.

I extend my appreciation to Gary Radford, James Gifford, Zach Nycum, and the entire staff at Fairleigh Dickinson University Press for their attentiveness and encouragement throughout the publication process.

My deepest gratitude goes to my family. Without their support this work would not have been possible. My parents, Tümay and Mehmet Üçok, my husband Akın Sayrak, and our daughter Özlem, are all part of this work in many different ways, and through their love and spirit. I am grateful for your presence.

And a special heartfelt thanks to all my teachers since graduate school and before; particularly to Dr. Kurt Bruder and Dr. Bud Morris, whose support and trust in me as a graduate student kept me going.

Deep gratitude to Thich Nhat Hanh, Gregory Kramer, Jon Kabat-Zinn, and Saki Santorelli, whose spiritual guidance allowed this work to breathe.

I would like to express my special appreciation to Tümay Üçok for the beautiful drawing she generously shared for the cover page.

Many thanks to Eva-Maria Simms and Michael Simms for their translation of a favorite poem by Rainer Maria Rilke. Thank you for this gift!

Special thanks to Thomas P. Pickett for his inspiring poetry!

Thank you, all my students, for being my teacher all along.

And thank you, Ricky, our cat, for your invaluable presence and quiet teachings of inhabiting life fully!

I dedicate this work to my family: my husband, Akın; our daughter, Özlem; my mother Tümay Üçok and the memory of my father Mehmet Üçok; my sister, Sevinç; and my brother, Doğan, and his family, Nüvit and Derviş.

Introduction

Being Reminded of Roots

This book aims to serve as a reminder, of roots and rootedness, as an interruption of a naive absorption in a disembedded reality that ignores the larger communicative environment, and of our deep connectedness to a sphere of life beyond individual autonomous being. This project frames existential rootedness as an orientation immersed in a communication ethic that recognizes the embeddedness and participation of the human being in her surroundings along with others, as well as her exposedness and struggle in a world that oscillates between disruption and harmony, tension and rest. Rather than a fixed state to be achieved, this book offers a conception of rootedness as an ongoing dynamic in human experience that moves in between the sensible and the intellectual, closeness and distance, contemplation and action, and silence and speaking. Finally, and importantly, a distinctive feature of this dynamic orientation that I refer to as existential rootedness is attentiveness, which involves a sense of in touchness, responsiveness, and responsibility that is both engaged and regarding (in the sense of maintaining a distance that respects the alterity and the solitude of the other).

In a chapter titled "The Radiance of the Lotus," Laycock (2001) writes about the luminous lotus flower, the symbol of the awakened mind, that is so absorbing in its presence that its rootedness gets ignored. Yet the lotus is rooted in muddy water, and being reminded of its roots is an interruption of this absorption, a wake-up call to the wholeness of the reality of the lotus that draws its nourishment from the depths.

> The lotus communicates in its wholeness, in its organic indissociability from the turbid ooze of the reality in which it is rooted, and as an expression of all-that-is, only when we find ourselves quiet and still among beings (inter esse), with an

"inter/est" which is no idle curiosity, nor even the insistent passion to "know," but an openness, a wonder. (Laycock 2001, 3)

Two main points stand out from this quote that connect to the heart of this book. First is the part (figure)–whole (ground) relation that Laycock (2001) highlights in the first two sentences that offers perspective on the ground in which the lotus is rooted that is inseparable in making sense of the lotus itself. The ground matters; it sustains life in all its diverse forms. Yet, in the context of the fast-paced, progress-oriented rhythms of modern life that promote the autonomous individual, the ground and the rootedness of existence gets forgotten or left unattended by many.

The second point relates to the attitude and orientation through which we attend to the lotus; a quiet wondering that is *letting*—not imposing even our desire to know—that makes space for the lotus to disclose itself. The lotus resists conceptual grasping that is reductive in pursuit of "knowing"; it refuses to be contained. It communicates "only when" . . . we release ourselves (*Gelassenheit*) in between beings, quiet and still, with a sense of wonder and openness.

In *Red Skin, White Masks: Rejecting the Colonial Politics of Recognition*, Coulthard (2014) writes about the place-based cultural foundation and ethics of the Indigenous peoples in Canada that underline their struggle and resistance against dispossession and colonialism. He explains that the profound importance of land or place to Indigenous cultures is not simply its material dimension although this too is significant. Land, or place, is a relational field, or a "system of relations" (Coulthard 2014, 61) that humans are a part of as much as animals, plants, lakes, rocks, and other elements, and facilitates a way of knowing who we are in relation to others. In this sense, land has an ontological significance in addition to being a material resource that facilitates survival. This ontological understanding of land is deeply connected to an ethics based on the interdependency of all elements of the land as well as an acknowledgment of the agency of nonhumans. Land signifies relational existence, teaching us about "living our lives in relation to one another and our surroundings in a respectful, nondominating and nonexploitative way" (Coulthard 2014, 60). Coulthard refers to this ethical framework along with its place-based practices and knowledge as "grounded normativity" (60), which resonates with the perspective taken in this project based on the themes of relational existence, and a nondominating, nonexploitative relation to the land as "a relational field" (61) through which practices and knowledge emerge.

In the following, I first offer background on the historical moment (in response to) in which this project comes into being. Next, I draw connections to the existing literature on rootedness and highlight the contributions and the significance of this project in connection to communication ethics and particularly to academic discussions on "moral blindness" (Bauman and Donskis 2013) and "modernity's amnesia" (Arnett 2013). Finally, I discuss the framework of aesthetic ecology as an environment of interconnected elements and themes that recognize the interplay of immediate sense experience along with the intellectual/interpretive as part of human existence and meaning making endeavors in the world. This discussion on aesthetics is informed and inspired by (1) Hans Georg Gadamer's (1975/2004) discussion of horizon, participation—or, *methexis*—(Gadamer 2007) and aesthetic attentiveness as part of Gadamer's "hermeneutical aesthetics" (Davey 2013); (2) Hans Ulrich Gumbrecht's (2004) discussion of the productive tension and oscillation between presence- and meaning-based relations in aesthetic experience; and (3) John Dewey's (1958) theory of the aesthetic as embedded in the struggles of everyday life.

MUDDY WATERS

Around the time this book is being written the world is faced with threats of terrorism, random shootings in various public places on a global scale, increased school violence especially in the United States, increased racial, ethnic, religious tension worldwide, as well as global forced displacement of people due to violence and human rights violations. In 2016, the United Nations Refugee Agency reported that we have reached the highest levels of displacement on record; 65.3 million people were forcibly displaced from home due to conflict or persecution in 2016. We, human beings around the world, do not live with a sense of safety, security, and peace but with fear, confusion, and disorientation in the twenty-first century.

In *The Sense of the World,* Nancy (1997b) states that "the women and men of our time have, indeed, a rather sovereign way of losing their footing without anxiety" (2). Living with anxiety, constant preoccupation, a sense of dissatisfaction, uneasiness, and a lack of presence have become the default of the lives of modern humans who seek *existential traction* through consumerism, workaholism, frantic sexuality, substance abuse, antidepressants, social media, and in general, constant busyness. "The homeless modern" (Mitchell 2006) is both bored and uneasy "despite incredible affluence, comfort, entertainment, and security" (13) and "rootless because we have traded a commitment to a particular place for the promise of a better job, a better standard of living, a better climate" (15).

In the context briefly sketched above on the "uprootedness of the modern man," this project turns attention to an examination of *existential rootedness* as a particular orientation to and inhabiting of life, and the accompanying contemplative and communicative practices that are attentive to self, other, and their dwelling ground. Rootedness as existential attentiveness serves to remind us of our essential connectedness in the larger environments we inhabit, as well as our vulnerability, and facilitates the construction of ethical subjectivity. This study is a call for engaging dialogue on the possibility of rootedness that refuses to forget our basic human capacity to turn toward *being* human and human suffering, beyond individual autonomous existence.

CONNECTIONS

In his memorial address to celebrate the German composer and conductor Conradin Kreutzer's work, Heidegger (1959/1966) highlights that the flourishing of any genuine work of art depends on the rootedness of man in his native soil, which he states is being threatened at its core due to the spirit of the technological and atomic age. Heidegger writes about the "rootlessness" of human beings, referring specifically to the Germans, who either wandered off from their local home or stayed but got "chained to" the radio, television, and magazines that drove them further away from their immediate surroundings as well as their customs and conventions. "Is there still a life-giving homeland in whose ground man may stand rooted, that is, be autochthonic?" Heidegger (1966, 48) asks. He expresses concern about the future, asking whether everything will "fall into the clutches of planning and calculation, of organization and automation" (49), which characterizes the spirit of the age that is dominated by "calculative thought" (50). Heidegger (1966) explains that calculative thinking plans, computes, investigates new opportunities but never stops to collect itself to contemplate the meaning that underlies all action. Calculative thinking highlights a technical relation of man to the world, where nature and the earth is seen as objects, resources to use and manipulate. Progress without reflection as well as the speed of change and information sharing characterize a world that leaves man "rootless."

Toward the final pages of his memorial address, Heidegger (1966) moves away from his initial emphasis on native soil and homeland as part of his discussion on the rootlessness of modern man and inquires about a new ground for the rootedness of man even in the atomic age. Heidegger states that what is really uncanny about the speedy technical, technological, and scientific progress is not that "the world is becoming entirely technical" but "far more uncanny is our being unprepared for this transformation, our inability to confront meditatively what is really dawning in this age" (52). This is when Heidegger underlines the significance of a different kind of thinking than calculative thought: "Meditative thinking," could that not be the new "foundation and ground out of which man's nature and all his works can flourish in a new way even in the atomic age?" (53). Meditative thinking allows human beings to discern, to see what is nearest and thus can be hardest to perceive. Meditative thinking facilitates the contemplation of meaning that underlies all action and "demands of us that we engage ourselves with what at first sight does not go together at all" (53). Both calculative and meditative thinking are needed, Heidegger (1966) states, yet he warns that only by relearning to think meditatively can human beings reclaim a new ground for a new kind of rootedness and overcome the dangers of the modern technological age that reduce human beings and the world to a resource in service of technology and industry.

In "Roots Against Heaven: An Aporetic Inversion in Paul Celan," Liska (2004) discusses how the metaphor of rootedness as an idea of being organically connected to a soil became a significant and loaded issue in the twentieth century. Liska explains that the publication of *Les Deracines* (The Uprooted) in 1897, a novel by Maurice Barres that describes—with a nationalistic and anti-Semitic undertone—the destructive consequences of uprootedness due to urbanization in the lives of seven young people who moved to Paris from the countryside, triggered public debates. The idea of the necessity of being rooted in the soil got linked with conservative nationalism and a critique of modernity in relation to the isolation of the individual, loss of community and morals, loss of existential security, and reactions toward "foreign elements." "Under the regime of National Socialists, Barres's merely theoretical xenophobia will turn into the most murderous reality" (Liska 2004, 43).

The Need for Roots by Simone Weil (1952) offers a sharp contrast to the nationalistic tone in Barres's work. Weil writes about rootedness as "perhaps the most important and least recognized need of the human soul" which is also "one of the hardest to define" (43). Weil first wrote *The Need for Roots* in early 1943, as a report that was commissioned by the Free French in London on regenerating France after World War II. She wrote the book during her employment at French Headquarters in London. Simone Weil writes about rootedness not only in terms of geographical roots but also *moral* and *spiritual* roots. For Weil, active participation in the life of a community is essential to rootedness. She warns that the urgency to reroot one's country and community can lead to intense feelings of patriotism (as in the case of Barres's work discussed above.) Weil does not suggest an elimination of patriotic feelings—which she says would be disastrous in the midst of uprootedness—but calls for a new patriotism based on compassion for the country. Weil offers compassion as an alternative source for inspiration to the glory of patriotism, which acknowledges the fragility of life, whether it is children, the elderly, or one's country, and which carries a *tender warmth and vitality that does not take existence for granted*. The vital energy of compassion does not need a sense of magnificence to inspire. It inspires through the *awareness of the beauty of the transient and the fragile*.

The moral and spiritual dimensions of rootedness are also reflected in scholarship from Indigenous studies that underline an understanding of land as a source of knowledge and understanding as well as ethical land-based practices (Wildcat, Simpson, Irlbacher-Fox, and Coulthard 2014; Simpson 2014; Schreyer, Corbett, Gordon, and Larson 2014; Coulthard 2014). In their editorial for the special issue of *Decolonization: Indigeneity, Education & Society,* Wildcat et al. (2014, ii) ask "How do our relationships with land inform and order the way humans conduct relationships with each other and other-than-human beings?" "What does it mean to understand 'land'—as a system of reciprocal social relations and ethical practices—as a framework for decolonial critique?" They write about land as a "source of knowledge and strength" (Wildcat et al. 2014, II) and underline the need for land-based education that facilitates relationships *with* and *on* the land toward resurging Indigenous knowledges and regenerating Indigenous cultural, spiritual, and social practices. In her essay that is part of the same special issue of *Decolonization*, Simpson (2014), uses a Nishnaabeg story of a young girl who has embodied land-based knowledge; who has learned how to observe and learn from animal teachers, to tap maple trees and collect the sap as well as "how to interact with the spirit of the maple" (7). This Indigenous learning process is contextual, based on interactions with the land, and involves spiritual presence, emotion, wonder, humility, respect, and learning from the members of community (Simpson 2014).

Along these lines, in a special issue of the *Canadian Journal of Education* titled "Indigenous Education: Pathways to (Re)membering," Styres and Zinga (2013) write that understandings of self-in-relationship lie at the heart of Indigenous education, which "include Land, waterways, our animal relations as well as each other" (1). The collection of essays in this special issue address (re)membering ways of knowing grounded in Land and self-in-relationship based on ancient knowledges and pedagogies and bringing this awareness to contemporary educational contexts. Styres, Haig-Brown, and Blimkie's (2013) article, for instance, highlight "*Land* as sentient. . . . *Land* is a living thing. A river is a living thing. The air is alive" (37–38). They distinguish a pedagogy of Land based on Indigenous knowledge from dominant Western understandings of place or place-based education that does not acknowledge "Land as a living fundamental being" (Styres, Haig-Brown, and Blimkie 2013, 38). Indigenous studies scholarship honors the deep interconnectedness of human beings to the land, not only materially but also spiritually and ethically, and engages a decolonizing process of remembering ways of knowing and being in the world based on Indigenous traditions as well as teaching this cultural heritage to the younger generations.

Finally, Arnett's (1994) discussion of "existential homelessness" (230), which is characterized by a "loss of trust in existence," offers an entrance to discussions on rootedness/rootlessness in communication studies. Existential homelessness is encouraged by the lack of "common centers" and moral stories that guide people, resulting in feelings of not being at home (Arnett 1994). Implications of the loss of common centers include loss of a sense of direction, an absence of trust, a hermeneutic of suspicion and narcissism in interpersonal relations. Arnett (1994) suggests that acceptance of the loss of trust and our homeless state, and an active partnership in dialogue toward building havens of trust, supported by a courage to trust, are called for to reclaim our existential home that does not rest in old answers but in the hard work of extending the reach of dialogue to others. This current project on existential rootedness and communication ethics is a response to Arnett's (1994) call for dialogue on acknowledging and turning toward the uprootedness of the modern individual and exploring, as we listen deeply, an aesthetic ecology that supports our flourishing as human beings.

Earlier in this introduction, I started a part of this dialogue with a description of the current state of human affairs in our painfully globalizing world (please see the section titled "Muddy Waters"). In the following, I expand this dialogue by connecting to a discussion on "moral blindness" (Bauman and Donskis 2013) that acknowledges and highlights our own role and capacity in cultivating existential homelessness and suffering—whether we realize or not— through a forgetfulness of the larger sphere of life beyond the individual that we all belong to, and a lack of attentiveness and failure to respond. I connect "moral blindness" to Arnett's (2013) discussion of "modernity's amnesia" (62) that is characterized by a forgetfulness of the conditions of existence and the dwelling places that guide and sustain human beings due to an "endless search for progress" (4) disconnected from a "a sense of 'why' for human life" (Arnett 2010, 242).

"MORAL BLINDNESS" AND "MODERNITY'S AMNESIA"

The introduction of this essay started with a list of the manmade threats that human beings are faced with in our contemporary world that illustrate the uprooted state of the global human community despite all technological and scientific advancements. In *Moral Blindness: The Loss of Sensitivity in Liquid Modernity,* Bauman and Donskis (2013) are concerned with the insensitivity to human suffering and a failure to reply to the other in need as the "new evil" that is "not confined to war or totalitarian ideologies" (9). They highlight a common but less visible form of evil that "lurks in what we tend to take as normality and even as the triviality and banality of mundane life" (36). This "less visible form of evil," according to Bauman and Donskis, manifests itself in turning away from someone else's suffering and failing to recognize and respond to the other.

A common theme in *Moral Blindness* is insensitivity to human suffering and a lack of existential attentiveness. Existential attentiveness transforms forgetfulness of one's connectedness to a larger sphere of life beyond the individual. Arnett's (2013) discussion of "modernity's amnesia" refers to the "phenomenological foundations of the human condition, which are forgotten, bypassed, and eclipsed by modernity" (7), which is further discussed in the next section. As the upcoming chapters illustrate, this project explores the metaphor of "rootedness" as a phenomenological participation in the world tied to an embodied communication ethic of existential attentiveness that resists the forgetfulness of modernity.

Modernity's Amnesia

In *Communication Ethics in Dark Times: Hannah Arendt's Rhetoric of Warning and Hope*, Arnett (2013) explores the scholarship of Arendt in terms of her critique of modernity, warning about the "tragic consequences of modernity" (1). Arnett (2013) states that modernity is marked by an "endless search for progress" (4) and "a pursuit of the unattainable" (5), risking "welcoming dwelling places" (3) that provide a sense of direction. "In our commitment to an endless search for progress, we gave life over to an unquenched desire in which the end, the good, is always beyond our reach, thereby eclipsing the very places capable of offering a sense of direction in the human condition" (4).

The focus of modernity on doing more without ever arriving puts the dwelling places that guide and sustain human beings at risk. Dwelling places matter in supporting human life.

Doing more without a sense of dwelling results in a loss of contemplation (Arnett 2013) and "existential homelessness," which is "a sense of 'why' for human life" (Arnett 2010, 242). Without a sense of "why," meaningfulness of life is lost and doing becomes a mechanical act disconnected from the joy and contemplation of doing. Arnett (2013, 63) states that the tendency of modernity to dismiss the ground that supports human beings denies our "partnership with existence itself." It is this "forgetting of the conditions of existence" that the ideology of progress accompanied by individualism—that assumes that one can stand above history, tradition, culture, and the physical ground that offer an existential home—that Arnett (2013, 62) refers to as "modernity's amnesia."

The discussion on modernity's amnesia is related to the notion of moral blindness introduced earlier. In their discussion of moral blindness, Bauman and Donskis (2013) use the term "adiaphorization of behavior" in reference to "a temporary withdrawal from one's own sensitivity zone; an ability not to react, or to react as if something were happening not to people but to natural physical objects, to things, or to non-humans. The things happening are unimportant; they do not happen to us or with us" (37). They explain that *adiaphron* means unimportant, and "real is only what happens to me" (39). Among the causes of adiaphorization that Bauman and Donskis (2013, 38) list are "instrumental rationality; mass society and mass culture; and being in a crowd each and every moment (just think of television and internet); having the crowd in one's soul." Being crowded and "having a crowd in one's soul" refers to a loss of solitude and quiet time that is connected to the loss of contemplation discussed as part of modernity's amnesia. Instrumental rationality highlights the achievement of ends without a connection to a "sense of why," which fits well with the emphasis of modernity on progress, endless doing, and individualism that result in the disappearance of dwelling places.

This project calls for the necessity of recognizing the problematic discussed above in terms of moral blindness and modernity's amnesia, and highlights rootedness tied to a communication ethic of existential attentiveness as a response to the "moral vacuum" (Bauman and Donskis 2013, 7) of our times. I will end this section with an example from the context of the classroom that illustrates the disconnectedness that results from the endless emphasis on doing and "having the crowd in one's soul" (Bauman and Donskis 2013, 38).

In her written reflections following a mindful observations assignment a few years ago, one of my students shared her realization of being out of touch with her bodily experience in her everyday life and interpersonal relationships, which she characterized as "frightening." Imagine not noticing how hot the water is until your skin turns red, or having to wash your hair more than once since you do not remember that you washed it in the first place. Most of my students, then and now, can easily connect to this mode of not being in touch with one's surroundings and the present moment, "zoning out" and "disappearing into one's mind," that extends into one's interpersonal relationships and communication. In the digital age, people talk about "being connected" all the time; however, most are disconnected from their bodies, surroundings, and others around them. The shared experiences of my students and my observations in the classroom over the years deeply motivate this study in discussing rootedness as cultivated through existential attentiveness, which constitutes the ground for turning toward the Other. The aesthetic ecology framework I discuss below specifies the notion of existential attentiveness in connection to rootedness and communication ethics.

FRAMING AN AESTHETIC ECOLOGY OF COMMUNICATION ETHICS

In the opening pages to this introductory chapter, I highlighted the perspective this project takes on aesthetics as one that recognizes the interplay of immediate sense experience with the intellectual/interpretive. This approach is informed by (1) Gadamer's (2004) discussion of horizon, participation (Gadamer 2007), and "aesthetic distance" (Gadamer 2007) as part of his "hermeneutical aesthetics" (Davey 2013, 22); (2) Gumbrecht's (2004) exploration of presence- and meaning-based relations in aesthetic experience; and (3) Dewey's (1958) discussion of aesthetic experience as embedded in the struggles to maintain equilibrium with the environment. The chapters in this book are organized in a way that they constitute interconnected parts of what I refer to as an "aesthetic ecology." Throughout the chapters, I engage the concept of "aesthetic ecology" as an environment that involves material (earth, body), conceptual (signlessness, "weight"), and contemplative (breath, silence) elements that constitute and contribute to the dynamic between the sensual and the intellectual as part of our being-in-the-world-with-others, and facilitate an understanding of existential rootedness and communication ethics. In the following, I first present the aesthetic framework that underlines this work in three subsections. Next, I make connections between the discussion on the aesthetic and communication ethics, and finally offer a synopsis of each chapter as part of this ecology.

Horizon, Participation, and Aesthetic Attentiveness

Gadamer (2004) uses the term "horizon" that refers to the "the range of vision that includes everything that can be seen from a particular vantage point" (301). Horizon is not fixed; it moves and expands as the interpreter stays open to acquire the right horizon of inquiry that allows one to see the connection of the part to the larger whole.

> A person who has no horizon does not see far enough and hence over-values what is nearest to him. On the other hand, "to have horizon" means not being limited to what is nearby but being able to see beyond it. A person who has a horizon knows the relative significance of everything within this horizon, whether it is near or far, great or small. (Gadamer 2004, 301–2)

Being immersed in the sensual experience of the lotus flower in the introductory quote, or any other phenomenon, to the point of forgetting or ignoring its connections and continuities leads to narrowness of horizon, or to "horizonal blindness" (Laycock 2001, 41), which is "a naïve privacy uninformed by . . .

the sense of one's view as *a* view." The dangers associated with horizonal blindness correlates with Arnett, McManus, and McKendree's (2014, 5) discussion of Arendt's (1963/2006) notion of *thoughtlessness* "that does not take into account the complexity of the texture and connections between background and foreground action" and that "rests within a basic assumption: there is only one perception of background and foreground that shapes understanding. Thoughtlessness assumes there is only one perceptual gestalt: *mine*."

Gadamer's (2004, 305) discussion of the "fusion of horizons" disrupts horizonal blindness and thoughtlessness through the acknowledgment of the encounter of the perspective one brings (horizon of the present) and the historical horizon (horizon of the past) that allows for new and different meanings to emerge in each interpretive occasion. The cultural and linguistic horizons one is grounded in (as part of the historical horizon) bring in "traditions of meaning" (Davey 2013, 76) that shape the horizon of the present. As Gadamer (2004) puts it, the horizon is "something into which we move and that moves with us" (303). Thus, the horizon is not fixed but it is in motion. Along these lines, "To acquire a horizon means that one learns to look beyond what is close at hand—not in order to look away from it but to see it better, within a larger whole and in truer proportion" (304). The discussion of horizon is significant in moving beyond subjective preference that focuses on "me and mine," which fails to recognize one's *participation* in a broader communicative environment and cultural horizons.

In *Unfinished Worlds: Hermeneutics, Aesthetics and Gadamer*, Davey (2013) highlights that "participation is a condition of meaning's emergence" (104) in Gadamer's hermeneutics and his discussions on aesthetic experience. Meaningfulness arises through our participatory involvement: "By virtue of its participation, the part is both informed by the semantic horizons in which it is placed and informs those same horizons when engaged with its meanings" (Davey 2013, 104). There is a mutuality regarding the notion of participation in the part–whole relationship that facilitates the emergence and continuous unfolding of meaning. Gadamer (2007) refers to the Greek word *methexis* in discussing participation, where the "syllable *meta* lends *methexis* the sense of 'being-with'" (314) and "belonging-together" (311). In describing participation as belonging-together, Gadamer (2007) uses terms such as giving oneself, being outside oneself, self-forgetfulness, and "devoting one's full attention to the matter at hand" (122). Being outside oneself, as Gadamer (2007) explains, does not mean "a negation of being composed within oneself" (122) but the "positive possibility of being wholly with something else" (122). In this sense, the self-forgetfulness of giving oneself over to that which one is attending fully is a practice of being present, a contemplative attentiveness. Gadamer (2007) highlights that "being present does not simply mean being there along with something else that is there at the same time" (121). As well, being present is not an absorption but involves a kind of attentiveness beyond goal-orientation that is set at an "aesthetic distance" (124) that "makes possible a genuine and comprehensive participation in what is presented before us" (124). What stands out from the discussion above on participation is a "doubled form of attentiveness" (Davey 2013, 80) that is both fully involved and present, and at the same time *regarding* in the sense of maintaining a differential distance. This doubled attention that Davey (2013) refers to as "aesthetic attention" (80) recognizes the interplay of sensory experience and the horizons of meaning that allows for the movement of understanding. Gadamer's critique of aesthetic sensationalism—reducing aesthetic experience to momentary sensual presence, pleasure, and perceptual immediacy— aims to free aesthetics from the confines of subjectivism that would blind the "transformative horizons of meaning" (Davey 2013, 72). This lies at the center of Gadamer's "hermeneutical aesthetics" (Davey 2013, 22) that recognizes the relationship between part and whole, and that "maintains a creative tension between sensibility and intellect" (24). It is this ongoing movement/tension between the sensory and the interpretive modes of experience that allows for an ongoing transformation and a broadening and deepening of understanding that makes possible to think and see differently.

In the next section, I connect the discussion on horizon, participation, and Gadamer's hermeneutical aesthetics to Gumbrecht's exploration of presence and meaning as an oscillation in aesthetic experience.

The Oscillation Between Meaning Effects and Presence Effects

Gumbrecht (2004) characterizes human contact with the things of the world in terms of both presence- and meaning-based relations that always appear together, especially in aesthetic experience, yet in a productive tension rather than in complementarity. Gumbrecht (2004) states that presence effects "exclusively appeal to the senses" (xv) *and* "they are necessarily surrounded by, wrapped into, and perhaps even mediated by clouds and cushions of meaning" (106). He highlights that the oscillation between meaning effects and presence effects, and their productive tension, is crucial such that neither side will bracket the other and make it disappear.

> Essential is the point that, within this specific constellation, meaning will not bracket, will not make the presence effects disappear, and that the—unbracketed— physical presence of things (of a text, of a voice, of a canvas with colors, of a play performed by a team) will not ultimately repress the meaning dimension. (Gumbrecht 2004, 108).

As important as it is to maintain the "aesthetic attentiveness" (Davey 2013, 80) discussed earlier that allows for the interplay of meaning and presence effects without diminishing one or the other, Gumbrecht (2004) alerts us that "modern (including contemporary) Western culture can be described [as] a process of progressive abandonment and forgetting of presence" (xv). Gumbrecht (2004) states that despite knowing he could not be fully present "in the full sense of my existence, if meaning were completely out of the question" (137), he shares his fear that "effects of meaning (at least an overdose of them) might diminish my moments of presence" (136) under the contemporary cultural conditions.

I share Gumbrecht's (2004) concern above and know by firsthand experience and observation in various relationships—with students, friends, family, colleagues—that our sensitivity and attentiveness to and through our bodily presence, and joint "participation" (Gadamer 2007) in different aspects of everyday life, get hijacked by meaning effects in our "so very Cartesian everyday lives" (Gumbrecht 2004, 107). In order to maintain and experience the productive tension of the oscillation between meaning effects and presence effects, Gumbrecht (2004) states that we need a specific framework instead of automatically bracketing the presence side. As a significant part of the framework he offers, Gumbrecht focuses on aesthetic experience that he highlights in terms of "moments of intensity" (97) such as "when a Mozart aria grows into polyphonic complexity and when I indeed believe that I can hear the tones of the oboe on my skin" (97) or the "feeling of having found the right place for one's body with which a perfectly designed building can embrace and welcome us" (98). Although Gumbrecht offers a few examples that are not directly related to art in discussing moments of intensity as part of aesthetic experience, such as tasting the first bite of great food or feeling elated by the swift movements of the American football players in his favorite college team as they pass or catch the ball, he distances aesthetic experience from the everyday worlds we inhabit. Gumbrecht (2004) states—as his opening hypothesis—that "what we call 'aesthetic experience' always provide us with certain feelings of intensity that we cannot find in the historically and culturally specific everyday worlds that we inhabit" (99). The appeal of aesthetic experience and our fascination with it, according to Gumbrecht, is that in moments of aesthetic experience "there is always something that our everyday worlds are not capable of offering us" (100).

Gumbrecht's (2004) description of moments of aesthetic experience point to a richness and fullness beyond our ordinary, habitual ways of being in the world, yet his characterization of aesthetic experience characterized by moments of intensity that excludes our everyday worlds can be problematized. What I am pointing to (as a communication scholar) is related to the emergence of our experiences through our encounters with the things of the world and others where *the ways* in which we meet, receive, and respond to the world constitute the quality of our experience as well as its intensity, and that is not limited to stumbling upon moments of aesthetic experience outside of everyday life (though that too is possible). In this sense, the framing of the aesthetic in this work resonates more with John Dewey's (1958) discussion of aesthetic experience as embedded in a world of things that I elaborate further under the next section.

Gumbrecht (2004) borrows Bakthin's concept of "insularity" (102) to describe the distance between aesthetic experience and everyday worlds as part of his "situational framework" (101) for aesthetic experience. Gumbrecht establishes "insularity" as a "structural condition" (103) of aesthetic experience summarized thus: "If aesthetic experience is always evoked by and if it always refers to moments of intensity that cannot be part of the respective everyday worlds in which it takes place, then it follows that aesthetic experience will be necessarily located at a certain distance from these everyday worlds" (101). The "situation of insularity" that distances aesthetic experience from everyday world is one of the main aspects of Gumbrecht's framework that aims to maintain the oscillation between meaning and presence effects. Rather than focusing on a situational condition (or conditions) that facilitate aesthetic experience such as "insularity," which distances aesthetic experience from the everyday, the approach I take in this project aligns with Dewey's (1958) discussion that aims to "recover the continuity of esthetic experience with ordinary processes of living" (11), which acknowledges that our interactions with the conditions of our environment "reach to the roots of the esthetic in experience" (14). Before turning to Dewey (1958), it is important to note that Gumbrecht (2004) reflects on a "*specific disposition*" (103, original italics) that goes along with the condition of "insularity." Writing about the two principal ways of entering situations of insularity that facilitate aesthetic experience, Gumbrecht refers to (1) the "sudden appearance of certain objects of perception" (103) that captures and diverts our attention from everyday routines and temporarily separates us from them. An example he offers is the first lightning in a thunderstorm. And the other way of entering situations of insularity Gumbrecht (2004) states is pointing to the presence of certain objects of experience and inviting an open but concentrated attention, a "composed openness" (104) that is focused but not effortful or tense. This resonates with the practice of contemplative attentiveness of allowing oneself to be with something or someone and receptively joining in the experience as one continues to attend, explore, and wonder without rushing to immediate interpretations. The second part of the disposition-related discussion that Gumbrecht integrates to his "situational framework" of aesthetic experience on "composed openness" (104) acknowledges the subject's role/position in addition to the situational condition of "insularity" he starts with. Still, Gumbrecht's discussion of aesthetic experience in relation to maintaining the productive tension of the oscillation between meaning effects and presence effects emphasizes the distance of aesthetic experience from the everyday worlds we inhabit. In the next section, I discuss Dewey's (1958) conception of the aesthetic that is embedded in the continual exchange of the living being with its environment in the context of everyday life, which offers an alternate perspective to Gumbrecht's (2004) discussion of the "insularity" of aesthetic experience.

The Aesthetic as Embedded in a World of Things

John Dewey (1958) discusses aesthetic experience as embedded in the struggles and undergoings of ordinary, everyday life, which takes place in an environment, and "not merely *in* it but because of it, through interaction with it" (13). In order to live, every creature needs to adjust itself to its surroundings. "At every moment, the living creature is exposed to dangers from its surroundings, and at every moment, it must draw upon something in its surroundings to satisfy its needs. The career and destiny of a living being are bound up with its environment, not externally but in the most intimate way" (13). Dewey highlights the deep, intimate connection of the living being with its environment, and its condition of being exposed. To stay alive and to satisfy its needs, the living creature is in a continual exchange with its environment where it goes through phases of life in which "the live being recurrently loses and reëstablishes equilibrium with his surroundings" (17). Although one might read the above as some obvious biological processes, Dewey states that "these biological commonplaces are something more than that; they reach to the roots of the esthetic in experience" (14). Dewey characterizes the transition from the loss of adjustment to the restoration of balance as "that of intensest life" (17) and the ground for aesthetic experience. "Because the actual world, that in which we live, is a combination of movement and culmination, of breaks and re-unions, the experience of a living creature is capable of esthetic quality" (17). Dewey (1958) locates the "moments of intensity" that Gumbrecht (2004) refers to in describing aesthetic experience—that was discussed in the prior section—in the context of everyday life rather than at a distance from it. "Because experience is the fulfillment of an organism in its struggles and achievements in a world of things, it is art in germ. Even in its rudimentary forms, it contains the promise of that delightful perception which is esthetic experience" (Dewey 1958, 19). Thus, for Dewey aesthetic experience is embedded in our interactions with the world, regardless of the level of sophistication of our engagements due to "the promise of that delightful perception." What stands out in Dewey's description above is the potentiality of aesthetic experience—"art in germ"—that rests within the struggles and achievements in ordinary everyday life that is evoked with "that delightful perception." As we see from these descriptions, Dewey focuses on the subject's experience and engagement of ordinary life rather than just the aesthetic object.

As Stroud (2014) writes, Dewey's discussion of aesthetics expands beyond the creation and perception of art objects to include our ways of seeing and attending to the world of everyday experience as aesthetic. Stroud highlights that our habits of attention and the quality of experience they create is a significant aspect of Dewey's pragmatist aesthetics. The orientation of an agent toward an object or an activity enables aesthetic quality. Stroud underlines two aspects of Dewey's discussion of (aesthetic) orientation, which both emphasize attentiveness to the present situation or object one is involved with. First, the present situation or object is conceived as "integrally connected to any future (or past) state, such as a goal or a cause" (Stroud 2014, 42). That is, the present is seen as part of remote state of affairs rather than separated from it. One can see this is an acknowledgment of how the future experiences emerge from the conditions of and our attentiveness (or lack thereof) to the present. Second, the present situation or object is valued at least as much as or more than remote state of affairs. The question is, if the future to be realized then is the present now, why should not they be equally valuable? Yet most people skip the present and focus on the desired results to be attained in the future. Dewey (1958) writes about the common tendency and habitual orientation to either be burdened by the past or apprehensive about what the future might bring.

> Even when not overanxious, we do not enjoy the present because we subordinate it to that which is absent. . . . Only when the past ceases to trouble and anticipations of the future are not perturbing is a being wholly united with his environment and therefore fully alive. Art celebrates with particular intensity the moments in which the past reënforces the present and in which the future is a quickening for what now is. (Dewey 1958, 18)

Not abandoning the present to the past or the future but being part of the immediate environment, attentive and fully alive is an important source of aesthetic experience for Dewey. The quote above highlights art specifically, yet as quoted earlier, the "delightful perception which is esthetic experience" (Dewey 1958, 19) emerges in the struggles and achievements of the living being in a world of things, and the orientation of one's attention matters. The aesthetic emerges in attentiveness to the present that is informed by the past and making way for the future.

CONNECTING THE AESTHETIC TO COMMUNICATION ETHICS

In the discussion above, I offered a framework based on the work of Gadamer (2007), Gumbrecht (2004), and Dewey (1958) that informs the conception of an aesthetic ecology for the purposes of this project that highlights:

1. A dialogic relation between our sensory and interpretive/reflective engagement of the world: Gadamer's (2007) discussion of horizon and participation in connection to the aesthetic that allows for the interplay of sensory experience and horizons of meaning, and Gumbrecht's (2004) framework of the oscillation between presence- and meaning-based relations in aesthetic experience that resists the undermining of one or the other.
2. The aesthetic as *embedded in everyday life* that emerges through our orientation and attentiveness to the present (which is informed by the past as well as informing the future): Dewey's (1958) pragmatist aesthetics.

Based on an understanding of the aesthetic that highlights a dialogic relation of the sensory and the interpretive in opening horizons as part of our sense making endeavors, and as an attentive orientation toward the present in the midst of the undergoings of everyday life, I now offer connections of this framework to communication ethics.

Attending to (the Image of) the (Cultural) Other

Given its richness in illustrating what I am to discuss here, I start this section with a recent classroom experience from my Exploring Intercultural Communication class and the reflections of a student that inspired the unearthing of the connection to the aesthetic in this project. Though a bit lengthy, this incident is well worth sharing and acknowledging as part of this book. First, a brief background to the actual story.

During class I notice a student sitting in the very back row reading a big book, which obviously does not look like the textbook. I take an internal pause and decide to attend to this issue at a time that is fitting. Next class, as the students take a few minutes to refresh their minds before the quiz, I notice the same student reading the same nontextbook. As others are studying, I slowly walk toward the back row and inquire in a soft voice whether his textbook arrived yet (this is at the beginning of the semester). The student responds that it should have but it is delayed. I inquire about the book he is reading and it turns out to be one from the Harry Potter series. Although Harry Potter can be adopted for this class in the future, at this point it was not, so I tell the student that the class is about to have a quiz and I do not want him to miss out. I suggest that he share the textbook of his classmate in the next seat and encourage them to sit closer to read together. They do.

This background primes what I am to share below, a reflection of the same student later in the semester in response to a class activity on cultural empathy. For this activity, I selected three photos of people from around the world (India and Africa in this case). The photos I picked were based on my assumption that these would be images of the "cultural other" for my students, based on their clothing, bodily decorations, facial expressions, the materials they were holding or carrying, and the physical background of the photo. This exercise was designed for practicing intercultural empathy, observing and reflecting on our relation with the image of the other, and the ways in which we respond and/or react that facilitate or diminish the empathy process.

The cultural empathy exercise consisted of three parts for each image observed. First, the students observed their thoughts, judgments, labels, as well as emotions, and memories (if any), as they took the time to attend to the first projected image for several minutes. Next, I instructed the students to take a pause in silence, close their eyes for a moment, and attend to what stays with them from the image. As the final step, as the students reopened their eyes, I invited them to relook at the same photo with a fresh state of mind, letting go of what they had seen before. This time around, I also instructed them to "enter" the picture, to find a spot in the picture to enter from and to imagine themselves in the picture. I asked such questions as "Where are you in this picture? What are you seeing, thinking, feeling, doing? Are you interacting with this person in the picture? What stands out for you?" After taking several minutes in this way, and repeating the same instructions for the three photos, students took another quiet pause and moved on to write in their journals.

Several students reflected in their journals stating that taking the pause and relooking at the images allowed them to feel connected with the people in the photos better, despite not knowing much about their culture. Some stated that they felt "transported into" their worlds as they took the time to attend to "her worn hands," "the weathered look of experience she has in her eyes," the "striking contrast of the patterns of her shirt with the plainness of her headscarf," "her age and weariness," "the sad look on her face." The descriptions of their experiences after the second half of the activity (where they imagined themselves in the picture) offer connections beyond immediate labels and judgments, and include affective and the sensory dimensions of relationality. But the striking response for me came from the Harry Potter reading student in the class where he wrote that taking the time to breathe and to focus allowed his judgments about these people to change substantially.

"Whereas before I would be more inclined to be *calloused and to care less* for the people that I saw, now I have much *greater sympathy* and feel substantially *freer*. It is like *stepping back* from your own perspective and looking at everything from an *aesthetic* perspective" [italics added].

What is the aesthetic perspective this student mentions above? As I kept asking this question to myself and processing it, I have come to realize that attending to this question constitutes the basis of connecting the aesthetic and communication ethics for this project. I was pleasantly surprised, excited, and a bit stunned by his use of the term "aesthetic" in characterizing his experience: "It is like stepping back from your own perspective and looking at everything from an *aesthetic* perspective." "Freer." This student (I will refer to him as S from now on) highlights a couple themes in his brief but rich paragraph quoted above. What stands out is S's characterization of his initial attitude as "calloused" and "caring less," from which he steps back (distanciation) and opens up to an "aesthetic perspective" where he feels "freer" and has "greater sympathy" for the other. It seems that pausing, connecting with one's bodily existence through breathing, attending to mental constructions (labels, judgments, stories, etc.) and releasing them to relook and to reengage facilitated the expansion of S's horizon beyond subjective preference and his habitual orientation.

Furthermore, and more important, having the opportunity to *participate* in the image through the senses ("what are you seeing? Hearing? Smelling?") as well as through the emotions ("how does it feel being in the picture? To be around this person, in this setting?") and cognitive processes ("What thoughts come to mind? Stories? Judgments? Labels?) seems to be powerful in enabling an aesthetic response that was liberating for this student. This resonates with the discussion earlier (as part of the "framing of an aesthetic ecology" section) on Gadamer's (2007) discussion of participation as belonging-together that involves a contemplative attentiveness that is both present and regarding. As part of this participation, we are reminded of the "aesthetic attention" that Davey (2013) highlights in his work on Gadamer's hermeneutic aesthetic that recognizes the interplay of sensibility and the intellect that resists narrowness of horizon.

The reflections of my students following the cultural empathy exercise show that they were able to connect with the culturally different other at a very basic human level, acknowledging the humanity of the other despite the cultural differences that are strange and unknown to them (we still need to work on this second part to be able to transform the "despite"). This is informative in connecting the aesthetic to communication ethics. Engaging the sensuous, bodily presence along with the intellectual—what Davey (2013) refers as "aesthetic attention"—facilitates participation (as *methexis*) in the world of the other and expands one's horizon, which might lead to the cultivation of an ethical subjectivity that is responsive to the other.

Furthermore, aesthetic attentiveness resists the "forgetting of presence" that Gumbrecht (2004, xv) writes about, that is dominant in contemporary Western cultural conditions that privilege the intellect and "effects of meaning" (136). Cultivating the aesthetic—as the class activity seems to have done without specifically intending to—allows for "the oscillation between presence effects and meaning effects" (Gumbrecht 2004, 108) without abandoning either dimension. As part of "stepping back from your own perspective and looking at everything from an *aesthetic* perspective," it might be that one is open to receive the emotional aspects in the photo such as noticing "her worn hands," or "the weathered look of experience she has in her eyes." Or one might step out of the story of poverty or strangeness and sense the joyful expression on the person's face in the picture along with the poor background. In connecting with the aesthetic in one's experience of the other, one might start to feel a warmer, less "calloused" inclination toward the other (as S described) that is liberating for both the self and the other.

Attending to the image of the other through the contemplative and participatory activity as discussed above allowed my students to be more receptive, present, and aware of their mental and emotional processes as they worked to relate and make sense of the other. Engaging the sensory and the emotional modes of interaction along with the cognitive, and assuming an orientation toward the images that is attentive to each image rather than moving onto the next task to be accomplished, seems to have led to a "delightful perception which is esthetic experience" (Dewey 1958, 19) that is responsive to the other. In a lecture titled "Ethics on a Global Scale," Butler (2011) spoke about "ethical responsiveness" that is needed before "ethical responsibility," that is "being capable of receiving the call [of the other] before actually answering it" (brackets added). Learning to resonate with the other through the interplay of the sensory, emotional, mental processes and a present-centered orientation rather than being absorbed in the past (such as preestablished labels, ideas, judgments, etc.) or the future (what is next in the to-do list) seems to make space for a sensibility that resists "moral blindness" (Bauman and Donskis 2013).

In *Communication Ethics Literacy: Dialogue and Difference*, Arnett, Fritz, and Bell (2009) highlight learning from difference that resists the "imposition of telling" (xiv) as the first principle of communication ethics in an era of difference that we live in. They explain that learning involves "withholding the impulse to tell until one understands the context, the topic, and the persons" (xiii). At the very beginning of this chapter, I started with the metaphor of the lotus flower that is rooted in muddy waters. To make sense of the lotus, one needs to recognize and attend to the ground that gives life to it. We all begin our lives in some place, with some people, that constitute our ground. Learning involves "the importance of knowing one's own ground and the ground of others" (Arnett, Fritz, and Bell 2009, xvii) that informs what matters to people. Based on the discussion above on the connection of aesthetics to communication ethics, this project underlines that the aesthetic opens up space for learning from difference by sparking our sensibilities to turn toward the other.

As stated at the beginning of this section, I use the concept of "aesthetic ecology" to refer to an environment that involves material (earth, body), conceptual ("signlessness," "weight"), and contemplative (breath, silence) elements that are part of the ongoing dialogue, or the "oscillation" (Gumbrecht 2004), between our sensuous and interpretive engagements in/with the world. Each chapter in this book explores an aspect of this aesthetic ecology in facilitating existential rootedness in connection to communication ethics.

ORGANIZATION OF THE CHAPTERS

The combination of philosophers and contemplatives that inform and guide this study reflects a commitment to the construction of knowledge through intellectual inquiry informed by contemplative insight, offering culturally diverse perspectives that honor a way of knowing grounded in the revelatory as well as the intellectual.

The first chapter "The Poíētic Sense of Meaning" highlights the poíētic/aesthetic sense of meaning in the experience of human beings that facilitates existential rootedness and opens up possibilities for dwelling in the world. In connection to the aesthetic ecology framework, this chapter highlights two material elements, the body and the earth, as part of the interplay between the sensible and the intellectual. This chapter grounds the discussion in the introduction chapter on the aesthetic in the study of communication through Pat Arneson's (2014) work on "communicative engagement," which recognizes that "human communication works in the wholistic space of theoria-poíēsis-praxis" (Arneson 2014, 53). Informed further by Giorgio Agamben's (1999) distinction of the "poietic status of man on earth," and Anna-Teresa Tymieniecka's (1995; 2000; 2001; 2004) exploration of the human creative function in her *Phenomenology of Life*, I examine some of the autobiographical narratives of Viktor Frankl (1984) based on his experiences in Nazi concentration camps as a prisoner. Overall, this chapter shows that creative-communicative practices that emerge through the interplay of the poíētic, the intellectual, and the moral senses enable human beings to reroot themselves even when external structures function to make people lose hold and to facilitate holistic insight in responding to communicative situations and engaging the world.

The second chapter "The 'Weight' of Meaning" focuses on Jean-Luc Nancy's (1997a, 1997b) discussion of sense as exposure to meaning beyond closure, completion, and appropriation. Nancy (1997a, 1997b) states that we are thinking as well as weighty beings who not only produce meaning but who are exposed to meaning. To wonder as a philosophical virtue and act today, according to Nancy, is being exposed to meaning at the limit, without being able to hold onto a system of signification. This chapter is a conceptual and phenomenological exploration of being exposed to meaning as an "event of opening" (Nancy, 1997a, 78) and learning to be suspended over meaning and letting thought weigh. I highlight Nancy's (1997a) "weight" of thought as part of the aesthetic ecology and show that the weight of meaning moves the oscillating dynamic between "presence- and meaning-based relations" (Gumbrecht 2004, 107) with the things of the world. To illustrate the discussion on the weight of meaning, I offer a phenomenological reflection based on my experience of reading Jean-Luc Nancy that examines the practice of *reading as weighing*: reading as an embodied exposure to exteriority—in this case, the text— that turns into aesthetic experience.

Chapter 3, "Signlessness," continues and expands the discussion in chapter 2 on the emergence of meaning at the limit of signification—through exposure to existence—from a non-Western perspective. Specifically, I discuss three themes from the writings of Vietnamese Buddhist monk, writer, poet, and peace activist Thich Nhat Hanh that are grounded in Buddhist teachings that focus on "simply existing" in connection to existential rootedness: interdependent co-arising, emptiness (nonself and signlessness), and impermanence. Hanh's (1999) discussion of signlessness as a way of knowing, and as an ontological and communicative practice, involves an acknowledgment of signs—the forms through which phenomena appear; however, Hanh warns us not to be caught by the signs. This chapter shows that signlessness, as the dialectic and practice of touching the world beyond signs in and through the world of signs, facilitates existential rootedness through a continuous surrendering of the self to experience toward "letting" oneself simply exist in a way that is in tune with the interconnected nature of all things that assumes responsibility for the other. Overall, the Buddhist teachings on interdependent co-arising, emptiness (nonself and signlessness), and impermanence provide a cultural context for ontological inquiry that is grounded in exteriority and otherness. In the final part of the chapter, I analyze a Zen koan titled "The Sound of Rain" that involves a dialogue between a Zen master and a student to illustrate the conceptual discussion and connect the practice of signlessness to the framework of aesthetic ecology. I argue that through the practice of signlessness, one cultivates aesthetic attentiveness (Gadamer 2004), stimulates the oscillation between presence- and meaning-based relations with the world (Gumbrecht 2004), and facilitates an aesthetic orientation and experience as part of everyday life (Dewey 1958).

Chapter 4, "Learning to Be (in Con/tact)," expands the discussion on existential rootedness to the experience of the body in illness. We rely on our bodily existence to make contact with the world and with others, yet the body is impermanent. Learning to inhabit one's constantly changing body is a fundamental aspect of human life through growing up, aging, illness, and the final stages of our existence. This chapter highlights that one's contact with and through her impermanent body is the foundation for existential rootedness. It is through contact with one's bodily presence in the world, with its struggles and challenges, and engaging the sensible, that one cultivates a "presence-based relation" (Gumbrecht 2004, xv) to the world and an aesthetic orientation. Informed by Merleau-Ponty's (1968) discussion of visibility and "intertwining," I first examine selected self-narratives, including a small sample of self-reports of breast cancer survivors, on encountering one's visual reflection to discuss the process of seeing as contact that facilitates existential rootedness. The excerpts of three breast cancer survivors illustrate the challenges of making contact with one's altered bodily appearance as a result of treatment. One way of coming to terms with and learning to inhabit one's changing or radically changed body is possible through becoming a "participation" (Merleau-Ponty 1968) in the family of visible things beyond dualistic thought. Overall, this chapter shows that existential rootedness is facilitated by *contact*, a dwelling in one's present bodily experience—including the experience of one's bodily appearance—rather than a quick consumption of one's visual reflection as something that he or she likes/wants or not. Guiding our habits of attention that ordinarily skip the present moment experience toward inhabiting it, the practice of mindfulness facilitates an aesthetic orientation in the midst of the struggles of everyday life that Dewey (1958) highlights in *The Art of Experience*.

Chapter 5, "Attending to the Breath (of the Other)," is an intercultural exploration of, and a call for, a subtle attentiveness to the breath, and to the breath of the other, that expands the ongoing discussions in the field of communication ethics regarding "a visual or an audio-ethic" (Arnett 2017, 17). Rather than a biological perspective on the breath as a process that oxygenates the blood and the organs, this chapter focuses on the breath as a phenomenological element of human experience that facilitates a way of being in direct contact with one's bodily participation in the world along with others who share this breath. I first offer some historical and intercultural context on the principle of air as the first principle of nature (based on Anaximenes's theory of air, one of the first pre-Socratic philosophers of the sixth century) and on the understanding of air/breath as prana (universal life energy) in Indian thought and yoga philosophy. Following this discussion, I explore Gaston Bachelard's (2002) work on the life-giving role of the breath in relation to words, as well as Luce Irigaray's (1999) important work on the ethics of breathing and being. This chapter shows that attending to and cultivating the breath facilitates *methexis* (Gadamer 2007), a sense of belonging together and presence. Being in touch with one's breath and the breath of the other invites an aesthetic sensibility that engages the senses, enabling a present-moment orientation that is receptive, responsive, and in Dewey's (1958) terms, aesthetic. I conclude this chapter with a discussion on an *aesthetic ethic of speaking* that emerges in connecting the breath with speech, making space for the coming together of the "will to speak" (Bachelard 2002, 243) and the "poetic will" (244). Speech that is immersed in the silence of the breath, and awakened by the breath, is not self-focused, but responsive to the breath of the other.

Chapter 6, "Silence, Solitude, Reverence," explores Thomas Merton's contemplative communicative perspective, focusing on four themes that include solitude, creative silence, inhabiting space, and reverence. For Merton, it is through the practice of silence and solitude that one roots herself in existence and cultivates reverence for life. I show that this reverential attitude toward life facilitates the cultivation of "presence effects" (Gumbrecht 2004, xv) along with "meaning effects" (108) and the "delightful perception which is esthetic experience" (Dewey 1958, 19). Finally, I explore the pedagogical implications of Merton's work in the classroom, focusing specifically on "inhabiting space" and "reverence."

In closing the introduction, I offer Rilke's (1918) poem "When Something Falls from My Window" that reminds us of our resistance and arrogance as human beings and getting in the way of ourselves only to be left confused, alone, and uprooted. This book is a gentle invitation "to learn from things like a child," as Rilke puts it, and to listen, deeply, beyond self-centeredness and arrogance.

> When something falls
> from my window
> (even the smallest thing)
> the law of gravity rushes
> like an ocean storm
> to bear ball and berry
> into the core of the world.
>
> Every thing is protected
> by a grace ready for flight,
> every stone and flower
> every child at night.

Only we, in arrogance, thrust
Out of peace
into space.
Not giving ourselves
to the mind of the world
to rise like trees.
Leaving the path
we're in knots;
abandoning bonds,
we're namelessly alone.

You who thought
to best birds in flight—
learn from things
like a child.
They are close
to God's heart:
never leave him,
able to fall,
patiently
at rest in gravity.

—Rilke (2019)

REFERENCES

Agamben, Giorgio. 1999. *The Man Without Content*. Translated by Georgia Albert. Stanford, CA: Stanford University Press.

Arendt, Hannah. 2006. *Eichmann in Jerusalem: A Report on the Banality of Evil*. NY: Penguin Classics. First published 1963.

Arneson, Pat. 2014. *Communicative Engagement and Social Liberation: Justice Will Be Made*. Teaneck, NJ: Fairleigh Dickinson University Press.

Arnett, Ronald C. 1994. "Existential Homelessness: A Contemporary Case for Dialogue." In *The Reach of Dialogue: Confirmation, Voice and Community*, 229–46. Cresskill, NJ: Hampton Press.

———. 2010. "Embeddedness/Embedded Identity." In *Encyclopedia of Identity*, edited by Ronald L. Jackson, 241–44. Thousand Oaks, CA: Sage Publications.

———. 2013. *Communication Ethics in Dark Times: Hannah Arendt's Rhetoric of Warning and Hope*. Carbondale: Southern Illinois University Press.

———. 2017. *Levinas's Rhetorical Demand: The Unending Obligation of Communication Ethics*. Carbondale: Southern Illinois University Press.

Arnett, Ronald C., Janie M. Fritz, and Leeanne M. Bell. 2009. *Communication Ethics Literacy: Dialogue and Difference*. Los Angeles: Sage Publications.

Arnett, Ronald C., Leeanne M. Bell McManus, and Amanda G. McKendree. 2014. *Conflict between Persons: The Origins of Leadership*. First edition, Dubuque, IA: Kendall Hunt.

Bachelard, Gaston. 2002. *Air and Dreams: An Essay on the Imagination of Movement*. Dallas Institute of Humanities and Culture: Dallas Institute Publications.

Bauman, Z., and L. Donskis. 2013. *Moral Blindness: The Loss of Sensitivity in Liquid Modernity*. Cambridge: Polity Press.

Boothroyd, Dave. Touch, time, and technics: Levinas and the ethics of haptic communications. *Theory, Culture & Society* 26, no.2–3 (2009): 330–345.

Brady, B. V. On the meaning of the Catholic Intellectual Tradition. *Journal of Catholic Higher Education* 32, no. (2013): 189–205.

Butler, J. 2011. "Ethics on a Global Scale." Video file retrieved from http://www.egs.edu/faculty/judith-butler/videos/ethics-on-a-global-scale.

Catholic Intellectual Tradition. (n.d.). Retrieved from http://duq.edu/about/centers-and-institutes/catholic-intellectual-tradition.

Coulthard, Glen Sean. 2014. *Red Skin, White Masks: Rejecting the Colonial Politics of Recognition*. MN: University of Minnesota Press.

Davey, Nicholas. 2013. *Unfinished Worlds: Hermeneutics, Aesthetics and Gadamer*. Edinburgh: Edinburgh University Press.

Dewey, John. 1958. *The Art of Experience*. New York: Capricorn Books.

Engelhardt, James. 2008. "Rooted and rootless: Writing from Place in a Mobile Society." *The Journal of the Midwest Modern Language Association* 41(1): 88–97.

Frankl, Viktor E. 1984. *Man's Search for Meaning: An Introduction to Logotherapy*, 3rd ed. Translated by Ilse Lasch. New York: Pocket Books.

Gadamer, Hans Georg. 1977. *Philosophical Hermeneutics*. Edited and translated by David E. Linge. Berkeley: University of California Press.

———. 2004. *Truth and Method.* Translated by Donald G. Marshall and Joel Weinsheimer, 2nd ed. London: Continuum. First published 1975.

———. 2007. "The Universality of the Hermeneutical Problem." In *The Gadamer Reader*, edited by R. E. Palmer, 72–88. Evanston: Northwestern University Press.

Gumbrecht, Hans Ulricht. 2004. *Production of Presence: What Meaning Cannot Convey.* Stanford, CA: Stanford University Press.

Hanh, Thich Nhat. 1999. *The Heart of the Buddha's Teaching: Transforming Suffering into Peace, Joy & Liberation: The Four Noble Truths, the Noble Eightfold Path, and Other Basic Buddhist Teachings.* New York: Harmony Books.

Heidegger, Martin. 1966. *Discourse on Thinking.* Translated by John M. Anderson and Hans Freund. New York: Harper & Row. First published 1959.

Irigaray, Luce. 1999. *The Forgetting of Air in Martin Heidegger.* Texas: University of Texas Press.

Laycock, Steven, William. *Nothingness and Emptiness: A Buddhist Engagement with the Ontology of Jean-Paul Sartre.* Albany, NY: SUNY Press, 2012.

Liska, Vivian. 2004. "Roots Against Heaven: An Aporetic Inversion in Paul Celan." *New German Critique* 91: 41–56.

Merleau-Ponty, Maurice. 1968. *The Visible and the Invisible.* Translated by Alphonso Lingis. Edited by Claude Lefort. IL: Northwestern University Press.

Mitchell, Mark T. 2006. "The Homeless Modern." *Intercollegiate Review* 41 (1): 13–22.

Nancy, Jean-Luc. 1997a. *The Gravity of Thought.* Translated by Francois Raffoul and Gregory Recco. Atlantic Highlands, NJ: Humanity Books.

Nancy, Jean Luc. 1977b. *The Sense of the World.* Minneapolis: University of Minnesota Press.

Rilke, Rainer Maria. 2019. *Das Stundenbuch.* Leipzig: Insel Verlag. Translated by Eva-Maria Simms and Michael Simms. Pittsburgh, PA: Vox Populi.

Schreyer, Christine, Jon Corbett, Nocole Gordon, and Colleen Larson. "Learning to talk to the land: Online stewardship in Taku River Tlingit territory." *Decolonization: Indigeneity, Education & Society* 3, No. 3 (2014): 106–133.

Simpson, Leanne Betasamosake. "Land as pedagogy: Nishnaabeg intelligence and rebellious transformation." *Decolonization: Indigeneity, Education & Society* 3, No. 3 (2014): 1–25.

Smith, David L. 2008. *Born to See, Bound to Behold: The History of Duquesne University's Simon Silverman Phenomenology Center.* Pittsburgh, PA: Simon Silverman Phenomenology Center, Duquesne University.

Stroud, Scott R. 2014. "The Art of Experience: Dewey on the Aesthetic." In *Practicing Pragmatist Aesthetics: Critical Perspectives on the Arts*, edited by Wojciech Malecki, 33–46. Amsterdam: Rodopi.

Styres, Sandra, Celia Haig-Brown and Melissa Blimkie. "Towards a Pedagogy of Land: The Urban Context." *Canadian Journal of Education* 36, no 2 (2013): 34–67.

Styres, Sandra and Dawn Zinga. "Opening the Circle: Welcoming Brother Sun." *Canadian Journal of Education* 36, no 2 (2013): 1–3.

Tymieniecka, Anna-Teresa, ed. 1988. *Logos and Life: Creative Experience and the Critique of Reason: Introduction to the Phenomenology of Life and the*

Human Condition. Analecta Husserliana: The Yearbook of Phenomenological Research 24.

———, ed. 1995. *The Elemental Passion for Place in the Ontopoiesis of Life: Passions of the Soul in the Imaginatio Creatrix. Analecta Husserliana: The Yearbook of Phenomenological Research* 44.

———, ed. 2000. *Logos and Life. Analecta Husserliana: The Yearbook of Phenomenological Research* 70.

———, ed. 2001. *Passions of the Earth in Human Existence, Creativity, and Literature. Analecta Husserliana: The Yearbook of Phenomenological Research* 71.

———, ed. 2004. *Imaginatio Creatrix: The Pivotal Force of the Genesis/Ontopoiesis of Human Life and Reality. Analecta Husserliana: The Yearbook of Phenomenological Research* 83.

van Manen, Max. 2014. *Phenomenology of Practice*. Walnut Creek, CA: Left Coast Press.

Weil, Simone. 1952. *The Need for Roots*. New York: Routledge & Kegan Paul.

Wildcat, Mathew, Mandee McDonald, Stephanie Irlbacher-Fox, and Glen Clouthard. "Learning from the land: Indigenous land based pedagogy and decolonization." *Decolonization: Indigeneity, Education & Society* 3, No. 3 (2014): I–XV.

Chapter One

The Poíētic Sense of Meaning

A distinctive and fascinating aspect of our humanly existence lies in our creative-communicative capacity to engage and respond to the conditions of life in which we find ourselves. This chapter grounds the discussion in the introduction chapter on the aesthetic in the study of communication through Pat Arneson's (2014) work on "communicative engagement" which recognizes that "human communication works in the wholistic space of theoria-poíēsis-praxis" (Arneson 2014, 53). Informed further by Giorgio Agamben's (1999) distinction of the "poíētic status of man on earth" and Anna-Teresa Tymieniecka's (1988; 2004) exploration of the human creative function in her *Phenomenology of Life*, I highlight the poíētic/aesthetic sense of meaning in facilitating existential rootedness in the experience of human beings and opening up possibilities for dwelling in the world even when the external conditions are not supportive. Specifically, I examine some of the autobiographical narratives of Viktor Frankl (1984) based on his experiences in Nazi concentration camps as a prisoner. Three main ideas that emerge from the analysis are as follows: (1) The poíētic sense of meaning working together with the intellectual and moral capacities enable humans to approach life beyond already established narratives that can be limiting in guiding people; (2) Creative-communicative practices that emerge through the interplay of the poíētic, the intellectual, and the moral senses enable human beings to reroot themselves even when external structures function to make people lose hold, and facilitate holistic insight in responding to communicative situations and engaging the world; (3) Liberation is possible through rootedness in one's lived experience and the environment he or she exists in even when—especially when—the conditions are not likable, preferable, or supportive.

The next section offers a discussion of Arneson's (2014) communicative engagement based on her exploration of Myrtilla Miner's life that was dedicated to bringing racial equality in education in a social environment where slavery was normalized and justified.

COMMUNICATIVE ENGAGEMENT AND MULTIPLE MODALITIES OF MEANING

In her discussion of communicative engagement throughout her book, Arneson (2014) highlights communication as a *reasoning art* grounded in the integrated and interactive working of theoria-poíēsis-praxis. Resisting the separation of these orientations in academia advocated by Plato following the death of Socrates—and pursued further by Aristotle and later on by Marx—Arneson's (2014) project expands Calvin O. Schrag's (1969) discussion of communicative praxis by reuniting theoria-poíēsis-praxis, which makes space for the fullness of communication in shaping lived experience. "Recognizing that *praxis* is necessarily united with theoria and poíēsis, human communication works in the wholistic space of theoria-poíēsis-praxis" (Arneson 2014, 53). Exclusion of the poíētic function of meaning or pushing it to the background has overwhelming consequences in the organization of human life and human communication, as it is shown through the examples offered in this chapter. Disconnected from the creative force of poíēsis, theoria-praxis function to narrow down the ways in which we interpret and create social worlds and *can easily result in the creation and legitimation of social structures that violate the dignity of human life*.

Arneson's (2014) discussion and exploration of communicative engagement acknowledges "multiple modalities of meaning discerned in one's lived experience" (41). In her discussion of the modalities of meaning in lived experience, Arneson refers to Tymieniecka's (1983) discussion of the three "meaning-bestowing faculties" in the experience of human beings: aesthetic (poíētic), moral, and intellective. The intellective sense "enables an intelligibility of the basic structures of human life" (Arneson 2014, 43). It provides a reference system in making sense of the forms, categories, and principles of social life. The aesthetic (poíētic) sense of meaning works together with the moral and the intellective functions. It is the capacity of human inventiveness that "allows a person to transcend social schemas (that function in their framing to limit the expansion of life) and open possibilities for 'unfolding a meaningful existential script within the intersubjective network of life'" (43). It is through engaging the poíētic sense of meaning in relation to one's lived experience that humans are able to approach life beyond already established narratives that can be limiting in guiding people. The intelligibility enabled by the intellect connects with the poíētic sense that opens possibilities along with the moral sense highlighting the ground of freedom and common interest of other beings.

I illustrate the discussion on multiple modalities of meaning in communicative engagement below through the life story of Myrtilla Miner that Arneson (2014) examines in her book. In chapter 5 of *Communicative Engagement and Social Liberation: Justice Will Be Made,* Arneson introduces Myrtilla Miner, a white American woman who lived in the mid-1800s and fought against racial inequality in education. Miner accepted a teaching position in southwestern Mississippi in response to the call from Southern educational reformers, which is when she was exposed to the practice of human slavery. Arneson (2014) writes, "Miner's physical, emotional, and mental health was deeply affected—an existential mood of dissatisfaction arose. . . . Miner's felt-meanings were so intense that unless she could directly help abolish slavery, staying in the South was likely to become impractical for her" (102). Arneson (2014) explains that at the same time dominant racial theories such as the ones produced by the scientist and physical anthropologist Samuel George Morton made claims about race, skull capacity, and intellectual ability. Morton claimed superiority of white people over black people in terms of intelligence and this line of scholarship continued. Louisiana physician Samuel A. Cartwright attributed two mental disorders to black people: *Drapetomania*, which he claimed was a running away disease that a black person who fled slavery suffered from, and *Dysaethesia Aethiopica,* which was claimed to be a lack of work ethic commonly seen in many slaves with symptoms such as disobedience and refusing to work. "Cartwright's research justified enslavement as a medical and moral responsibility of white slave owners, prescribing 'whipping the devil out of them' as a 'preventative measure' against disease" (Arneson 2014, 102). The seemingly logical, scientific arguments for slavery opposed Miner's lived-experience and felt-meanings and she questioned the narratives and practices of slavery. She discerned the disconnections between theoria-poiēsis-praxis. Miner devoted her whole life to establishing a school to teach black young women in the North, which she eventually accomplished after facing many difficulties and obstacles. Through education, she persisted in her endeavors to resist slavery and worked to change the attitudes and structures that normalized and perpetuated its practice.

Cut off from the "Energy of Poiēsis"

Separation of the multiple modalities of making sense of the world can be devastating. Disconnected from the creative force of poiēsis, one's lived experience, and felt meanings, theoria-praxis, function to narrow down the ways in which we interpret and create social worlds. Arneson (2014) writes, "*Praxis* is generally considered to be theory-informed action. This truncation excludes *poíēsis*—or at best relegates *poíēsis* to a secondary or tertiary background in experience. Scientific theories about the inferiority of people with darker skin color were taken as a reason and an ethical responsibility for enslaving black people. Legislation of the time reinforced this thinking" (103). Theoria-praxis disconnected from the *visceral* understanding offered by the poíētic sense can easily result in the creation and legitimation of social structures that reinforce one type of thinking that functions to perpetuate itself. "Poíēsis is the force that compels the creative act of expression" (Arneson 2014, 22). The creative potential of poíēsis allows one to approach and interpret the world otherwise.

Referencing Ramsey's (1998) work on liberation politics, Arneson (2014) connects Ramsey's discussion on dissatisfaction and change to poíēsis: "Dissatisfaction arises when one is frustrated by the perceived limits of tradition and desires to do otherwise" (62). Furthermore, "the existential mood of dissatisfaction provides an opening to the possibility for which one yearns. When one experiences dissatisfaction, her interpretive abilities *poíētically* open possibilities within that situation" (63, original emphasis). Dissatisfaction in the experience of Myrtilla Miner illustrates the opening of poíētic possibilities toward expanding social justice in the South.

In the following, I offer an example that illustrates the consequences of being cut off from the "energy of poíēsis" as well as the role of poíētic sense in allowing human beings to create possibilities even in miserable external conditions. In *Man's Search for Meaning,* Viktor Frankl (1984) writes about his experiences as an ordinary prisoner in a concentration camp in Auschwitz as prisoner #119,104. He focuses on the everyday struggles and sacrifices made to survive rather than major heroic acts. The following section focuses on one specific scene Frankl describes vividly in connection to the discussion above on poíēsis and its separation from theoria-praxis.

After travelling for several days and nights by train with fifteen hundred prisoners who expected that they were being taken to a munitions factory for forced labor, Frankl describes an instance where "a cry broke from the ranks of the anxious passengers, 'There is a sign, Auschwitz!'" when "everyone's heart missed a beat at that moment" (27). After arriving at the station, they were told to leave their luggage on the train and follow a line based on their sex after passing a senior SS officer. With a kind of courage surprising to himself, Frankl hid his haversack under his coat and straightened his body as he approached the officer so as not to have his load noticed. Frankl (1984) writes about his encounter with the officer:

> Then I was face to face with him. He was a tall man who looked slim and fit in his spotless uniform. What a contrast to us, who were untidy and grimy after our long journey! He had assumed an attitude of careless ease, supporting his right elbow

with his left hand. His right hand was lifted, and with the forefinger of that hand he pointed very leisurely to the right or to the left. None of us had the slightest idea of the sinister meaning behind that little movement of a man's finger, pointing now to the right and now to the left, but far more frequently to the left. (30)

The image of the tall officer looking slim and fit in sharp contrast to the prisoners, and the leisurely movement of his finger pointing to the left or right—determining the destiny of the prisoners as the reader learns later—not only appeals to the intellect but also affects the body and touches the heart. The story pulls one into the scene through vivid descriptions of the contrast between the polished appearance of the officer and the messy and filthy condition of the prisoners, facilitating a visualization of the "careless ease" in which the officer holds his body and the leisurely movement of his forefinger pointing to the right or the left. We find ourselves walking side by side with Frankl; suspended. Unlike Frankl, however, being familiar with the context based on its history, we can guess the "sinister meaning" and have a sense of the terrifying condition of the prisoners. But, reading along, we slow down to match our rhythm with Frankl's. He goes on:

> It was my turn. Somebody whispered to me that to be sent to the right side would mean work, the way to the left being for the sick and those incapable of work, who would be sent to a special camp. I just waited for things to take their course, the first of many such times to come. My haversack weighed me down a bit to the left, but I made an effort to walk upright. The SS man looked me over, appeared to hesitate, then put both his hands on my shoulders. I tried very hard to look smart, and he turned my shoulders very slowly until I faced right, and I moved over to that side. (30)

Waiting for things to take their course, suspended and exposed, Frankl worked hard on his self-presentation to look acceptable. Feeling his shoulders being turned to the right and slowly moving toward what showed up as the path, Frankl allowed things to take their course. Later on, he learns about the "finger game" where the prisoners who were sent to the left went straight to the crematorium that had the word "bath" written over its doors.

Focusing on the "felt meaning" of Frankl's account and one's own bodily experience upon reading it, one might notice a sense of being disturbed, of being out of sorts. This is an emotionally charged text that invites shock, disturbance, helplessness, and a cry for justice. Now, let's go back to the image of the tall officer and the leisurely movement of his finger pointing to the left or right: what would it take to be able to be there, in that role, having assumed that identity, and moving on with the duty as it is? No sense of disturbance, dissatisfaction, or terror at the face of sending people to death, one after another, with an attitude of ease and the leisurely movement of one's forefinger? Earlier, it was discussed that separation of the multiple modalities of making sense of the world has overwhelming consequences as illustrated by the discussion on slavery and Miner's experience in Arneson's (2014) book. *Disconnected from the creative force of poiēsis, one's lived experience, and felt meanings, theoria-praxis function to narrow down the ways in which we interpret and create social worlds and can easily result in the creation and legitimation of social structures that violate the dignity of human life and in destruction.* Frankl's account serves to illustrate this point and supports the main idea shared through Miner's life story in a different historical context and time period.

More important, however, as one reads on, Frankl's book shows how even in such terrifying conditions, human beings can maintain the creative capacity to respond by taking on the tasks that life offers. Rather than asking the question about the meaning of life in the brutal conditions they had to survive, Frankl (1984) states, "We had to learn ourselves and, furthermore, we had to teach the despairing men, that it did not really matter what we expected from life, but rather what life expected from us. . . . Life ultimately means taking the responsibility to find the right answer to its problems and to fulfill the tasks which it constantly sets for each individual" (98). Frankl's quote highlights the deep existential connection of human beings with life itself, our "partnership with existence itself" (Arnett 2013, 63), that acknowledges the larger container in which we survive. Frankl shifts the focus of attention from the individual and his or her expectations from life to the larger container of life that the individual is part of and turns the individualistic question of what one expects from life to what life expects from the individual. Thus, the question of the meaning of life becomes a question of how one responds to the needs and expectations of the conditions in which one finds herself and taking responsibility for one's response. It is through our creative-communicative response that we *make* our lives and our selves, as also exemplified by Miner's story discussed in the prior pages.

Following the next section on Agamben's (1999) discussion of the poetic status of man on Earth, I will further examine Frankl's account of his specific experiences in the concentration camp in connection to the creative-communicative making of life and the possibility of rerooting one's self even when the external structures are designed to function to make people lose hold.

THE POETIC STATUS OF "MAN" ON EARTH

In *The Man Without Content*, Agamben (1999) asks "What does it mean that man has on earth a poetic, that is, a pro-ductive status?" (59). Agamben explains that today pro-ductive activity is understood as praxis, "production of material life" (59), and "manifestation of a will that produces a concrete effect" (68). The distinction between praxis and poiēsis is blurred: "When we say that man has a productive status on earth, we mean, then that the status of his dwelling on earth is a *practical* one" (68). This blurring of praxis and poiēsis eclipsed the sphere of poiēsis to the point that all productive activity is interpreted as praxis, which highlights the voluntary and willful production of material life. To the ancient Greeks, however, "central to poiēsis was the experience of production into presence, the fact that something passed from nonbeing to being, from concealment into the full light of the work (Agamben 1999, 68–69) and "building a world for man's dwelling on earth" (70). Different from praxis as willed action, Agamben explains that the essential character of poiēsis is pro-duction, which brings something into presence that is something other than itself. Poiēsis as pro-duction has its end and its limit *outside itself,* whereas praxis as willed action/doing reaches its own limit and brings *itself* to presence in the end (willed action moves, reaches its limit, and remains inside the circle). Agamben highlights that for the Greeks, praxis as willed action is distinct from pro-duction; the will is not-productive as it brings only itself into presence.

Poiēsis as pro-duction that has its end and its limit outside itself can be understood as a way of making sense of the world that "brings forth possibilities that are withheld" (Arneson 2014, 64). In contrast to calculative thinking that functions to narrow down and limit possibilities toward predictable, orderly, and singular interpretations of the world, meditative thinking and releasement—as part of the poiētic function—allow for "distanciation" (45), which is a stepping back and suspending of the normative assumptions and customs that condition ways of thinking, speaking, and acting. In this critical space, one can question, disagree, and consider possibilities of interpretation. Keats's (1951) notion of "negative capability" seems fitting as part of this discussion on poiēsis as pro-duction that brings into presence something other than itself, along with meditative thinking and distanciation. Negative capability is the ability of "being in uncertainties, mysteries, doubts, without any irritable reaching after facts and reason" (Keats 1951, 29) to let the truth reveal itself. Negative capability allows one to attend to and contain complexities of life without jumping into quick judgments and conclusions, "without the armor of systematic certainties" (29), and without having to make up one's mind to stay open. Negative capability then is a creative capacity that resists "enframing" (Arneson 2014, 64) that reinforces a singular interpretation of the world. Along with meditative thinking, releasement, and distanciation, negative capability cultivates and brings to the foreground the poiētic mode of theoria-praxis-poiēsis in communicative engagement. As discussed earlier, poiētic ways of engaging the world guided and encouraged Miner to continue attending to the problem of slavery despite the major obstacles she faced including her health condition. Arneson (2014) explains that the bed rest required due to her health allowed her to distanciate herself and engage in meditative thinking. Miner continued her work to bring educational reform, making it her life work to articulate the disconnections between theoria-poíēsis-praxis in the context that she lived.

CULTIVATING EXISTENTIAL ROOTEDNESS THROUGH THE POÍĒTIC SENSE OF HUMAN COMMUNICATION

The discussion above on poíēsis based on Agamben's (1999) work highlights the essential character of poíēsis as bringing something into presence that is something other than itself. Agamben further connects poíēsis to "building a world for man's dwelling on earth" (70). In an environment that restricted certain freedoms to certain people and imposed narrowed down versions of being, thinking, and acting, Miner's struggle was to build a dwelling that ended social injustice; to build a space, a physical and social space, that allowed black people to receive an education so they too could dwell on earth and build a life. Miner worked toward building a world where she also could dwell differently along with others; she was not at home in a world where she could not teach black people. The poem, writes Frost, "begins with a lump in the throat, a homesickness or a love-sickness. It is a reaching-out towards expression; an effort to find fulfillment" (Frost 1979, 224). What Frost states about the written poem also manifests itself through the creative act of bringing-forth toward building a dwelling place in the world. Miner started with a restlessness, a "lump in the throat," a homesickness, and worked to create the conditions in which she could dwell with others differently. In her lived, bodily experience Miner felt the existential ties with the community that she shared life with. Hammarskjold wrote:

> So rests the sky against the earth.
> The dark still tarn in the lap of the forest.
>
> —Hammarskjold 1966, 77

Just as the sky rests against the earth, human beings stand on the earth. Like the dark still tarn in the lap of the forest, we exist in the lap of our relationships, or long for it. Existentially, we depend on our physical, social, cultural environment to survive. We do not exist independent of our surroundings. We rely on the air we breathe, the right temperature, the right amount of food and nourishment, including social and "communicative nourishment" (Fritz 2013, 174), attention, and love. The poet knows and lives in this existential rootedness:

> Breath, you invisible poem!
> Pure, continuous exchange
> with all that is, flow and counterflow
> where rhythmically I come to be.
>
> —Rilke, *Sonnets to Orpheus II, 1*
> (in Barrows and Macy 2016)

The philosopher knows it too. In *Experience and Being*, Schrag (1969) writes about the "field notion of experience," which includes the "interlacing constituents" of *experiencer-experiencing-figure-with-background,* with intentional hyphens that draw attention to "the bonds or connective tissues within experience" (18). Although one might conventionally and habitually foreground the experiencer and disregard the rest in our everyday existence, thinking that we exist as independent individual selves, one cannot go on without the connective tissues. Connective tissues matter, especially when they are threatened.

A heart-wrenching and intense experience of the destruction of connective tissues is exemplified in the autobiography of Viktor Frankl where he writes about his experiences in the concentration camp that is specifically designed to cut people loose from any connective bonds. As Frankl describes, undernourishment in all possible ways and brutality led to the experience of a *subhuman* existence. In the preface to *Man's Search for Meaning,* Allport (1984) writes, "In the concentration camp every circumstance conspires to make the prisoner lose his hold" (12): daily and hourly beatings, ten and a half ounces of bread and very watery soup served once a day, extremely heavy work, constant humiliation, brutality, disgust, apathy, intense longing for the loved ones, and feelings of lifelessness due to what Frankl (1984) calls "provisional existence" with regards to not knowing when they might be released and not having any future related goals (91). Still, Frankl warns the reader/outsider not to get a wrong conception of life in a concentration camp "mingled with sentiment and pity" and highlights the "hard fight for existence" and "unrelenting struggle for daily bread and for life itself, for one's own sake or for that of a good friend" (22). Frankl further states that "it is possible to practice the art of living even in a concentration camp, although suffering is omnipresent" (65). The art of living that Frankl writes about was practiced by the prisoners through various poiētic engagements such as developing a sense of humor, cultivating a sense of curiosity, contemplating images of loved ones, deepening one's religious or spiritual life, or catching glimpses of the beauty of nature. Such poiētic ways of engaging life allowed a prisoner to approach and relate to life differently and made it possible to dwell even in the worst of conditions. For instance, after surviving the initial selections upon arriving at the camp, prisoners lined up to get into the shower after getting completely undressed in the two minutes they had, and were then completely shaved to the point of not being able to recognize each other. They were stripped from all they had. Frankl (1984) writes,

> Thus the illusions some of us still held were destroyed one by one, and then, quite unexpectedly, most of us were overcome by a grim sense of humor. *We knew that we had nothing to lose except our so ridiculously naked lives.* When the showers started to run, we all tried very hard to make fun, both about ourselves and about each other. After all, real water did flow from the sprays! (33–34; emphasis added)

In addition to the strange sense of humor, Frankl writes about a sense of curiosity that allowed the mind to assume a detached observer role, which had a protective function. "We were anxious to know what would happen next; and what would be the consequence, for example, of our standing in the open air, in the chill of late autumn, stark naked, and still wet from the showers. In the next few days our curiosity evolved into surprise; surprise that we did not catch cold" (35).

On another occasion that Frankl describes, his group was marching to their work site on one early morning in the cold weather, stumbling over the stones and the puddles in the dark as the guards kept shouting at them and pushing them with the backs of their rifles. Prisoners with very sore feet supported themselves on their neighbor's arm. Frankl heard the man next to him whisper that he hoped their wives were better off in their camps, which brought thoughts of his own wife to mind. And as they walked stumbling on, slipping on ice, supporting and dragging each other, Frankl had the image of his wife in his mind. He writes about how through contemplating his wife, he was able to create a place of dwelling even for a few moments. The strength of his love for his wife helped him keep going. Even when his thoughts were interrupted when someone stumbled, fell, and got whipped, after a few moments Frankl reconnected with his wife in his mind and continued conversing with her. Frankl did not know whether his wife was alive at that point; however, he states that it did not matter. "There was no need for me to know; nothing could touch the strength of my love, my thoughts, and the image of my beloved" (1984, 58). Frankl found refuge in the image of his beloved in the midst of desolation. Frankl writes about this intensification of the prisoner's inner life in relation to the spiritual poverty of his existence and its significance in giving life to a person when all hope was lost.

Frankl writes about another time when he was working on icy ground and all around was grey; grey sky, grey rags of the prisoners, grey faces, grey snow.... He was conversing with his wife in his mind, and struggling to find the reason for his sufferings and slow dying. Gradually, her presence grew stronger and stronger, and Frankl was filled with a transcendent inspiration. His doubts and questions about the ultimate purpose of existence were lifted up as he continued to hack at the icy ground feeling the presence of his beloved. At that moment, a bird quietly flew down and stood on the top of the soil that Frankl dug up and looked at him steadily.

Contemplation and imagination became a way of surviving for Frankl. He built a dwelling place through such creative engagements. He was not alone in these endeavors. A fellow prisoner, for instance, drew attention to the beauty of nature or the sunset as they worked next to each other. Frankl writes about how they experienced the beauty of nature more deeply as their inner life got intensified. He writes about one evening when his team was dead tired, resting on the floor in the hut and having soup, a fellow prisoner rushed in and asked them to run out to see the sunset. They stood outside in silence, watching the glowing clouds in the sunset and the whole sky became alive with the changing colors, and one of the prisoners said, "How beautiful the world could be!" (Frankl 1984, 60).

Despite the conditions in which they lived and the apathy that emerged as a protective mechanism to survive in the midst of the terror, the prisoners still found beauty, and made an effort to share it. They could still discern the beauty of nature, and the colors in the sky, in the midst of the lifeless conditions they had to survive in. Arneson (2014) highlights Tymieniecka's discussion of *imaginatio creatrix,* "the prime force inspiring human endeavors" and ontopoiēsis, "the vital creative impulse that generates the formation of life . . . that inspires people to shape particular meanings in their words and deeds" (22). These creative forces function beyond intentionality. Poiētic possibilities open up through the inventive function of *imaginatio creatrix*. One is able to discern beauty in the midst of everything grey, or one is able to contemplate a loved one and be filled with life and love in the midst of the misery of a concentration camp. As Arneson (2012) puts it, "The creative function of human beings gives life its significance" (158).

All three examples discussed above—finding humor in the midst of desperation, contemplating and conversing with the image of a loved one, sharing and enjoying the beauty of nature—illustrate the creative-communicative making of life even when the external structures are designed to function to make people lose hold. It is through such creative-communicative acts that allowed the prisoners to reroot themselves in the camp even for brief moments. Arneson (2014) states that "the everyday world is *made* through communication," including the sociopolitical structures that we operate in, the selves we become, and the kinds of meanings we create (21). Arneson (2012) highlights Tymieniecka's (2000) discussion of creative interpretation that allows human beings to transcend "*deciphering already ciphered script*" and to "*dwell in the ciphering itself*" toward reaching the fullness of life (as qtd. in Arneson 2012, 163; original emphasis). In interaction with others, people share and explore each other's meanings, creating ideas, objects, and aspects of self that make it possible to expand one's world and one's self. Arneson (2014) refers to "existential self-expansion" (42) that "can only be accomplished through communicative interactions" (43) through the poíētic faculty in human experience. "The inventive function (*poíētic* sense) allows a person to transcend social schemas (that function in their framing to limit the expansion of life) and open possibilities for 'unfolding a meaningful existential script within the intersubjective network of life'" (43).

The discussion above shows that poíētic engagement in human communication makes way for existential rootedness in addition to existential self-expansion. Frankl and his fellow prisoners were able to reroot themselves and to dwell together even in brief moments in the concentration camp through creative-communicative interactions. Despite all challenges, Miner was able to continue rerooting herself toward accomplishing her mission as she created her whole life around it. Neither Miner nor Frankl and his friends dismissed their "partnership with existence itself" (Arnett 2013, 63) even when the conditions of life were miserable and inhumane. Questioning, wondering, contemplating, finding humor and beauty, and distanciation allowed for continued exploring of hermeneutic possibilities that allowed for dwelling meaningfully in the worst of conditions.

The next section focuses on Anna-Teresa Tymieniecka's *Phenomenology of Life* that highlights the human being as a *homo creator* that is connected to the web of life and situated in the unity-of-everything-that-is-alive. Tymieniecka (2000) sees cognition as a "specific modality of human creative genius" and the creative act as an energy that pushes the limits of the human cognitive grasp allowing us to directly participate in the progress of life and of the universe (189). Using the creative act as the entry point in exploring the human condition, Tymieniecka's *Phenomenology of Life* focuses on the workings of life in and through the human being and further textures the discussion on the poíētic function of human sense-making and acting in the world.

THE HUMAN CREATIVE FUNCTION IN THE "PHENOMENOLOGY OF LIFE" OF ANNA-TERESA TYMIENIECKA: THE PASSIONS OF THE EARTH, THE PASSION FOR PLACE, AND "MAN'S SELF-INTERPRETATION-IN-EXISTENCE"

In her discussion of the creative function of the human being, Tymieniecka (1988) highlights imaginatio creatrix as "the means, *par excellence*, of specific human freedom; that is, freedom to go beyond the framework of the *life-world*, the freedom of man to surpass himself" (26). Tymieniecka places the human creative imagination as the focal point of phenomenological inquiry and the *homo creator* as "the living being with *the-unity-of-everything-there-is-alive*" (Tymieniecka 2004, xii). The creative act emerges out of a dissatisfaction of the human being, the "*human-being-in-conflict*" with the present state of things, with the reality that "the present phase of the constituted world" offers (Tymieniecka 1988, 26–27). Through her creative participation in the world, the human being is able to go beyond a submissive absorption with survival only—animality—and transform the already existing conditions giving them new form and meaning. Thus, the creative function distinguishes the human being from the animal, and it is to be recognized "as a basis of the fundamental human condition . . . that *to be human means to be creative*" (26).

In *The Creative Act as the Point of Phenomenological Access to the Human Condition*, Tymieniecka (1988) states that in privileging cognition and cognitive constructivism, classical phenomenology—including Husserlian and post-Husserlian phenomenology—while making an extraordinary contribution to our knowledge of the givenness of man, limited a "radical investigation of the universe of *human existence in the unity of all*" (6). Tymieniecka (1988) proposes a larger phenomenological framework that aims to expand and unite the focus on the *constitutive function* of rational consciousness in classical phenomenology with the *creative function* of the human functioning system that "reaches deeper into the nature of man's complete functioning" (344). The human creative process is attentive to all the "voices of sense" including the moral, aesthetic/poetic, and the intellectual, with the aim of "revealing the *creative orchestration of man's self-interpretation-in-existence*" (17).

Tymieniecka (2001) highlights the "passions of the soul" (1) that originate as an aesthetic response to the elementary conditions of existence—including light, air, the sea, soil, place—which have a vital role in investigating a "specifically human significance of life" (1) at the deepest level. In her essays titled *The Triumph of Imagination in the New Critique of Reason* (2004) and, *The Passions of the Earth* (2001), Tymieniecka explains that with the great advances of science and technology, humanity has acquired an enormous amount of knowledge and mastered more and more conditions of life; however, the pace of technological progress has also disoriented contemporary human beings who are "breathlessly trying to adjust to these transformations" (Tymieniecka 2004, xi). Furthermore, "Old visions of the 'whole' that we humans had entertained and within which we felt englobed like a butterfly in a chrysalis have collapsed. We feel estranged from previously familiar surroundings. We feel uprooted as if thrown into thin air, incapable of finding our bearings and our compass" (Tymieniecka 2001, 1). In this disoriented state, Tymieniecka (2001) explains that it becomes crucial to inquire into the deepest sphere of human functioning that takes into consideration the human condition in relation to the most elemental ties that sustain us within the unity-of-everything-that-is-alive. The "elements" stated in the paragraph above inspire generative and vital passions that Tymieniecka (1990; 2001) refers to as the "passions of the soul" in connection to the human realm. These passions that emerge as a response to the elements of nature-life facilitate the distillation of the human significance of life. Tymieniecka (1990) terms the meeting place of the life-promoting elements of existence and the human universe the "subliminal sphere" (xi). The interplay between the elements and the passions of the soul takes place in the subliminal sphere of functioning where creative imagination takes the lead. In this subliminal sphere, the human being attends and responds to the elementary factors "by drawing them into and through the networks of imagination creatrix" and "transmutes the wild numb strivings that blindly strike out when vitally provoked into aim-oriented, concentrated powers that initiate and actuate elevated human endeavor" (Tymieniecka 1990, xi). It is through the "passions of the soul" in response to the elements of existence that culture originates.

In the following, I focus on two of the "elemental passions" that Tymieniecka discusses; the passions of the earth and the passion for place that texture the prior discussion on communicative engagement, poíēsis, and existential rootedness.

The Passions of the Earth

Tymieniecka (2001) states that "the silencing of the passions and the atrophying of our existential roots and tentacles that bring to us the power of life-promoting passions of the earth" is "the crucial weakness of our present day human predicament" (12). In the following, I discuss rootedness and the passion for "grounding" as part of Tymieniecka's framework of the main spheres of the passions of the earth.

As human beings we have an essential bond with the earthly existential conditions whether we realize it or not. Tymieniecka (2001) explains that before we realize that the earth upon which we walk is a planet positioned in space among other planets we develop a deep and mute familiarity with it. It is through the interplay of our humanly experience of existence and the earthly conditions that our passions of the earth emerge. We establish ties with the soil, climatic conditions, and magnetic field of the mother earth and root ourselves in the "womb of life" (Tymieniecka 2001, 5). Thus, *rootedness* is one of the main spheres of the passions of the earth in Tymieniecka's phenomenology of life, which reminds us "we are not suspended in a void, within undifferentiated matter. Nor are we abandoned to ourselves in a neutral medium" (Tymieniecka 2001, 4). Rather, we "throw hooks" upon the earth that supports our existential condition and rise out of that life-promoting ground.

A related passion for the earth that Tymieniecka (2001) discusses is the *passion for grounding*, which is connected to our direct contact with the earth, the solid ground that the earth offers upon which we walk and to which we can rely on. Our experience of living "upon" the earth where we walk, build, dwell, plant crops, dig up minerals and stones creates an inner impression that consists of mental concepts, meanings, tendencies that are significant for human life. We are able to assume and rely on a solid ground on which we can exist, work, and build a dwelling that offers us a sense of solidity.

The Passion for Place

Tymieniecka's (1995) exploration of the elemental passion for place relates to the efforts made by the human being who "seeks to establish and fortify his/her foothold in existence . . . among other beings within the space of the natural, social cultural fabric of existence" (ix). Tymieniecka (1995) places the aesthetic sense of the human condition at the center of the passion for place for in addition to its role in situating the human being in the vast network of life, the passion for place simultaneously mediates the spacing and individualizing functions of life in the human universe, which will be explained in the following section. She explains that at the same time with seeking to situate itself, the human being looks for expanding its spacing toward transformative freedom, which characterizes the "specifically human 'style' of dwelling upon the planet earth" (Tymieniecka 1995, ix). "We attach ourselves to a 'place' in order to long to leave it. . . . We have to be chained in order to shake ourselves free" (x).

Tymieniecka (2000) draws attention to the contradictory relation between the human being and its sphere of existence—its territory, its soil—suggested by such expressions as "inhabiting the earth" or "dwelling upon the earth" as if the human being and earth *"were two separate spheres, the one of individual life, the other of an indifferent 'entity,' a planet. It is as if the living being could also inhabit or dwell elsewhere, on some other planet, in an unknown neutral sphere"* (409). Tymieniecka states that these expressions—juxtapositions—raise some basic questions of life regarding "life's foundation, grounding, elementary conditions, on the one side, and its most complex manifestation, freedom from them, on the other" (409). This is an essential point in Tymieniecka's exploration of the "human passion for place"; the intricate relation between the need for grounding, to have a place to establish oneself, and to be free from these conditions. That is, the relation between the movement of rootedness and the movement of liberation.

Tymieniecka's (2000) inquiry into the passion for place starts with the *human experience* of the world where "we envision everything as lying either 'within' or 'around' us; we, living persons, being the 'centers' of these inquiries" (410). In contrast to the postmodern assumption that denounces centralized organization, Tymieniecka (2000) states that in the investigation of the human significance of life and the universe around it, the human being is a "center" around which the world is organized "within the unity-of-everything-that-is-alive" and it is from its center that the "living beingness reaching out establishes its existential realm" which also meets other "centralizing life-processing agencies" along the way (411).

Tymieniecka's discussion of "spacing" highlights the expansion of the living being in situating itself in a place, the spreading of the tentacles of the living being that, on the one hand, stretch to the cosmic laws, and to the specific human sphere on the other. It is through the aesthetic function that the human significance of life expands and "spaces" itself. The aesthetic/creative sense is at the center of Tymieniecka's inquiry into the passion for place. Through the "human aestheticizing function of our experience" we create the places we call "home," the human nest (Tymieniecka, 2000, 420).

Tymieniecka writes about the "human nest" distinguishing it from the nest of animals as being "more than a place to be nurtured or to seek retreat from danger, cold, tempest, etc." (2000, 418). For animals, Tymieniecka explains, the nest is a place for protection and growth where "the animal family keeps mutually 'warm'" and it is abandoned until the conditions such as inclement weather necessitates its reconstruction (419). The human nest on the other hand "is an enduring reality for the human being who unfolds from within a much vaster area of meaning, of existential self-interpretation-in-existence.

The human being makes its nest 'for keeps,' does not abandon it after seasonal use, or use it intermittently" (419).

For the human being, the nest-home is a long-term ground upon and through which the meaning of its being is constructed. *The human nest is not just a physical space but also an existential ground for building a life.* The nest-home of a human being is an aesthetic interpretation of its existence and a "spacing" of its experience that allows for self-expansion and expression (Tymieniecka 2000, 419). The "aesthetic atmosphere of the home" involves objects and materials that human beings surround themselves with and reflects attitudes, habits, tendencies, tastes, morals, and preferences of the self (420). It is a place where "we surround ourselves with all that we enjoy, where we retreat to refuel, to find repose, security, healing . . . a place for intimacy . . . one to relish and share with others" (419). Thus, the human nest-home is not a neutral space but it is "'marked' as a special place by the natural unfolding of the individual's functioning." In short, "nature's nest aestheticized by the human being becomes his home" (419).

As we can see from the quotes above, Tymieniecka highlights the aestheticizing function in the human experience in relation to the human being's passion for place and in the building of the human home. The human "passion for place" transforms the animal instinct to build a nest for shelter and comfort toward "the working out of our very own interpretation of existence, for finding a place to anchor our very own means, talents, desires in the fully creative crystallization of the Human Condition . . . to get our bearings within life's expanse" (Tymieniecka 2000, 420). It is through our connection with a place that we establish our grounding, physically, existentially, and aesthetically. The connection to a place is the most powerful passion of the soul in Tymieniecka's discussion.

Reconnecting back to our earlier discussion on poiēsis, dwelling, and existential rootedness in relation to Frankl's account of his experiences in Nazi concentration camps, which are strategically designed to cut the prisoners off from any connections to any life-promoting elements, Tymieniecka's (1995; 2000; 2001) discussion of the passions for the earth—rootedness and grounding—and the passion for place offers insight. It shows how deeply human beings are interwoven with their surroundings and demonstrates the importance of existential ground for human life.

Disconnected from the passions for the earth and passion for place in their uprooted state, the prisoners in the concentration camps lost the "why" for their lives. They experienced a "provisional existence" (Frankl 1984, 91) not knowing when or whether they might be released, with no future goals, no connection to their surroundings outside of the camp, and no connection to their families or friends. Not having a future and not having a goal in life resulted in feelings of lifelessness and loss of meaningfulness for most: "I have nothing to expect from life anymore" (Frankl 1984, 98) was a common theme that got expressed before giving up on one's life. The loss of the passion for place, the connection to life that offers a "why," loss of a sense of orientation and meaning also resulted in the loss of the person, spiritually first, and then physically.

In addition to the examples offered earlier that illustrate reconnecting with the passions of the earth and place even for brief moments, such as appreciating the beauty of the sunset with others for a few moments (passions of the earth) or contemplating the image of a beloved one (passion for place/earth) that allowed Frankl to find meaning, faith, and strength, one final example stands out in relation to the discussion on the passions for the earth and place. It shows how one female prisoner was able to recover the essential bond with life in the miserable conditions of a concentration camp through her receptiveness to the life of a tree branch with two blossoms that she could see from the window of her hut. It is through her connection to this tree that she was able to maintain her existential ground and her "inner hold" (Frankl 1984, 90). Frankl writes about his encounter with this young woman who knew that she would die soon but who was cheerful and expressed her gratefulness for her fate in her conversation with Frankl. She explained to Frankl about her spiritual growth in the camp and her relation to the chestnut tree she befriended—her only friend:

> "I often talk to this tree," she said to me. I was startled and didn't quite know how to take her words. Was she delirious? Did she have occasional hallucinations? Anxiously I asked her if the tree replied. "Yes." What did it say to her? She answered, "It said to me, 'I am here—I am here—I am life, eternal life.'" (Frankl 1984, 90)

As part of the discussion on the passions for the earth, it was discussed that we establish ties with the earthly existential conditions and root ourselves in the "womb of life" (Tymieniecka 2001, 5). We "throw hooks" upon the earth that supports our existential condition and rise out of that life-promoting ground. Responding to the life of the tree, this young woman supported herself, strengthening the connection to life in herself, and she could dwell in this existential ground. She could maintain a "foothold in existence" (Tymieniecka 1995, ix) through connecting to the "eternal" life in and through the tree. Not only she was able to root herself, to draw strength and spiritual nourishment and create a place she could dwell, but she was also able to free herself from the life-destroying conditions around her by connecting to the eternity of life. Earlier under the discussion of the passion for place, it was stated that the aesthetic/creative sense is at the center of Tymieniecka's (2000) inquiry into the passion for place and that it is through the human aestheticizing function that human life expands and "spaces" itself interpreting its self in existence. The role of the aesthetic sense in facilitating the existential self-interpretation of the human being and transcendence of the limiting external conditions of life can be seen in the story of the young prisoner above. The way in which a prisoner in the concentration camp responded to the external circumstances of camp life and took up his or her suffering is part of the aesthetic function of human life through which one created the meaning of life and made choices about how to suffer and what to make of suffering. Frankl (1984) explains that the way a prisoner took up his suffering "gives him ample opportunity—even under the most difficult circumstances—to add a deeper meaning to his life. . . . Here lies the chance for a man either to make use of or to forgo the opportunities of attaining the moral values that a difficult situation may afford him. And this decides whether he is worthy of his sufferings or not" (88). Frankl's statement connects the aesthetic sense to the moral sense in terms of the interpretation of suffering as part of life and as one's fate that one responds to. In the experience of Frankl and a few other prisoners, turning suffering into a task, into a responsibility to suffer with dignity became their anchor.

Tymieniecka (2000, 420) states that "our outlook on life, our bents and attitudes, our very personality contribute to the "aesthetic atmosphere" of the home; a home breathes and exhales an aesthetic atmosphere." The creative-communicative practices discussed in this essay including sharing humor in the midst of desolation, enjoying the beauty of nature together, contemplating and conversing with the image of a loved one or a tree, allowed the prisoners to reconnect with the passions of the earth and the passion for place which enabled them to orient and anchor themselves even for brief moments, to have some contribution to the "aesthetic atmosphere" of their "provisional existence," and to "suffer with dignity" maintaining their "inner hold" rather than passively vegetating and giving in. Tymieniecka's (2004) *Phenomenology of Life* contributes to our understanding of the human condition through its consideration of the human being as a *homo creator* that is connected to the web of life situated in the unity-of-everything-that-is-alive. Furthermore, by exploring the passions of the soul that complements the intellective functioning of the human being on earth, Tymieniecka expands the ways in which we approach human sense-making and her existential self-interpretation in the world. Over and over again, through the examples of Miner's and Frankl's life stories, we have seen that the poiētic function allows human beings to reroot themselves in the midst of disorienting and terrifying external conditions, and to create a response that open up possibilities for being and dwelling that liberate self and others (even momentarily).

Implications for Aesthetic Ecology of Communication Ethics

At the beginning of this chapter, I highlighted Arneson's (2014) discussion of multiple modalities of meaning as part of communicative engagement, stating that the aesthetic (poíētic) sense of meaning works together with the moral and the intellective functions. Through an exploration of Miner's and Frankl's life experiences, I showed that engaging the poíētic sense of meaning in relation to one's lived, felt experience allows for existential rootedness that anchors human beings in the large container of life beyond the individual and offers a sense of connection that guides people in relation to the "why" of their lives.

As part of the aesthetic ecology framework I presented in the introduction, John Dewey's (1958) discussion of aesthetic experience underlines the struggles and undergoings of human beings in everyday life in an attempt to adjust to their surroundings. Dewey highlights the deep, intimate connection of the living being with its environment and its condition of being exposed. Aesthetic experience emerges in one's orientation and attentiveness to the present that is part of the continuum of the past and the future. Miner's and Frankl's experiences illustrate Dewey's discussion of the art of living beyond the ordinary struggles of everyday life and in the midst of inhumane conditions. Not knowing if he could survive in the next moment, or what awaited him and other prisoners, Frankl turned toward what life offered him in the desolate conditions of the concentration camp—suffering—and made choices about how to suffer and what to make of his suffering. He chose to participate in and respond to the experiences that were violently imposed upon him, and his presence and response allowed him to stay rooted, existentially and aesthetically. Miner's deep felt meanings against human slavery empowered her to keep exploring ways in which she could create a life-promoting space for the education of young black women in the midst of structures that normalized and perpetuated the practice of slavery. The life experiences of Miner and Frankl powerfully illustrate how the ways in which we attend to and participate in the present, through "belonging together" (Gadamer 2007, 311), that integrate the sensible and the intelligible, lead to the emergence of the aesthetic.

Arnett, Fritz, and Bell (2009) connect communication ethics to communicative practices through which one seeks to protect and promote that which matters—the good—in a historical moment. Beyond a fixed understanding of what is right or wrong, the "good" refers to "a central value or set of values manifested in communicative practices that we seek to protect and promote in our discourse together" (2). Multiplicity of goods that are competing is a defining characteristic of the postmodern historical moment that we live in. Arneson's (2014) discussion on the poíētic engagement of life as part of theoria-praxis that is essential to human communication is part of the goods that are central to this chapter. Creative-communicative practices in the experiences of Miner and Frankl allowed for cultivating and maintaining rootedness in destructive external structures. This chapter emphasizes poiētic/aesthetic function of communication as a good to be protected and promoted as part of the reasoning arts of theoria-poiēsis-praxis. As stated earlier, *disconnected from the creative force of poiēsis, theoria-praxis function to narrow down the ways in which we interpret and create social worlds and can easily result in the creation and legitimation of social structures that violate the dignity of human life and in destruction.*

Furthermore, existential rootedness as a good is discussed in a couple different ways throughout the chapter. One is highlighted through Frankl's quote: *"We knew that we had nothing to lose except our so ridiculously naked lives"* (Frankl 1984, 33–34; italics added). At the most concrete level, existential rootedness can be seen as the nakedness of being alive, just being alive, and our efforts and struggles to maintain it on an everyday basis. Basically, we all work to maintain our own *ridiculously naked lives*, nothing less nothing more. Frankl's narratives serve as reminders of this fact, this existential connection, that most usually forget or ignore. Awareness of preciousness and nakedness of life, no matter what form, color, or shape, can serve as an anchor in attending to life beyond limited and destructive ways, and poiēsis plays a significant role in this.

Another way in which existential rootedness is discussed as a good in this chapter is through Tymieniecka's (1995; 2000; 2001) discussion of the passions for the earth—rootedness and grounding—and the passion for place that shows how deeply human beings are connected to the life-promoting elements of the earth, and how this connectedness becomes part of the human creative process in facilitating *"man's self-interpretation-in-existence"* (Tymieniecka 1988, 17). It is through the passions of the earth and place that human beings orient and anchor themselves in the network of existence and create a dwelling, a home. The poiētic function is at the heart of the human being's passion for place and in the building of the human home (Tymieniecka 2000) and facilitates existential rootedness not only physically but also spiritually and morally.

Tymieniecka (2000) highlights the moral sense, the extension toward the other, as a function of the poiētic/aesthetic sense. She locates the roots of the moral sense in the subliminal realm of the passions that emerge from the depths of the human soul. The "passional promptings" have diverse tendencies that can be oppositional such as sharing–holding back, attracting–repelling, generosity–greed, and so forth, which requires a harmonizing principle (370). In Tymieniecka's (2000) *Logos and Life*, this harmonizing principle in the system of the "individual human-self-in-its-world-of-life" is the moral sense (373). The harmonizing principle functions to balance the inner passions as well as the internal tendencies and the external world. It is through the harmonizing of the inner and the outer that the "awareness of the self-in-its-world-of-life" (Tymieniecka 2000, 438) emerges.

With the release of the moral sense, three transformational moments take place in the life of the individual: the recognition of the "experience-of-oneself-and-the-other" (532), the attribution of equivalence to the other in the sharing of the vital significance of life (equivalence of the rights of the other), and the "*gesture*" as the action that transcends itself, the "*trans-action*" (532). Trans-action indicates a transgression of the individuals who enter into it, which opens out to societal sharing in life and through which the individual becomes fully human. To be capable of entering into a constructive trans-action with others in a way that is sensitive to the needs, sufferings, and feelings of others, human beings need to maintain an inner balance of attitudes, reactions, and opposing tendencies. Sharing-in-life with others is "always in the hands of individual persons" (Tymieniecka 2000, 590) beyond institutional rules and regulations, laws and the government.

> If the person who is expected to perform such or other function in the care and distribution of services and goods to people is not adequately balanced and sensitively attuned to the needs, joys, sufferings of others while at the same time capable of overcoming reactions of personal revulsion, antipathy, real misgivings, discouragement, apathy, loss of heart, or just laziness, no laws or institutions will be able to secure an honest sharing-in-life for their tutees. (Tymieniecka 2000, 590)

As we see from the long quote above, moral sense as the harmonizing principle is at the heart of constructive trans-action with others, and this harmonizing principle is a good to be protected and promoted along with the poiētic sense that drives it. Along these lines, Arnett, Fritz, and Bell (2009) highlight that "communication ethics does not live in codes and principles, but in the willingness of communicators to show up for the communicative task of protecting and promoting a given good" (6). The willingness of communicators to show up and attend to what matters—the moral sense—is a good that is to be protected and promoted and which is supported and facilitated by the interrelated goods of poiētic/aesthetic function of communication and existential rootedness.

REFERENCES

Allport, Gordon. 1984. Preface to Viktor E. Frankl, *Man's Search for Meaning: An Introduction to Logotherapy*, 3rd ed. Translated by Ilse Lasch. New York: Pocket Books, 1984.

Agamben, Giorgio. 1999. *The Man Without Content*. Translated by Georgia Albert. Stanford, CA: Stanford University Press.

Arneson, Pat. 2012. "A Creative Turning: Communicative Participation in Tymieniecka's Logos of Life." *Empedocles: European Journal for the Philosophy of Communication* 4(2): 153–67. doi:10.1386/ejpc.4.2.153_1.

———. 2014. *Communicative Engagement and Social Liberation: Justice Will Be Made*. Teaneck, NJ: Fairleigh Dickinson University Press.

Arnett, Ronald C. 2013. *Communication Ethics in Dark Times: Hannah Arendt's Rhetoric of Warning and Hope*. Carbondale: Southern Illinois University Press.

Arnett, Ronald C., Janie Harden Fritz, and Leeanne Bell. 2009. *Communication Ethics Literacy: Dialogue and Difference*. Los Angeles: Sage Publications.

Barrows, Anita, and Joanna Macy. 2009. *A Year with Rilke: Daily Readings from the Best of Rainer Maria Rilke*. New York: Harper Collins.

———. 2016. *In Praise of Mortality: Selections from Rainer Maria Rilke's Duino Elegies and Sonnets to Orpheus*. Brattleboro, VT: Echo Point Books & Media.

Dewey, John. 1958. *The Art of Experience*. New York: Capricorn Books.

Frankl, Viktor E. 1984. *Man's Search for Meaning: An Introduction to Logotherapy*, 3rd ed. Translated by Ilse Lasch. New York: Pocket Books.

Fritz, Janie M. Harden. 2013. *Professional Civility: Communicative Virtue at Work*. New York: Peter Lang.

Frost, Robert, David Bradley, and Dewitt Jones. 1979. *Robert Frost, a Tribute to the Source*. New York: Henry Holt & Company.

Gadamer, Hans Georg. 2007. "The Universality of the Hermeneutical Problem." In *The Gadamer Reader*, edited by R. E. Palmer, 72–88. Evanston, IL: Northwestern University Press.

Hammarskjöld, Dag. *Markings*. 1966. Translated by Lief Sjoberg and W. H. Auden. New York: Knopf.

Keats, John. 1951. Letter 32 in *Selected Letters of John Keats*. New York: Farrar, Straus and Young.

Ramsey, Ramsey Eric. 1988. *The Long Path to Nearness: A Contribution to a Corporeal Philosophy of Communication and the Groundwork for an Ethics of Relief*. Amherst, NY: Humanity Books.

Schrag, Calvin, O. 1969. *Experience and Being: Prolegomena to a Future Ontology*. Evanston, IL: Northwestern University Press.

Tymieniecka, Anna-Teresa, ed. 1983. "The Moral Sense: A Discourse on the Phenomenological Foundation of the Social World and of Ethics," in A-T. Tymieniecka (ed.) *Analecta Husserliana: The Yearbook of Phenomenological Research* 15, 3–78.

———, ed. 1988. *Logos and Life: Creative Experience and the Critique of Reason: Introduction to the Phenomenology of Life and the Human Condition. Analecta Husserliana: The Yearbook of Phenomenological Research* 24.

———, ed. 1990. *Poetics of the Elements in the Human Condition. Part 3: The Elemental Passions of the Soul. Analecta Husserliana: The Yearbook of Phenomenological Research* 28.

———, ed. 1995. *The Elemental Passion for Place in the Ontopoiesis of Life: Passions of the Soul in the Imaginatio Creatrix. Analecta Husserliana: The Yearbook of Phenomenological Research* 44.

———, ed. 2000. *Logos and Life. Analecta Husserliana: The Yearbook of Phenomenological Research* 70.

———, ed. 2001. *Passions of the Earth in Human Existence, Creativity, and Literature. Analecta Husserliana: The Yearbook of Phenomenological Research* 71.

———, ed. 2004. "The Triumph of Imagination in the New Critique of Reason", in A-T. Tymieniecka (ed.) *Analecta Husserliana: The Yearbook of Phenomenological Research* 83, 11-18.

Chapter Two

The "Weight" of Meaning

This chapter explores Jean-Luc Nancy's (1997a, 1997b) discussion of sense that resists the enclosure and appropriation of meaning within a system of signification that serves its own agenda. "There is today an imperious, strident demand to stop surrendering meaning, without further ado, to signification" (Nancy 1997a, 65). Nancy (1997a) highlights the emergence of meaning not through the process of signification but at the limit of signification through exposure. The exposure to exteriority maintains the necessary opening that suspends signification and allows meaning to "weigh." It is this concept of weight that I connect to the discussion of existential rootedness in this chapter since what weighs is the excess of meaning, the surplus, in other words, the "simplicity of existence" (Nancy 1997a, 81); the joy and the tears, the turbulence, and trembling. . . . The existence of our being—its exposedness—involves being in *touch* with the sense of the world where signification is suspended, or "ruptured" (Nancy 1997a, 59). It is this *in-touchness* as exposure to existence that breaks open the absorption and closure of meaning, and that allows the ongoing arrival of meaning without completion that I connect to being rooted in existence.

In the following, I first explore Nancy's (1997a, 1997b) discussion of sense and weight of meaning as exposure. For Nancy, sense is possible only as a relation to something outside, in a "*being-to* relation" (Nancy 1997b, 7) that resists the closure of meaning. The weight of meaning resists completion and appropriation. Furthermore, Nancy (2003) questions and rejects the idea of an originary self that precedes exposure to existence and proposes the "singular plural" constitution of being, which I explore as the second main point in this chapter (under the section "Being Singular Plural and 'Coessentiality'"). Third, I discuss Nancy's (2008) conceptualization of the body as an "open space" (15) or "a space that opens" (17) and as a place of existence. As the final section of this chapter, I offer a phenomenological reflection of *reading* Jean-Luc Nancy that illustrates the discussion on the weight of meaning. Through this reflective analysis I show that the weight of meaning moves the oscillating dynamic between "presence- and meaning-based relations" (Gumbrecht 2004, 107) with the things of the world (that was discussed in the introduction chapter as part of the aesthetic ecology framework). Three main phenomenological themes that emerge in the analysis of reading Nancy include (1) reading as interruption; (2) reading as suspension, dwelling, becoming; and (3) reading as weighing. I conclude by stating that *reading as weighing* is an embodied exposure to exteriority—in this case, the text—rather than an isolated weighing of ideas in the mind. In this sense, reading is to let oneself "simply exist," to be exposed, to be displaced, and to coappear with the text, which I highlight as *aesthetics of reading*.

SENSE, BEING-*TO*, AND THE WEIGHT OF MEANING

In *The Sense of the World*, Nancy (1997b) states that "the women and men of our time have, indeed, a rather sovereign way of losing their footing without anxiety" (2). The ironic paradox in this sentence points to a serious issue in the lives of modern men and women who work hard to find *existential traction* by constantly and anxiously busying themselves, and whose lack of presence have become the default of life. Nancy further states that today we are beyond a "crisis of sense" that was still possible to speak about not long ago. Today, "all sense has been abandoned" and "it is precisely this exposition to the abandonment of sense that makes up our lives" (Nancy 1997b, 2). And, Nancy adds, *"This makes us a little faint"* (2; italics added).

Nancy's project in underlying the "abandonment of sense," is a critique of Western philosophical thought that is caught up in and enclosed within a system—or, "regime" (1997b, 5)—of significations that appropriates meaning and serves its own agenda. It is this closure of meaning, the circular movement of thinking that returns back to itself that Nancy problematizes, thus announcing the *"end of the sense of the world,* which is the *end of the world of sense* in which we had—and still have, day by day—all the points of reference we need in order to continue to manage our significations" (5). One way to respond to this loss of sense, according to Nancy, is to give way to the demand for and the expectation of sense, which sets "fearful traps" to provide some reassurance such as identity, security, and certainty. "Those who give way to the demand for sense . . . demand of the world that it signify itself as dwelling, haven, habitation, safeguard, intimacy, community, subjectivity" (Nancy 1997b, 3). But this approach does not give a chance for sense other than circling back the "regime of signification" (5) that is already available to us and within which we are enclosed.

For Nancy, sense is possible only as a relation to something outside/other, "elsewhere," so that it maintains a necessary opening. Sense exists only in a *being-to* relation, "as *being-toward*-something, this something evidently always being 'something *other*' or 'something *else*'" (1997b, 7). Without this opening, there is no sense. Nancy explains that the other response to the "*end of the sense of the world*" is to attend to this loss without necessarily re-creating further significations that appropriate, recapture, and close off meaning (1997b, 5). For Nancy, what arises at the exhaustion of signification is not a communication of meaning but *being exposed to meaning*, which "borders the meaning of significations in all discourse" (1997a, 57). Nancy brings our attention to the world of meaning before and beyond all the production of meaning, meaning at the level of our existence, which does not have signification by itself. "Before all exchanges of meaning, our existence presents itself to us as meaning" (1997a, 62). Nancy offers discussion of our exposure to the world through our senses, feeling pleasure, pain, and love; exposure to language, to space, to atrocities, which is not a matter of signification but "meaning at the limit of signification" (1997a, 58). The existence of our being—its exposedness—involves being in *touch* with the sense of the world where signification is suspended, or "ruptured" (59). This exposure to meaning without returning to signification takes place at the limit of signification, which is where one cannot settle down, or appropriate meaning. "One must always let the limit present itself anew, and it always presents itself anew" (Nancy 1997a, 67). To wonder as a philosophical virtue and act today, according to Nancy, is being exposed to meaning at the limit, without being able to hold onto a system of signification. Wondering and contemplating this "opening of meaning or the opening to meaning" (Nancy 1997a, 65), thought needs to be "passible" (69) to meaning, to receive and undergo the act of meaning, "being capable of receiving the shock of meaning" (70).

Why the "shock of meaning" one might wonder? Being exposed to meaning, which "always has the sense of the noncompleted, nonfinished, of the yet-to-come," is to be exposed to "meaning as the event of an opening" (Nancy 1997a, 78). It is an exposure to that which cannot be closed, completed, or appropriated. As Raffoul states in the preface to *Gravity of Thought*, "This exposure to an inappropriable is understood by Nancy in terms of materiality under the names of 'weight,' 'heaviness,' or 'gravity.' What *weighs* is precisely this inappropriable, the impact or the shock that the event of meaning imparts to thought. . . . It is the exposure to the inappropriable limits of signification that weighs upon thought" (Nancy 1997a, xxvii). So the "shock of meaning" is the "weight of meaning" that thought weighs.

Undergoing the event of meaning is a weighing, and as Raffoul (in Nancy 1997a) puts it, a "suffering" (xvii). *What the thought cannot appropriate weighs*; it is the excess of meaning. And to wonder is to let go of the habit of appropriation, and "working toward a *letting*" (Nancy 1997a, 81), letting existence resist the appropriation of thought, and *"having weight at the heart of and in spite of thought: of being the breast, the belly, the guts of thought"* (81; emphasis added). The weight of thought as the breast, the belly, the guts of thought, interrupts appropriation. The breast, the belly, the guts of thought is inappropriable and it weighs. What weighs is the excess, the extension, the "ex-scription" that cannot be absorbed into signification (Nancy 1997a, 79). Nancy tells us,

> Meaning needs a thickness, a density, a mass, and thus an opacity, a darkness by means of which it leaves itself open and lets itself be touched *as meaning* right there where it becomes absent as discourse. Now, this "there" is a material point, a weighty point: the flesh of a lip, the point of a pen or of a stylus, any writing insofar as it traces out the interior and exterior edges of language. It is the point where all writing is *ex-scribed*, where it comes to rest outside of the meaning it inscribes, in the things whose inscription this meaning is supposed to form. (1997a, 79)

Right at the point where meaning becomes absent as discourse it comes to presence as a weighty, material, thickness. This weighty "place" or "location" is at the edge of language; it is the outside of inscribed meaning. Meaning emerges not through the process of signification but at the limit of signification, in touch with a weighty exteriority where signification is held back. Nancy refers to this process as a "letting," letting meaning weigh, and the "letting-come of existence" (Nancy 1997a, 81). And he asks, "Are we (we who keep saying to ourselves that we arrive so late, so much at the *end*), in the end, going to let ourselves be presented with this constantly renewed gravity? Are we—with difficulty and serenity—going to let ourselves simply exist?" (82). To let ourselves exist is to be presented with the weight of meaning beyond signified meaning. It is to be exposed to exteriority that is inappropriable and to "simply exist."

To be exposed to the "simplicity of existence" (81), to the joy and the tears, to its turbulence, thickness, trembling. . . . We are presented with the weight, the excess of meaning that is constantly renewed in and through this exposure without closing the "event of meaning" (78). It is through weighing that meaning does not coincide with itself and stays open.

Thus, for Nancy (1997a), meaning is an "event of opening" and "always has the sense of the noncompleted, nonfinished, of the yet-to-come, and in general of the *to*" (78). The "–to relation" is at the heart of Nancy's (1997a) discussion of meaning, sense, and being which creates a spacing, an opening that resists a tautology of meaning and/or being. Being –to or –toward maintains the distance of otherness that is essential for the existence of sense. As Nancy (2003) puts it, "Sense depends on relating to itself as to another or to some other" (6). Nancy's own experience of going through a heart transplant discussed below is illustrative.

In *The Intruder*, Jean-Luc Nancy (2000b) wrote about his experience when his heart failed and he needed a heart transplant. He felt the presence of his heart when it failed, which initially was "as absent as the soles of my feet while walking" (162). Until that point, his heart was familiar, and thus, absent, not sensed. Nancy writes: "Up to this point, it was strange by virtue of not being even perceptible, not even being present. From now on it fails, and this strangeness binds me to myself" (163). Before his heart failed, it was a "stranger" due to its familiarity. It was through the interruption of the imperceptible connection he had with his heart that Nancy actually realized the presence of his heart, when his own heart became a stranger to him, an "intruder." This strangeness connected him *to* himself, his heart was no longer absent. Nancy found himself exposed, intruded, separated from the familiar, and yet in touch through this separation and estrangement. It is this distance of otherness that allows for contact (which will be further discussed later in the chapter) and sense. As Nancy put it, "Sense is the openness of a relation *to* itself" (Nancy 2003, 6) where the *to* "is first and foremost the fissure, the gap, the spacing of an opening" (7) that resists the reabsorption of sense. This resistance of sense to appropriation through the opening created by the relation of being –towards is at the heart of Nancy's radical ontology.

In *A Finite Thinking* Nancy (2003) writes about being as a "being-to-the -self" (7).

> Through the spacing of the *to*, being refuses to come back to itself, it does not coincide itself. There is sense only once this being-to itself no longer belongs to itself, no longer comes back to itself. Only once it *is* this not-coming-back-to itself: this restless refusal to come back to itself in such a way that it does not simply "remain" outside, either in the sense of a lack or in the sense of a surplus, but as itself the *to* of being to itself, the open of its openness. (8)

Sense depends on nonclosure; it exists only when an opening is maintained. Nancy refers to this opening as a relation of "*to* itself," where the *to* is the spacing. Sense of being then is a being-to or being-to-the-self and not just being. The self that is to-itself is open; it cannot be appropriated or reabsorbed; it *is* openness. And nothing lacks or remains outside when being is this open-ended movement, a being-to. Nancy (2003) also highlights that the self that is to-itself does not indicate that there is initially a self that is then opened. "Being *is* open." It is "openness as such" (Nancy 2003, 7).

Groundlessness: The *"Without-Essence* of Existing"

In relation to his discussion of being as "openness as such" Nancy (2003), uses the term "groundlessness" (*Abgrundlichkeit*). Groundlessness refers to "being's reference to nothing, either to a substance or to a subject, not even to 'being,' unless it be *to* a being-to, to itself, to the world as openness, the throw or the being-thrown of *existence*" (9). What Nancy underlines by "groundlessness" is being's relation to exteriority/otherness where being is a being –towards, beyond a fixed ground that closes or appropriates this movement of being (–to). Nancy's project is to push being beyond an essence, or a subject/self-identity that is not exposed to the outside, toward the *"without-essence* of existing" (9). For Nancy, the idea of an originary self that precedes exposure to existence is senseless. Self cannot exist without being-other to itself, or being-to-the-self. Thus, it cannot be completed or reabsorbed. Being exposed to existence weighs and puts itself in excess of any content of signification. Groundlessness, in the framework of Nancy (2003), assures inappropriability of being.

Nancy problematizes a philosophy "of the subject" since the subject is enclosed in-itself and exists for-itself. "There has never been, and never will be, a philosophy 'of the subject' in the sense of the final [*infinite*] closure in itself of a for-itself" (Nancy 2000a, 29). Nancy proposes the "singular plural" constitution of being, which highlights that existence is coexistence of singularites, a being-with where the "with" is not "an addition to some prior Being; instead the 'with' is at the heart of Being" (Nancy 2000a, 30). Nancy questions and critiques the subordination of "being-with" to being throughout the whole history of philosophy including Heidegger's order of discussion where *Mitsein* followed the originary character of *Dasein*. Nancy aims to "reverse the order of ontological exposition" (31), highlighting that philosophy begins with the thinking of being-with. Nancy underlines over and over again that "Being does not preexist its singular plural. To be more precise, being absolutely does not *preexist*; nothing preexists, only what exists exists" (Nancy 2000a, 29). Thus, there is no prior substance or essence of being. Existence is no other than coexistence, it is co-originary. To philosophize about the essence of being for Nancy is to establish co-essentiality as the heart of being, which is discussed further in the next section.

BEING SINGULAR PLURAL AND "CO-ESSENTIALITY"

To begin, the concept of the singular is not to be confused with the individual. The individual is not concerned with the other or the exterior; it is autonomous—an "immanent totality" (Nancy, 2000a, 32) that is perfected without an other. The singular, on the other hand, is "indissociable from its being-with-many" (32) yet distinct from other singularities. Singulars are not enclosed beings, which then "relate" and share to create a commonality. "In its very being, as its very being, singularity is exposed to the outside" (Nancy 1991, 28). The existence of the singular being as exposed, on the limit, is central to Nancy's discussion of singularity. Singular beings are exposed to the outside, to each other, and "co-appear" (Nancy 2000a, 67). Co-appearing "is not a question of coming out from a being-in-itself in order to approach others. . . . It is to be in the simultaneity of being-with, where there is no 'in itself' that is not already immediately 'with'" (67–68). Thus, *singularities are constituted in their exposition and co-appearing*. There is no prior being-in-itself before the co-appearing; therefore, being-with (*Mitsein*) is essentially a "co-essentiality" (30) or a "being-with-the-without" (Nancy and Schuback 2013, 51), *Ohnesein*. That is, being-with is being-without a prior essence. Thus, rather than privileging a discussion of the question of being over being-with, being singular plural highlights being as being-with-one-another, a being-with-many of singularities. The singularity of being then is plural.

Togetherness of Singular Beings: "To Touch without Touching"

The being-with of the singularities, that is, the togetherness of singulars does not take place on the condition of unification or fusion but a "plural unity" (Nancy 2000a, 39), or an "excess of unity" (40). Singular beings are neither in "relation" nor "linked" but they touch. "In the touching, there is no link, there is proximity but no link" (Nancy and Schuback 2013, 15). This proximity of the "with" in being-with-one-another is "the closeness, the brushing up against or the coming across, the almost-there [l'à-peu-près] of distanced proximity" (Nancy 2000a, 98). The proximity of singular beings is to be understood through the distance or the spacing that maintains their singularity.

In *On Touching—Jean-Luc Nancy,* Derrida (2005) states that Nancy's discussion on touch breaks away from the focus in haptocentric discourses toward continuity, indivisibility, and homogeneity. Derrida (2005, 47) highlights "tact" that is essential to the tactile experience: "For there is a *law of tact.* . . . One must touch without touching" (66). To touch without touching: to *regard,* to keep at an attentive distance, "to guard against touching, affecting, corrupting" (67). Singular beings touch with tact, never completely overlapping.

In "Rühren, Berühren, Aufruhr," Nancy (2011) offers discussion on the semantic family of *ruhr* in German that correspond to *move, agitate, touch* in English, highlighting the link in German between movement—physical and emotional—and touch, which he states is missing in the French *toucher* and English *touch*. "To touch sets something in motion. As soon as I approach my body to another body—be it inert, made of wood, stone or metal—I displace the other—be it ever so slightly—and the other displaces me, while holding me in some way." (Nancy 2011, 10) It is this double—and seemingly paradoxical—movement of touch that is a central theme in Nancy's discussion on touch: "No contact without displacement" (Nancy 2008, 57). Entering into contact through the sense of touch is not just a coming together for Nancy but involves a movement of distancing at the same time that makes space for the bodies to distinguish themselves. So the movement of touch is a movement of proximity and distance, since "only a separate body is capable of touching" (Nancy 2011, 11).

The next section on the ontology of being-with as an ontology of bodies highlights Nancy's (2008) conception of the body that expands the traditional Western thought on this matter.

BEING-WITH AS AN ONTOLOGY OF BODIES

In his 2008 book *Corpus,* Nancy questions the long Western philosophical tradition of thinking about the body as something closed up, full, and grounded in itself. Nancy (2008) offers a philosophy of the body as "a space that opens" (17). "Bodies aren't some kind of fullness or filled space (space is filled everywhere): they are open space, implying, in some sense, a space more properly spacious than spatial, what could also be called a place. Bodies are places of existence, and nothing exists without a place" (Nancy 2008, 15). As opposed to the traditional Western conceptualization of the body as a filled space, Nancy highlights that the body is an open, spacious space. Moreover, the body is not just any open space but is a place of existence. As part of his discussion that "the body makes room for existence," Nancy underlines that the body makes room "for the fact that the essence of existence is to be without any essence" (Nancy 2008, 15). The body as a place of existence does not have a substance, essence, or being prior to itself. Rather, "the body is the being of existence" (15). Thus, in *Corpus,* Nancy (2008) establishes the ontology of the body as ontology itself expanding on his discussion in *Being Singular Plural* (2000a), which highlights ontology of being-with as an ontology of bodies, including bodies that are inanimate, animate, speaking, thinking, and *weighing*. So in Nancy's (2008) work there is a return to the concept of weight that I discussed earlier in the chapter based on his (1997a) work discussing the weight of meaning. As part of his ontology of bodies, Nancy (2008) uses the term "weight" in highlighting the exposition of bodies to one another. He highlights that "a body doesn't have a weight: even in medicine, it is a weight. It weighs on, it presses against other bodies, right up against other bodies" (Nancy 2008, 93). Bodies are exposed to one another through their weight. Bodies don't just have weight, nor do they weigh by themselves, but they are weighed by other bodies. In other words, the weight of bodies is extended; "it isn't concentrated 'inside,' within 'itself'" (Nancy 2008, 93–95). The weighing of bodies against each other and the discussion on weight as being extended resonates with the earlier discussion on the body as "a space that opens" (Nancy 2008, 17). It seems that by weighing each other, bodies make space. Rather than being concentrated in themselves and weighing by themselves against gravity, bodies are exposed to each other through weighing against the other, and in doing so they "make room for existence" (Nancy 2008, 15).

Up to this point, based on Nancy's (1997a, 1997b, 2008, 2011) writings on sense, weight of meaning, and the body, I have discussed weighing as (1) the exposition of bodies to one another and (2) the exposition of meaning to exteriority (earlier in the chapter). I now share reflections of my own lived experience of reading Jean-Luc Nancy and show how reading can be seen as an act of "weighing," that is, as a bodily exposure to exteriority—in this case, the text—rather than an isolated weighing of ideas in the mind. I focus on my reading experience first as an *interruption*, next as *suspension and dwelling*, and finally as *weighing*. Based on this analysis, I highlight that reading Nancy has been a journey of being exposed, being displaced, and co-appearing with the text, which I refer to as *aesthetics of reading* in the last part of the chapter.

A PHENOMENOLOGICAL REFLECTION OF READING JEAN-LUC NANCY

In the first chapter of *Writing in the Dark*, van Manen (2003) describes an experience when he was sitting at his keyboard, staring out of the window barely aware what he is doing so, and thinking about some words to finish a text. His son walks into the room and asks him what he was doing to which van Manen responds "I am writing." His son teases him saying that he is just looking out of the window, not writing. This experience makes van Manen wonder when he is actually writing and if there is an actual moment where he can say, "Now.

Now I am writing!" (van Manen 2016, 1). This story is informative in understanding phenomenological research, which aims to examine the meaning of prereflective experience, that is, experience as we live through it.

> Prereflective experience is the ordinary experience that we live in and that we live through for most, if not all, of our day-to-day existence. Whether we are eating a meal, going for a walk, driving a car, gardening, daydreaming, texting a message, hugging a loved one . . . these are all prereflective experiences from a phenomenological point of view. (van Manen 2014, 28)

The examples in the above quote are ordinary, everyday occurrences that are mostly taken for granted, and thus, not paid attention to. In doing phenomenology, one is inspired by a sense of wonder, or a "wondering attentiveness" as van Manen (2005, 36) put it. In the opening story above, van Manen wonders about the writing experience, "when does one actually write?" When fingers are typing on the keyboard or holding the pen and moving it on a page making marks? We realize that phenomenological inquiry of the experience of writing is not focused on the factual occurrence of writing but the "phenomenon" of writing. The phenomenological question in this case could be posed as: "What is the actual *experience of writing* like?" or "How does one live through an actual incidence of writing?" Furthermore, "Phenomenology asks, 'What is the nature, meaning, significance, uniqueness, or singularity of this or that experience as we live through it or as it is given in our experience or consciousness?' 'How does this experience present itself as a distinguishable phenomenon or event?'" (van Manen 2014, 39).

In the introductory story on writing, van Manen wonders about writing as a phenomenon and recollects an experience of writing. He starts to describe writing as seeking and entering a certain kind of space, a textual space—a space of words and a world that opens up through words—where the familiar, personal self retreats or steps back and becomes "'one' who writes" (van Manen 2015, 4). In describing the experience of writing, van Manen connects writing to the experience of reading where one first needs to find a physical space that is conducive to reading and writing, and then enters the textual space through the words. We see that writing as lived experience is more than the moment of typing words or making marks on a page; it is a transformative experience of entering and dwelling in the space of the text where one gains insight and invites the reader to read/write her text as she dwells in that interpretive space.

In the following, I offer a phenomenological account of reading, and specifically my experience of reading some of Jean-Luc Nancy's books. Why a phenomenological inquiry on reading Jean-Luc Nancy? "A phenomenological question may arise any time when we had a certain experience that brings us to pause and reflect" (van Manen 2014, 31). Reading Jean-Luc Nancy's books have been an interruption of my habitual, taken-for-granted ways of reading. In reading Nancy's texts, I experienced disorientation, uncertainty, frustration, resistance, fascination, and most of all, wonder. Being challenged by not having access to the text in ways that I am used to, I became curious: what is this experience?

Van Manen (2005) writes about the sense of wonder—which is different from curiosity—as key to initiating phenomenological research. He states that wonder is "the unwilled willingness to meet what is utterly strange in what is most familiar" (223). Furthermore, "Wonder is the stepping back and let things speak to us, an active-passive receptivity to let things of the world present themselves on their own terms" (223). My initial curiosity about my reading experience was later transformed into wonder, or a "wondering attentiveness" (224), which is part of the phenomenological attitude as well as a basic preparatory element of phenomenological reduction (heuristic reduction). The heuristic reduction in the sense of wonder is a gesture of stepping back from—or suspending, bracketing—the taken-for-grantedness of the phenomenon and awakening to the strangeness of it. The ordinary becomes extraordinary through the sense of wonder.

In addition to bracketing the attitude of taken-for-grantedness in phenomenological inquiry, one needs to be critically aware of and bracket the preunderstandings, preoccupations, assumptions, interpretations, and emotional inclinations that obstruct the actual experience of the phenomenon. This is the hermeneutic reduction, which is a "practice of radical openness" (van Manen 2014, 224) to the phenomenon. In my experience of reading Jean-Luc Nancy's books, bracketing my initial disorientation, frustration, and fascination with the reading experience as it gives itself, and to be in contact with experience as I live it, is part of the hermeneutic reduction process. Furthermore, noticing and suspending one's ideas about being a good/bad, competent/incompetent reader or any judgments about the author is important to maintain openness to the reading experience. Thus, the practice of hermeneutic reduction involves an opening to not knowing rather than privileging the assumption that one knows and waiting attentively until the conceptual and emotional layers clear out and the phenomenon starts to show itself.

Up to this point in this section, I have repeated the term "experience" often as the focal point of phenomenology and highlighted the exploration of prereflective experience as it is lived through in phenomenological research. Van Manen (2005) states that "experience is what presents itself immediately, unmediated by subsequent thought, image, or language. . . . Experience is a kind of immediate awareness that is not (yet) aware of itself" (225). Thus, we are always late in capturing the experience as it is; the moment we are inclined to capture it, the living moment of experience has already passed. Van Manen explains that we can only access experience through thought, image, or language. He further states that it is this impossibility of capturing the present that makes phenomenology so fascinating, necessary, demanding, and a radical approach to the study of life as we experience it. It is the sense of immediacy in describing human experience that is key to phenomenological reflection. "So phenomenology focuses on lived experience, but phenomenological reflection only begins in earnest when it tries to grasp reflectively the lived meanings of this prereflective experience" (van Manen 2014, 226). Accordingly, the third preparatory element of phenomenological reduction is the experiential reduction that aims to bracket and examine all theoretical and abstract meanings or conceptualizations that hide experiential reality (van Manen, 2014). Applied to this study, one might start by bracketing definitions and focus on reading as it is experienced, which I illustrate later through the lived experience descriptions (LED).

Cambridge English Dictionary defines reading as "the skill or activity of getting information from books." The Google definition of reading is to "look at and comprehend the meaning of (written or printed matter) by mentally interpreting the characters or symbols of which it is composed," which highlights visual reception (over tactile reception, for instance) and mental processing. The Foreign Language Teaching Methods site, a professional development resource for foreign language teachers, offers a definition of reading as "a process undertaken to reduce uncertainty about meanings a text conveys" ("Methods, Modules, Reading," https://coerll.utexas.edu/methods/modules/reading/01/). Furthermore, "The process results from a negotiation of meaning between the text and its reader." The site also explains that knowledge, expectations, and strategies a reader uses to uncover textual meaning play an important role in the negotiation of meaning. Some themes emerging based on the three sources above include getting information, mental interpretation and comprehension of meaning, and reducing uncertainty about a text. Although the above definitions and their comparative discussion along with others can serve as useful initial resources for a study of reading, in a phenomenological inquiry of the experience of reading they need to be suspended for the sake of capturing the phenomenological meanings in one's actual reading experience. As it will become clear in the next section, the themes that emerged based on my reading experience of Nancy are very different from the themes I summarized above based on the dictionary, Google, and Foreign Language Teaching Methods site.

In addition to bracketing and examining the assumptions, abstractions, and other "intoxications" (van Manen 2014, 222), one needs to be aware of the methodological approaches in doing phenomenological research, including the organization and writing of the phenomenological text. A "flexible narrative rationality" (227) is needed that allows the richness of the phenomenon being researched to be presented. This is the methodological reduction that aims to invent a creative scholarly approach that is most appropriate in giving access to the lived experience of the phenomenon being explored.

Interruption, Suspension-Dwelling, and Weighing: Toward an Aesthetics of Reading

In the following, I share two "lived experience descriptions (LED)" (van Manen 2005, 314) of my earlier and later experiences of reading two of Jean-Luc Nancy's (JLN) books, *The Sense of the World* and *Corpus*. Following each LED, I explore the main themes (phenomenological reduction) in each description of the lived experience of reading in an attempt to capture the phenomenological meanings in these thematic expressions about the actual experience of reading in a singular instance: "What may this phrase/sentence/narrative reveal about the phenomenon being described?" Finally, I offer a reflective writing on the themes (interpretation) that explore the phenomenological experience and significance of reading based on the emergent themes.

In writing LEDs the phenomenologist tries to describe her experience "as much as possible in experiential terms, focusing on a particular situation or event" (van Manen 2014, 313), avoiding casual explanations or abstract explanations. Based on the LEDs, one can construct phenomenological anecdotes by editing "the redundant material and retaining theme-relevant material" (van Manen 2014, 254). The following is the first anecdote based on my initial lived experience of reading *The Sense of the World* by Jean-Luc Nancy. For analytical purposes, I use the third person pronoun in interpreting the LEDs and refer to myself as O.

Reading as Interruption

> I remember the first time I started reading Jean-Luc Nancy. I picked up *The Sense of the World* that has been standing on my desk in my office. After reading a few lines I needed to pause . . . and to reread, sometimes more than a couple times to start making some sense. As I kept reading, I noticed that I could not move on with the reading as I usually do. I had to pause often, and my usual reading experience got *interrupted*. I needed to slow down the habitual pace of reading. . . . Initially, I felt resistance to this interruption; I did not welcome it. Felt the urge to move on. "Time passing, got to get this done." "Do I continue or let go?" The next day, I checked out more books by the same author from the library.

What lies at the heart of this excerpt, as a whole, is the experience of interruption in reading (and this person's response to it.) The interruption emerges in the relation of the reader (O) to the text where her taken-for-granted experience of reading and making sense of a text becomes problematic. O is unable to continue reading as she is used to. Her initial reaction to this interruption is not one of appreciation but of resistance. The need for slowing down the pace of reading and feeling the pressure to continue and to complete the task arise as competing demands. The reader reaches a significant turning point in her reading experience where a decision needs to be made about the continuity of her relation with the text. Then the decision is made, she takes up the challenge of reading further.

This excerpt is a description of what we might refer to as a "difficult reading" experience, which is characterized above as an interruption of one's ordinary, nonproblematic mode of relating to and making sense of a text. The need for frequent pauses, rereads, slow pace of reading, and lack of immediate access to the meaning of the text serve as important indicators of a way of reading a text that is not familiar to this reader. A new and unfamiliar relationality to the text is called for, one that is not defined by "immediate consumability" (Anton 2005, 68). Access is not granted until one dwells in the text for a while, a long while, with frequent visits, attentive listening, and an openness to learn without turning the text to what is already known. The anecdote based on the second lived experience description I share below elaborates on the reader's experience of learning to relate to the text in new ways as part of her reading experience after a few months of her early readings.

Reading as Suspension, Dwelling, Becoming

> Reading *Corpus* is a dip into the unknown and the mind/body is alert, stimulated, then exhausted, only to become alert again. . . . *Corpus* does not lend itself easily and I am learning to enjoy this. . . . Reading *Corpus* requires a patient attentiveness for meaning to emerge. Nonrushing, thoughtful, contemplative; both engaging and staying with the text and observing what comes out of this contact. This experience is more like dwelling in the text rather than reading on to complete it. I do not mind what is still not clear; let go of the urge for clarity and learn to be with the responding to and processing of what comes. Contemplating *Corpus* in this way opens up ways of seeing, thinking, feeling, being. Spending a couple days on a few pages that I would ordinarily read in a few minutes, I feel *suspended*, noticing time going by, and not moving on yet. *Not yet.* . . . Stay. Stay a little more. A little more. . . . Stay, allowing the text to *touch* you.

The main theme in the above reading experience is the feeling of being suspended in relation to the text in a way that one takes the time to patiently attend to and receive the text, to dwell in the textual space, and to observe what emerges in her contact with the text without coming to quick conclusions. This reading experience suggests a careful, slow, tactful relation to the text where one is receptive to the uncertainty of the process and the emerging meanings. The reader states that she is learning to enjoy the challenge of making sense of the text in this way. This reading experience is characterized as contemplative where the reader is in contact with the text. That is, there is a meeting of the reader's world and the world of the text. It is out of this meeting that new "ways of seeing, thinking, feeling, being" emerge rather than the reader consuming the text and imposing herself on it. An important part of the reading experience is highlighted as "staying with text" without moving on to the next idea or chapter, staying and listening, and the reader adds: "Allowing the text to *touch* you." Thus, rather than being just an intellectual or abstract process, there seems to be a more direct/intimate experience of the text in this meeting of the inner and outer worlds. Compared to the first excerpt, the reading experience described in the second one above is not characterized as an "interruption" but as a *suspension* where the reader is learning to live in the textual space with uncertainty, allowing for continued contact with the text rather than quick closure of meaning. In this suspended space, meaning emerges in the meeting of the reader and the text as the reader continues to contemplate and dwell. This process seems to be transformative as it gives way for the emergence of new ways of thinking, seeing, and being.

This anecdote offers experiential insight to the philosophical discussion offered at the beginning of the chapter on the weight of meaning, being-to(ward) the other, and the co-appearing of singular beings. As we have seen in the first half of the chapter, Nancy's philosophical project problematizes the appropriation of meaning into a system of signification, which is a closure of meaning. He offers the concept of weight to refer to what cannot be appropriated; the weight of thought as the excess of meaning that can't be enclosed. To let ourselves to be presented to the weight of thought is to wonder and to be exposed to meaning at the limit of signification, which is an exposure to existence, "to the joy and the tears, to its turbulence, thickness, trembling" (Nancy 1997a, 81). It is to be exposed to "meaning as the event of an opening" (78). In the second anecdote, the reader shares her experience with the text in terms of a "contact" with the text where she patiently listens to what emerges in her meeting with the text, rather than consuming and making it a part of what she already knows. She lives in the uncertainty of the textual space allowing and exploring new ways of thinking, relating, and being to emerge. Through this process, she lets meaning weigh. She "simply exists" (Nancy 1997a, 82) *toward* the text, which allows for an opening for meaning. The last line of the anecdote "Stay, allowing the text to *touch* you" illustrates the exposure to exteriority (in this case, the text) through which not only meaning emerges but the reader is constituted in this process as well. As she touches the text and the text touches her, they co-appear. What stands out here about the phenomenological experience of reading is this co-emergence of meanings about the text and the reader through the process of dwelling in the text and being-toward the text. The process of reading emerges not as a consumption of information or meaning, but as a process of entering and staying in the textual space, of being exposed to the text and to co-appear with it, each time anew.

Clearly, the kind of reading discussed above requires effort (an effortless effort?) and patience but "the context today is impatience" (Anton 2005, 68). Anton explains that compared to the little effort required by other media such as the television or the internet, difficult reading seems to be "not worth the effort" (67). Students question why the authors can't just get to the point as if reading is about the transfer of information from the author to the reader. "It is obvious that they don't think of a text as a place to dwell or as a shaping stone against which to forge themselves. Most students, perhaps most people in the society at large, impatiently take information to be a thing, some kind of stuff to be delivered over or added to their 'knowledge base'" (Anton 2005, 68).

Reading, as described in the above quote, is practiced as an information seeking process and as a means to an end rather than as a process in itself. As Anton (2005) explains further, this approach does not allow readers to grow in their abilities for expression, comprehension, discovery of new ideas and of who they are/might be, and to engage in dialogue. As the second anecdote analyzed above illustrates, however, reading a good, difficult book and the labor that it might require opens up space for becoming. The last line of the second anecdote states, "Stay, allowing the text to *touch* you." Touch refers to the encounter with the text, the meeting of the text and the reader as a transformative moment where a change takes place. The reader is not the same after this encounter. In the contact between the reader and the text, something shifts. There is an effect. The text touches the reader, there is contact, and at the same time a change is produced. The reader is displaced. A new perspective might emerge, a slightly different way of seeing or thinking. One does not occupy the same place anymore; her positionality has shifted.

Reading as Weighing

A final interpretive frame that I will offer to the discussion of the two anecdotes above highlights the experience of reading a (difficult) text as "weighing." Earlier in this essay, I have discussed my reading experience as interruption, suspension, dwelling, and becoming. Nancy's (1997a) discussion on the "weight of meaning" inspires and informs the interpretation of my reading experience as weighing that serves as a comprehensive theme building on the earlier themes discussed—interruption, suspension, dwelling, and becoming. Nancy's (1997a) discussion of the weight of thought as the excess of meaning that can't be enclosed or appropriated has been a repeated theme in this chapter. The weight of meaning is the resistance of existence to the closure of meaning, a reversal of signification. It is a "staving in" (Nancy 1997a, 81), a rupture that opens up to existence. As a reader, I felt interrupted and suspended over the meaning of Nancy's writing, and I experienced the resistance of the text to my immediate appropriation of it. The text did not allow me quick access. As Anton (2005) stated, the "natural resistances" offered by good books require effort, patience, and devotion (71). Moreover, "their difficulties provide for us; they are winds or even sails" (73).

The experience of reading became a process of weighing such that in each attempt to make meaning I encountered resistance of the text to disclose itself in the ways that I was familiar. This led to the realization that there is more to it, more than I could appropriate right away. I could make sense of bits and pieces but meaning became an "event of an opening" (Nancy 1997a, 78), an ongoing process that resisted completion. Gradually, I learned to dwell in this textual space without searching for closure, but living, playing, dancing in and with the text, and enjoying the ongoing dialogic experience and being transformed by it. Reading as weighing in this experience is learning to stay with the text, allowing it to speak and even sing to you, without demanding closure. It is letting the song of the text to go on regardless of "getting it," and learning to match your movements to its rhythm. It is open-ended listening and exploring, arriving at local, transitory moments of understanding and continuing the journey.

This dwelling in and with the text is not necessarily a smooth, pleasant process despite the singing and dancing metaphors I used above in characterizing it. It is being exposed to the text, a bodily exposure. Earlier in the section on "Being-With as an Ontology of Bodies," I discussed that the body, for Nancy (2008), is a place of existence that makes possible the experience of weighing. "The body makes room for existence" (15) and, accordingly, makes room for the taking-place of the experience of weighing. Reading as weighing is an embodied exposure to exteriority—in this case, the text—rather than a weighing of ideas in the mind. It is to be exposed to the disorientation, confusion, joy, interruption, suspension, suffering, exhaustion, and wonder. As Nancy (2008) states, "The body's place is the taking-place of sense" (119). Reading as weighing is to let oneself "simply exist," to be exposed, to be displaced, and to co-appear with the text. It is to "stop surrendering meaning . . . to signification" (Nancy 1997a, 65) and "being the breast, the belly, the guts of thought" (81). Weight of meaning, then, is the *ongoing rooting of meaning in existence*, in our exposedness to existence in excess of signification. It is the abandonment of meaning that inclines to return to itself and to anchor meaning in exteriority.

IMPLICATIONS FOR AESTHETIC ECOLOGY OF COMMUNICATION ETHICS

Based on the above discussion on the ongoing rooting of meaning in existence, I conceptualize an *aesthetics of reading* facilitated by the weight of meaning. In the introduction of this book, I discussed the oscillating dynamic between "meaning effects and presence effects" that Gumbrecht (2004 xv, 108) highlights as part of aesthetic experience. It seems that the weight of meaning pushes or moves this movement by resisting the undermining or forgetting of "presence effects" (Gumbrecht 2004) based on the bodily exposure to existence. Presence effects highlight our bodily participation with the things of the world. As part of my lived experience descriptions (LEDs) in the above section, I offered examples of being exposed to Nancy's texts that illustrate "presence effects" such as feeling disoriented and interrupted, having to slow down the pace of reading, learning to be in touch with the text patiently, and to be exposed to it. Gumbrecht (2004) also offers some examples on presence effects from his experience, such as being attentive to "the ways in which my body relates to a landscape (while I am hiking, for example) or to the presence of other bodies (while I am dancing)" (144) that allows for contact, or in Nancy's terms "exposure" (1997a). Overall, I argue that weighing as being exposed to existence maintains the productive tension between "meaning- and presence-based relations" (Gumbrecht 2004) to the world, opposing the bracketing of either side. This tension helps maintain the process of meaning as an "event of opening" (Nancy 1997a, 78), as arriving beyond completion or closure. Furthermore, the ongoing arrival and renewal of meaning maintains the relation of *being -to* or *-toward* that was discussed earlier in the chapter, where the *to* is the spacing that is essential for the existence of sense. As Nancy (2003) put it, "Sense depends on relating to itself as to another or to some other" (6) and exposure to exteriority facilitates this "distanced proximity" (Nancy 2008, 98) that is necessary for tactful contact. In my reading experience of Nancy's writings, I have come to live through the oscillation between meaning effects and presence effects (Gumbrecht 2004) through the resistance of the text in unfolding itself. I had to learn to attend to it as an other, through being interrupted, suspended, and to reengage by waiting, dwelling, and being exposed. Learning to coexist with the text in this embodied way, *undergoing* the text rather than conquering or consuming it, became a lesson in "touching lightly" or to "touch without touching" (Derrida 2005, 66) that I present as part of the aesthetic ecology of communication ethics.

A NOTE ON A CHAPTER THAT RESISTS CLOSURE

It is probably only natural for a chapter on Nancy to resist closure! I thought I was done with this chapter. To check a passage from Nancy's *A Finite Thinking* (2003), I opened the book and was immediately drawn in—sucked in—to a couple lines. I share my experience below without any further analysis, leaving it to the reader to weave their reading of it to the rest of this chapter that resists closure.

> As my eyes dance on and around the lines, I have a feeling of my body whirling as it is seated on the chair and lean closer toward the book. I enter a space where I am neither I nor the other, I am in between, and whirling like a dervish. Reading, learning, making sense, letting go (un-making sense), transcending, being transformed, and feeling the joy and the struggle of it all. In other words, experiencing the "weight of meaning."

REFERENCES

Anton, Corey. 2005. "The Practice of Reading Good Books: A Plea to Teachers and Students." *Explorations in Media Ecology* 4(1): 65–77.

Derrida, Jacque. *On Touching—Jean-Luc Nancy*. 2005. Translated by Christine Irizarry. Stanford, CA: Stanford University Press.

Foreign Language Teaching Methods. "Methods, Modules, Reading." Last accessed May 1, 2017. https://coerll.utexas.edu/methods/modules/reading/01/.

Gumbrecht, Hans Ulrich. 2004. *Production of Presence: What Meaning Cannot Convey*. Stanford, CA: Stanford University Press.

Nancy, Jean-Luc. 1991. *The Inoperative Community*. Translated by Peter Connor, Lisa Garbus, Michael Holland, and Simona Sawhney. Minneapolis: University of Minnesota Press.

———. 1997a. *The Gravity of Thought*. Translated by Francois Raffoul and Gregory Recco. Atlantic Highlands, NJ: Humanity Books.

———. 1997b. *The Sense of the World*. Minneapolis: University of Minnesota Press.

———. 2000a. *Being Singular Plural*. Translated by Robert Richardson and Anne O'Byrne. Stanford, CA: Stanford University Press.

———. 2002. L'Intrus. Translated by Susan Hanson. *The New Centennial Review*, 2 (3), 1-14. https://muse.jhu.edu.

———. 2003. *A Finite Thinking*. Edited by Simon Sparks. Stanford, CA: Stanford University Press.
———. 2008. *Corpus*. Translated by Richard Rand. Kindle Edition.
———. 2011. "Rühren, Berühren, Aufruhr." Translated by Roxanne Lapidus. *SubStance* 40(3): 10–17.
Nancy, Jean-Luc, and Marcia Sa Cavalcante Schuback, eds. 2013. *Being With the Without*. Stockholm: Axl Books.
van Manen, Max. 2014. *Phenomenology of Practice: Meaning-Giving Methods in Phenomenological Research and Writing*. Walnut Creek, CA: Left Coast Press, Inc.
van Manen, Max, ed. 2015. *Writing in the Dark: Phenomenological Studies in Interpretive Inquiry*. New York, NY.: Routledge.

Chapter Three

Signlessness

Chapter 2 explored Jean-Luc Nancy's project on the emergence of meaning at the limit of signification through exposure to existence. This chapter explores this main idea from chapter 2 from a non-Western perspective, that is, Nancy's emphasis on "letting" meaning weigh and the "letting-come of existence" (Nancy 1997a, 81) beyond continued attempts of signifying meaning in this "crisis of sense" that we find ourselves. The following quote is worth repeating here: "Are we (we who keep saying to ourselves that we arrive so late, so much at the *end*), in the end, going to let ourselves be presented with this constantly renewed gravity? Are we—with difficulty and serenity—going to let ourselves simply exist" (82)? It is right at this juncture of asking this existential question on letting ourselves be exposed to existence and to the weight of meaning—this gravity that pulls us down to meet existence—that the Vietnamese Buddhist monk, peace-activist, writer, and poet Thich Nhat Hanh (1999; 2006; 2008; 2009) offers us insight.

To let ourselves "simply exist" is not so simple for human beings. Rather than inquire into the why of this existential condition, in this chapter I offer three main themes from Thich Nhat Hanh's writings grounded in Buddhist teachings that focus on "simply existing" in connection to existential rootedness: interdependent co-arising, emptiness (nonself and signlessness), and impermanence. Through a nondualistic perspective in making sense of all phenomena (including the mental and the physical), these teachings provide a context for ontological inquiry that is grounded in exteriority and otherness. Any one entity becomes what it is through their relation to everything else rather than assume an independent existence. The self becomes itself only through nonself elements; it is grounded in everything else other than the self. After an exploration of these themes above, this chapter shows that the *practice* of these concepts lies at the heart of existential rootedness examined from a non-Western perspective. In the final part of the chapter, I analyze a Zen koan titled "The Sound of Rain" that involves a dialogue between a Zen master and a student to illustrate the conceptual discussion and connect the practice of signlessness to the framework of aesthetic ecology. I argue that through the practice of signlessness, one cultivates aesthetic attentiveness (Gadamer 2004), stimulates the oscillation between presence- and meaning-based relations with the world (Gumbrecht 2004), and facilitates an aesthetic orientation and experience as part of everyday life (Dewey 1958).

INTERDEPENDENT CO-ARISING

A major coordinate of the Buddhist teachings is interdependent co-arising (*pratitya samutpada*) that highlights the multiple causes and conditions that give rise to the existence of mental and physical phenomena that is expressed by the Buddha as

> This is, because that is.
> This is not, because that is not.
> This comes to be, because that comes to be.
> This ceases to be, because that ceases to be.

(Hanh 1999, 221)

As the name of the teaching highlights, interdependent co-arising, or dependent co-origination, underlines the relational nature of existence where all phenomena (mental or physical) emerge through the coming together of multiple conditions and causes. Thus, nothing exists in and of itself independent of the conditions that make it possible. As Hanh (1999) states: "This is like this, because that is like that" (221). The teaching of interdependent co-arising is clearly illustrated in Hanh's (2009) discussion of *interbeing* where he writes about looking deeply at a sheet of paper and seeing all the "non-paper elements" in it such as the clouds, sunshine, rain, the logger, the trees, and even ourselves. Without a cloud, there is no rain; without the rain, tree cannot grow; without the trees, there is no paper. This is not an intellectual exercise that Hanh offers, but we can observe and experience interbeing in our own experience and existence. Without air for instance, we cease to exist. We need air, the right temperature, food, to exist. Without the sunshine, rain, clouds, plants, and animals we would not have food. And we can go on listing how "This comes to be, because that comes to be." Everything that exists depends on multiple causes and conditions, co-appearing and co-existing with each other.

When interdependent co-arising constitutes the background for ontological inquiry, then this dialectic that Hanh shares from the *Diamond Sutra* might not come as a surprise: "A is not A. That is why it is truly A." The flower example Hanh offers is helpful:

> A flower is not a flower. It is made only of non-flower elements—sunshine, clouds, time, space, earth, minerals, gardeners, and so on. A true flower contains the whole universe. If we return one of these non-flower elements to its source, there will be no flower. That is why we can say, "A rose is not a rose. That is why it is an authentic rose." We have to remove our concept of rose if we want to touch the real rose. (Hanh 1999, 129)

From the quote above, we see that it is only in relation to exteriority and otherness that one can make sense of a flower or any other phenomena. It is in relation to everything else that any one entity becomes what it is. It is through the "non-self" elements that the "self" truly becomes itself. Just like the rose, "a human being is made entirely of non-human elements" (Hanh 1999, 129). The perspective of interdependent co-arising offers a radically different view of being compared to the traditional Western conceptualizations that focus on independent, autonomous units of existence. Based on this Buddhist perspective, being is to be conceived as interbeing that highlights the deep, intimate participation of different elements of existence in constituting each other. I present the ethical implications of this ontology later in the chapter. The next section focuses on a related theme to the discussion above that highlights emptiness or nonself as the "ground of being" (Hanh 1999, 136).

EMPTINESS (NONSELF)

The teaching of interdependent co-arising involves teachings on nonself (emptiness). "Non-self means that you are made of elements which are not you" (Hanh 1999, 135). Nagarjuna, acknowledged as the most important Buddhist philosopher after the Buddha himself, connects interdependent co-arising and emptiness: "All phenomena that arise interdependently, I say that they are empty" (Hanh 1999, 226). Thus, emptiness does not mean nonexistence but being empty of a separate self. In a way, emptiness of self acknowledges fullness with nonself elements. Along these lines, Hanh (1999) writes about "discriminative perception" (*vikalpa*) and "nondiscriminating wisdom" (134). The insight of nondiscriminating wisdom allows us to see that "when we touch one thing, we touch everything" (136). It is through this deep looking practice that we are in touch with "the ground of being" beyond what is immediately visible on the surface. Furthermore, the ground of being (that Hanh refers to as Nirvana) is the "complete silencing of concepts" (136), including our notions of self, nonself, birth, and death. The complete silencing of concepts allows us to be in touch with things as they are beyond our ideas about them. As quoted earlier, "We have to remove our concept of rose if we want to touch the real rose" (Hanh 1999, 129). This is where the discussion on signlessness comes into play.

Signlessness

To better understand the notion of emptiness, it might serve to explore signlessness (*animitta*) in Buddhist philosophy. "'Sign' here means an appearance or the object of our perception. When we see something, a sign or image appears to us, and that is what is meant by 'lakshana'" (Hanh 1999, 148). Hanh refers to the representations that appear in our minds when we engage the world as signs. When we see a bird, for instance, the image of the bird becomes an object of our mind (a representation). Or, hearing the bird, the sound becomes the object of the mind. A fundamental point in Hanh's (1999) discussion of signs based on the Buddha's *Discourse on the Many Realms (Bahudhatuka Suttha)* is that our inability to see the "signless nature of things" (149)—the impermanent and interbeing nature of things—causes anxiety and suffering. Hanh offers the example of seeing water in various forms—liquid, solid, gas—in a square or round container, and warns us not to be caught by the signs to enter the "heart of reality." Hanh further explains that we enter the world of signlessness through the world of signs. "If we throw away the water, there is no way for us to touch the suchness of water" (149). It is through the practice of deep looking beyond the appearance (sign) of the water that we can see the *suchness* of water, its ground of being. If we see only water when we look at water, we are not in touch with "the wondrous nature of reality" (Tathagata) (Hanh 1999, 149).

> When we can see that the water *is* the sun, the earth, and the flower, that just by looking at the sun or the earth you can see the water, this is "the signlessness of signs." An organic gardener who looks at a banana peel, dead leaves, or rotting branches can see flowers, fruit, and vegetables in them. She is able to see the nonself nature of flowers, fruit, and garbage. (Hanh 1999, 150)

Hanh describes a way of relating to and experiencing phenomena beyond a dualistic vision that separates and categorizes them independently. He offers a way of seeing that acknowledges interbeing, which is at the center of a nondualistic ontology and epistemology. As a way of knowing, signlessness first acknowledges signs, the forms through which phenomena appear; however, it warns us not to be caught by the signs. "The flower cannot be limited to its briefest manifestation. Everything manifests by means of signs. If we get caught by the signs, we become afraid of losing that particular manifestation" (Hanh 1999, 151). Hanh states that signs allow for things to manifest, and highlights that the reality of a flower—and anything else—is not limited to manifestation. When we get caught by the reality limited to signs, we lose sight and fear loss. This is why the practice of signlessness and the practice of throwing away of signs are crucial. In a Dharma Talk he gave in June 2006 titled "Throwing Away," Hanh discussed signlessness as a practice and not just a description or a concept. The practice of signlessness is a contemplation of letting go:

> Skillfully, he practices breathing in, contemplating letting go.
> Skillfully, he practices breathing out, contemplating letting go.
>
> (Hanh 2006a, 7)

The monk contemplates letting go with each in-breath and out-breath. Hanh explains that throwing away is a very strong term, stronger than letting go, and that the *Diamond Sutra* highlights four signs to be thrown away: self, human being, living being, and life span (birth and death).

The first sign is the "self." Earlier I discussed interdependent co-arising along with the nondualistic ontology of interbeing. Hanh (1999; 2006) explains that the self is made of nonself elements; therefore, the notion of "self" as a separate, independent entity does not reflect the truth. Hanh further explains that the notion of self is a mental formation. There are physical formations such as a piece of paper, or a rose, mountain, and so on; mental formations such as anger, self, and nonself; and physiological formations such as my fingers or kidneys. All formations are impermanent and interdependent. They are always changing, aging, deforming, and transforming, and thus they are empty of a fixed identity. "Our concept of self arises when we have concepts about things that are not self. Using the sword of conceptualization to cut reality into pieces, we call one part 'I' and the rest 'not I.'" (Hanh 2011, 343). The "I" emerges through conceptualization of reality where we group things as "I" and "not I." Throwing away the notion of self, according to Buddhist philosophy, brings us closer to the nature of reality and is liberating. Hanh (2012, 7) highlights that removing the notion of self is crucial for peace; it is "the basic action for peace." Throwing away the notion of self allows one to see the interbeing nature of everything beyond discrimination and to realize that the suffering of the other is one's own suffering.

The second sign is "human being." Although conventionally most people separate humans from animals, minerals, rocks, and plants, Hanh (1999; 2006) explains that "human is made of non-human elements." Without the nonhuman elements, the human element cannot exist. Therefore, respect for all forms of life is essential. Hanh (2006) connects this discussion into the teaching on "deep ecology" that is at the center of the *Diamond Sutra*. When we destroy nonhuman elements, we also destroy human elements; therefore, to protect one we should protect the other. Throwing away the notion of human being liberates us from discriminating views of our relation to the larger environment that we live in and allows us to acknowledge our deep connection to nature. "With liberation from that notion, we become less proud, less arrogant as a species" (Hanh 2006a, 9).

In his 2015 encyclical "Laudato Si," Pope Francis repeatedly highlighted the urgency for a change in lifestyle and the creation of a culture that would address the crisis humans have created in damaging "our common home," the earth. "We have forgotten that we ourselves are dust of the earth (cf. Gen 2:7); our very bodies are made up of her elements, we breathe her air and we receive life and refreshment from her waters." Pope Francis refers to our forgetfulness of who we are in relation to what gives life and what makes life possible for us as human beings. He reminds us of our intimate connection with the earth that constitutes who we are. This resonates with Hanh's discussion of interdependent co-arising ("This comes to be, because that comes to be" that was introduced earlier) and interbeing. Both Hanh and Pope Francis underline our existential rootedness in the larger ecology that we live in that makes it possible for us to be, which has significant ethical implications.

The third sign that Hanh highlights to be thrown away is "living being." Hanh (2008) explains the distinction that is drawn between living beings and nonliving beings through the criteria of having sensations. Living beings have sensations. He goes onto state that living beings are made of nonliving elements similar to the discussion on the self being made of nonself elements. Living and nonliving elements inter-are. The Zen teacher John Daido Loori asks, "Where does the earth end and where do I begin?" (Loori 1999, 13). Loori challenges us to question the boundaries of the conventional self and to examine our relation to the earth. Loori (1999) writes about "being born as the earth" which is "to realize the world . . . to realize the mountains, the rivers, and the great earth as the mind and body of the Tathagata." Tathagata refers to "suchness," "rootedness in truth," or, one who has realized the teaching of nonself (Buddha) (Loori 1999, 14). One is to realize the Tathagata as one's own body and mind, which is to acknowledge the mountains and rivers and the great earth as one's self. Thus, the distinction between living and nonliving beings are blurred and thrown away to realize one's self in its suchness.

Finally, the fourth sign to be thrown away is "life span," which is "the period of time between our birth and death" (Hanh 1999, 152). Based on the perspective of Buddhism, Hanh highlights that birth and death are notions that do not necessarily reflect how things are. Life span refers to the ideas we have about the beginning and end of our lives. Hanh explains that conventionally, being born means we become something from nothing and that death means we become nothing from something. Hanh (1999, 137) questions this perspective through offering an example of a sheet of paper:

> When you look at this sheet of paper, you think it belongs to the realm of being. There was a time that it came into existence, a moment in the factory it became a sheet of paper. But before the sheet of paper was born, was it nothing? Can nothing become something? Before it was recognizable as a sheet of paper, it must have been something else— a tree, a branch, sunshine, clouds, the earth.

Hanh points to the interconnected continuity of life that is based on transformation rather than a clear-cut, dualistic sense of existence and nonexistence. Based on the prior discussion on interbeing, the paper already contains all the other elements. So, rather than understanding birth and death as coming into being and disappearing, the Buddhist framework offers the theme of "continuity," and the "world of no-birth and no-death" (Hanh 1999, 139). Hanh uses the example of the wave to explain no-birth and no-death. He states that we can see each wave in the ocean as having a beginning and an end but when we look deeply we also see that a wave is made of water and lives the life of water. If the wave in its relative truth does not see that it is also part of the world of water (absolute truth or its "true nature"), then it will not transcend the notion of life span; it will be imprisoned in the world of signs. Hanh explains that in the world of signs and relative truth, if we can also touch the world beyond signs, we touch the ground of being which leads to liberation.

As discussed earlier, the dialectic of touching the world beyond signs in and through the world of signs is reflected in the *Diamond Sutra* as "A is not A. That is why it is truly A." The wave is not a wave; this is why it truly becomes a wave (once it realizes its true nature as water). Releasing the four notions of self, human being, living being, and life span makes it possible to be in touch with life, others, and ourselves beyond our ideas. Throwing away notions is a kind of "bracketing" in phenomenological terms, to arrive at the suchness of things. Bracketing preconceived ideas of self/nonself, human/nonhuman, living/nonliving, birth/death is a practice of learning to see anew and learning to see deeply "the wondrous nature of reality," which is the world of signlessness (Tathagata) (Hanh 1999, 149).

Hanh (1999) explains that to see the signless nature of anything, water, mountains, a flower, one needs to look beyond the sign (of water, mountain, flower) and see that they are made of nonself elements (nonwater, nonmountain, nonflower elements). Looking at a flower, if you see that it is only a flower and think that it cannot be the sun, the water, the earth, and so on, then you are not in touch with its signless nature (true nature of interbeing) but you are caught by the signs. Hanh (1999) states that there are three phases in practicing the Concentration of Signlessness: "Water, not water, true water" (149). The first phase is based on a dualistic vision, a naive, "unsuspecting registration of manifest reality" (Laycock 2001, 37). The second phase is the realization that there is no independent, separate existence: A is not A. And the third phase is the realization of the "signlessness of signs" (Hanh 1999, 149) where one opens up to the "true nature of interbeing." She sees water in its boundless, expansive, unconditioned suchness. Laycock (2001) writes that for Buddhism "to be is to defer its own being, its own-being (*svabhavata*), to its conditions. Its 'self' is drained away only to reappear among the manifold factors which sustain its being" (21). Buddhist phenomenology, as Laycock states, is based on contingency, where nothing has a self-existence independent of conditions. Nothing exists in itself, rather "things exist 'outside of themselves'" (Laycock 2001, 112). This is the main point that I connect to existential rootedness, the realization of the rooting of our existence in exteriority, which is visibly clear when we observe the roots of a tree that holds on to the earth. We humans have invisible roots yet we need to look deeply beyond the world of signs to be able to "see" them.

Laycock (2001) further writes about the suspension of self-identification (A is not A) in Buddhist philosophy and "the dissolution, the 'emptying' of identity into difference" (11). This is a significant statement in offering insight into a common misunderstanding (by some Western scholars) regarding the signless, empty nature of the self in Buddhist philosophy that is based on the assumption that when the self is suspended or emptied, and one realizes that the self is made of nonself elements, differences get lost, and self and the other are merged where the other is absorbed into the sameness of self. As Laycock (2001) highlights in the above quote, however, the emptying of identity is not into sameness but into difference. Laycock offers a helpful example to illustrate the manifold conditions that make possible the existence of a *particular* book one is reading at a *particular* moment in time (in this case, his book, as the reader reads it) that constitute *this* "book."

> The existence of this book, in the always lacunary specificity of its detail, depends upon being printed by a particular press. But it also depends upon its being printed with a particular stock of paper, with a certain ink, and by a certain operator who happened to consume a particular cheese sandwich, with a particular slice of tomato and a particular dollop of mustard, for lunch. It depends, as well, upon the particular trees, felled by particular lumberjacks, in a particular grove with a particular soil density, humidity and reserve of nutrients, subject to particular atmospheric conditions, and enjoying a particular exposure to the sun. . . . Minus *any single one* of these conditions, the book in your hands would

have been different—not the same book *altered*, but *a different book*. (Laycock 2001, 112–13)

The self-existence of a book, its independent identity, is relinquished, emptied into its particular conditions. There is no book independent of its particular conditions. And this is also true for the particular conditions that depend on their conditions to exist (manifest). "Realization of the endlessness of ontological deferral is the great leap into emptiness" (Laycock 2001, 114). A is not A. This does not mean that A does not exist but "in abandoning itself to its conditions, its 'self' has been multiplied to infinity . . . its conditions scatter its presence everywhere" (113). Thus, the limited, narrow sense of self that considers itself to be independent of the larger container that it actually depends on for its existence, comes to realize a larger, wider, expansive existence where A is not A (and, "This is why it is truly A"). Furthermore, in each case, since the particularities of the conditions for any existence are different, and rather than being absorbed into a vastness that homogenizes each existence, difference is maintained where *this* book is not the same as *that* one.

I have discussed interdependent co-arising, emptiness, and signlessness as some of the main themes in Buddhist philosophy that are connected to our exploration of existential rootedness from a non-Western perspective. Before an explicit discussion on the connections of these themes to existential rootedness, it is important to highlight that in Buddhism, contemplation and direct realization (understanding) of emptiness, interdependent co-arising, and signlessness lie at the heart of one's practice. That is, these themes, among other Buddhist notions, are offered not just for conceptual understanding but, more important, to be embodied and practiced as part of one's life. In Zen training, for instance, silent sitting meditation and koan introspection are two practices that facilitate "direct realization" rather than intellectualizing of the words and concepts that describe reality. In the following, I examine a Zen koan and a Zen story that illustrate the discussion up to this point on interdependent co-arising, emptiness, and signlessness.

EMBODYING SIGNLESSNESS: CULTIVATING "BEING WITH"

A Zen koan is a "seemingly paradoxical statement or question that challenges our understanding of who we are, what the nature of the self is, and what the activity of our life expresses" (Loori 1988, xiv). Koans are *seemingly* paradoxical "because in reality there are no paradoxes; paradoxes exist in the language we use to describe reality. In the direct and intimate experience of reality itself, there are no paradoxes" (Loori 1988, 1). In addition to their function as a "vehicle for spiritual realization" in Zen training, koan stories or cases are rich resources in studying main themes in Buddhist philosophy, such as the ones discussed in this chapter— interdependent co-arising, emptiness, and signlessness. The use of language in the dialogue between a Zen master and a student is not conventional and might initially be confusing; however, an important part of koans is their function to "frustrate the intellectual process" (Loori 1988, 2) and linear, discursive thinking. Koans cannot be "figured out" by thinking, but they need to be "realized." "To realize a koan is to *be* it with the whole body and mind; to be it with the whole body and mind is to forget the self" (2). Thus, working with a koan is to release ideas and words, and to start experiencing it personally, in silence and with the assistance of a teacher who does not and cannot provide an answer because the student needs to make the koan her own. The teacher's role is to offer pointers until the student brings the koan into life in the reality of her own existence. Below I present a koan case titled "The Sound of Rain" that illustrates the themes discussed in this chapter: interdependent co-arising, signlessness, and emptiness. This koan case is part of a classic koan collection titled *Blue Cliff Record* that was originally compiled in China, to which American Zen teacher John Daido Loori (1988, 69) added pointers, verses, and modern commentaries.

"The Sound of Rain"
Blue Cliff Record: **Case 46**

Main Case:

> Kyosei asked a monk, "What is that sound outside the gate?" The monk said, "The sound of raindrops." Kyosei said, "Sentient beings are inverted, they lose themselves and follow after things." The monk said, "What about you, Teacher?" Kyosei said, "I almost don't lose myself." The monk said, "What is the meaning of 'I almost don't lose myself'?" Kyosei said, "Though it still should be easy to express oneself, to say the whole thing has to be difficult."

For analytical purposes, I present the case in dialogue format below with line numbers:

1. K: What is that sound outside the gate?
2. M: The sound of raindrops.
3. K: Sentient beings are inverted, they lose themselves and follow after things.
4. M: What about you, Teacher?
5. K: I almost don't lose myself.
6. M: What is the meaning of 'I almost don't lose myself'?

7. K: Though it still should be easy to express oneself, to say the whole thing has to be difficult.

As stated earlier, the language of koans and koan cases can be confusing and "strange" since they neither follow conventional language use nor aim to represent conventional understandings of self, other, and nature of reality. The questions teachers ask are to inquire and test the student's understanding. When Kyosei (K) asks about the sound outside the gate in this context of the teacher-student relationship, he is not making small talk about the weather, which becomes obvious in line 3 in his response to the monk's answer. When the monk offers a literal answer to K's question and does not demonstrate an understanding of the teacher's inquiry as an opportunity to show how he understands the sound of raindrops, Kyosei offers a teaching and a subtle warning: "Sentient beings are inverted, they lose themselves and follow after things." K's statement on sentient beings being inverted and losing themselves refers to not knowing who they truly are, including the monk whose response illustrates K's point. From this response, it is clear that K was inquiring about something else than what the sound actually is. K can hear and identify the sound and yet he asks. In his commentary, Loori (1988) writes that in the original footnote to the question "What is that sound outside the gate?" it says that the teacher "casually lets down a hook. He is out to catch a fish, and the fish is the monk" (70). The teacher (K) is fishing for a response that shows the alertness and the understanding of the student. The monk does not present a response that shows his understanding of the signless nature of the sound of raindrops. Rather, he offers a label, which presents a conventional, dualistic understanding of self and the other—the sound of raindrops, in this case. In his commentary to this case, Loori (1988) explains "the monk was separating himself. His head was filled with ideas about things" (71). How does the monk show his understanding of the sound? Loori states, "If you call it the sound of rain, then this is losing yourself and following after things. If you don't call it the sound of rain, then how do you turn around?" (77).

In the prior discussion of signlessness, I highlighted the three phases of signlessness through the example of "water, no water, water." The monk in this koan case seems to be stuck in the first phase, he states that "A is A." The teacher is not content with his answer and he points to being inverted, not knowing the self, and being attached to signs. This is when the monk performs another "bad move," when he turns the question over to his teacher on line 4 "What about you, Teacher?" Alternatively, he could have paused to reflect on his teacher's point, or he could have bowed and left to contemplate on the teaching K offers on line 3, but he continues to miss the point and pursues the matter intellectually and away from himself. As an alternative response I turn to Laycock (2001) quoting Dogen, the founder of the Soto Zen school in Japan: "Since I have no mind in me, when I hear the sound of raindrops from the eave, the raindrop is myself" (11). Dogen's response takes up Kyosei's challenge by referring to the interdependent co-arising of the mind and the sound of raindrops, where having no mind leads to not having the sound as a sign. Mind and sign coexist together, and Dogen's response highlights the "dropping of the mind" (which is one of his main teachings) that is a letting go or throwing away of the self as a sign (as discussed earlier) that causes the letting go of the sound of rain as a sign. What remains then is the signless nature of reality where there is no separation between the raindrop and the self; since they constitute each other, they take part in interbeing. Dogen's response basically underlines nonduality of self and the sound, no separation. In the conversation between Kyosei and the monk, K's response on line 3 "Sentient beings are inverted, they lose themselves and follow after things" could be read as sentient beings losing themselves in the world of signs, and becoming attached to signs. That is why they are inverted; they are unable to see the signless nature of reality that K's inquiry with M seeks by asking "What is that sound outside the gate?"

"The Sound of Rain"
Blue Cliff Record: **Case 46 continued**

4. M: What about you, Teacher?
5. K: I almost don't lose myself.
6. M: What is the meaning of 'I almost don't lose myself'?
7. K: Though it still should be easy to express oneself, to say the whole thing has to be difficult. (Loori 1988, 69)

On line 4, the question is turned to the teacher, and the opportunity for the monk to respond, to wake up to his teacher's initial probing is gone; he is "chasing after things." Kyosei continues to alert his student, "I almost don't lose myself." *Almost?* Why almost? K is pointing to the present conversation, which is being lost (in signs) because the monk continues to pursue it with no signs of waking up and Kyosei is being part of the conversation though not lost in it—but *almost*. The monk, still lost in pursuing, asks about the meaning of "I almost don't lose myself" on line 6. This is the third moment in the interaction that the monk could have paused and contemplated on the teacher's pointing. Rather, he takes the easy way by asking the teacher to feed him with answers. The teacher does not offer a direct response to the monk's question; he continues to "create complications along the way" as Loori (1988) puts in his commentary, inviting the monk to contemplate on them. In this last line, K makes a statement on expressing oneself and the challenge of "saying the whole thing" (76). Loori's commentary adds, "If you call it the sound of rain, you're blind. If you don't call it the sound of rain, what will you call it? Your feet need to be on the ground of reality, the ground of being, before you can get in here" (Loori 1988, 76).

With this koan, we are reminded of the ground of being, of existential rootedness, based on the Buddhist tradition: nonself, nonduality, and signlessness. The monk's response on line 2, and the teacher's initial question (line 1) and response on line 3, bring up the questions to be contemplated: What is the sound of the rain? What is the self? What is "being inverted?" The koan serves as a vehicle for contemplating and waking up to these questions. Loori (1988), explains in his commentary that "being 'upside down' means being deluded by the self, following after things. Where are the things to pursue? What are the things? They only exist outside ourselves when we place them there by the way we use our mind" (76). We construct and reify the separation between the world and ourselves through our use of signs: "A is A," reflects a self-existing being and dualistic ontology rather than pointing to an interdependent, nondual way of making sense of self and other. Over and over again, Zen masters point to our conditioning where "we separate ourselves, we lock ourselves in this bag of skin and call it a self, and place everything else outside it and call it 'other.' Self and other are not two" (Loori 1988, 77). Loori further states that when we free ourselves from this conditioning, we realize that we are as vast as the universe, which is the ground of being that is at the heart of Buddhist ethics, which I will explore further as part of the discussion of the next koan titled "Are You Awake?"

Taking responsibility for one's life in the Buddhist context is not to cut ourselves off from the "ten thousand things," and to realize that "circumstances are just yourself—that what you do and what happens to you are the same thing" (Loori 1988, 43). The koan titled "Are You Awake?" highlights that waking up to the reality of who we are leads to the realization that it is not the conditions but our *conditioning* that create our experience of life, which changes the way we live and relate to others. Loori (1988) discusses the "Are You Awake?" koan where Zen Master Zuigan calls out to himself, every day, asking whether he is awake and he answers himself, "Yes, I am." Then he tells himself, "Never be deceived by others—any day, any time," and follows with a response "No, I will not" (42). Loori (1988) explains that "others" refer to circumstances. Not being "deceived by others" is to realize and to remember that circumstances are not responsible for how one experiences life. Master Zuigan practices this remembering through the external conversation he holds with himself, calling himself out to make the commitment, every day, to take responsibility for his life. When we realize that we are responsible for how we respond to circumstances and that "what you do and what happens to you are the same thing" (Loori 1988, 43), this is taking responsibility for one's life. What we think, what we say, and what we do have consequences and create the experience of our life. In this worldview, the self, the conditions, and the world are not separate but they constitute each other (interdependent co-arising, as discussed earlier).

In "Dependent Co-arising: The Distinctiveness of Buddhist Ethics," Macy (1979) writes about the deep connection between ethics and worldview. Paraphrasing Clifford Geertz's (1968) work *Islam Observed*, Macy (1979) states that "worldview and ethics are inseparable, because they constitute a mutually conditioning system, each validating and reinforcing the other" (39). The ethical implications of a vision of reality that is based on co-dependent arising and the interdependent self shaped by "the flow of experience and the choices that condition this flow" (42) are radically different from a vision of reality based on the idea of an autonomous, independent self. "Possessed of no 'I' apart from what it feels, sees, thinks, does, the self does not *have* experience, it *is* its experience" (42). Accordingly, Loori (1988) discusses that without a separate "I," when one sees the guy lying in the street bleeding, she takes care of him "with no sense of separation and no sense of doing 'good.'" The same action takes place in relation to the earth and the environment. This is taking responsibility for one's life that is based on the activity of nonself.

To connect back to our earlier discussion of signlessness, nonself is the stepping into the signless, "I-less" nature of being. Nonself is to realize that there is no "I" that is having an experience separate from its experience. It is to realize that we are not locked up inside "this bag of skin" and that "we are as vast and as complete as the universe itself" (45). Loori offers the example of the great blue heron that visits the pond:

> It comes and it goes
> Leaving no traces at all
> Yet knows how to go its own way.
>
> (Loori, 1988, 45)

The great blue heron is clear about its path and is the master of its own life. So is the fly buzzing around, and the sun and the moon. As Hanh (1999) puts it, "The beautiful flower does not *become* empty when it fades and dies. It is already empty, in its essence" (147). The great blue heron, the fly, the flower, are all empty of a separate self; their existence is rooted in the flow of experience, and in the words of Watts (1995), they truly belong to the earth.

As Loori (1988) concludes his comments on the "Are You Awake?" koan, he urges us to deeply explore and experience the ground of our being and to live our lives out of this realization. This life, Loori (1988) states, "is too precious to waste" (45).

A crucial point to keep in mind regarding the realization of teachings such as interdependent co-arising, signlessness, nonself, and emptiness in the context of Buddhism is *practice*. The embodiment of the teachings can only take place through one's practice since it is not an intellectual endeavor. Nobody can tell about it or do it for another; one needs to explore and work through one's own conditioning, finding out for oneself. Whether one is engaging in the practice of silent meditation or koan introspection, the practice is a process of emptying the self, to let go of one's hold on concepts, positions, and ideas (Loori, 1988) and stay open to experience. When we are caught up in the ideas and words that describe reality, we miss reality itself. Just like Master Nansen said as he pointed to a flower, "People these days see this flower as though they were in a dream" (Loori 1988, 93), when we are occupied with mental activity, with the representation, we are separated from being in touch with the flower. Loori quotes Master Dogen, "To study the Buddha Way is to study the self. To study the self is to forget the self. To forget the self is to be enlightened by the ten thousand things" (96). Forgetting the self refers to the realization that the self is not separate from its experience, that there is no barrier between the self and the "ten thousand things." To think otherwise is to see the flower—and anything else—as if in a dream. But the point is not to "understand" this; it is to experience directly, which is cultivated through *practice*. Thus, one inquires about the nature of the self through deep looking and observation, not by standing outside but by "being with," by bringing and maintaining awareness on the object of inquiry (meditation). The following section explores this practice through Hanh's discussion and commentary on the Satipatthana Sutra that offers specific means for cultivating and maintaining attentiveness.

PRACTICING SIGNLESSNESS: IMPLICATIONS FOR AESTHETIC ECOLOGY OF COMMUNICATION ETHICS

In his commentary on the Satipatthana Sutra (The Sutra on the Four Establishments of Mindfulness), Hanh (2006b, loc 21) explains that the Pali word *sati* means "remembering," or "mindfulness." *Upatthana* means "place of abiding" or, establishing. Satipatthana Sutra is one of the main Buddhist teachings that offer specific instructions on the practice of being aware of the body, feelings, mind, and objects of mind that are the four establishments of mindfulness. It is through these four areas of mindfulness that one cultivates insight into the nature of self, mind, and phenomena. One starts with the awareness of the body, the anchor of our existence: "In the establishment known as the body, the practitioner is fully aware of the breath, the positions of the body, the actions of the body, the various parts of the body, the four elements which comprise the body, and the decomposition of the body as a corpse" (Hanh 2006b, loc. 345). The exercises that focus on the specific themes listed in the above quote put one in direct contact with the body, including its parts, actions, positions, and impermanence. It is through this direct contact with one's body that one is able to see the interdependent nature of the body, its impermanence, selflessness, and signlessness. The first practice listed above is the full awareness of breathing, which I focus on in the remaining of this chapter in connection to existential rootedness and communication ethics.

"When we breathe in, we know that we are breathing in. When we breathe out, we know that we are breathing out. Practicing in this way, our breathing becomes conscious breathing" (Hanh 2006b, loc. 366). Initially, this practice might seem so simple that one might have the tendency to disregard it; however, this simple practice can be transformative. Anyone who has tried conscious breathing practice knows that it is simple yet not easy. It is a very challenging practice given that the mind is easily distracted. To stay focused on breathing for more than a few breath cycles is a major accomplishment and creates a deep and direct connection with the body and a way of being and relating that is beyond the habituated, desensitized, and the taken-for-granted patterns of being and relating. As Hanh (2006b) puts it, as a result of conscious breathing "we come in contact with life in the present moment, the only moment we can touch life" (loc. 380). Thus, one follows the breath:

> Breathing in, I know that I am breathing in.
> Breathing out, I know that I am breathing out.
>
> (Hanh 1992, 8)

Focusing on the *sensations* of the breath in this way, one realizes her dependence on the breath to exist. At the beginning of this chapter interdependent co-arising was discussed as "This is, because that is. This is not, because that is not" (Hanh 1999, 221). As one continues to follow the breath, she realizes that "I am breathing" is replaced by the diminishing of the "I" where the breath is breathing you. There is no "I" separate from the breath, but there is breathing. *Simply* breathing: a letting oneself simply exist, to return back to Nancy's (1997a) inquiry that we revisited at the beginning of the chapter. A moment of signlessness and nonself, and direct contact with anything that arises whether it is joy, fear, anger, desire, repulsion, or else. When we belong to the breath, which is "impossible to appropriate" (Irigaray 2002, 79), and open our mouth to speak, who speaks? One might also contemplate: Who listens? Who acts? Meeting the breath consciously is a practice that opens the way for signlessness and, in Nancy's (1997a) words, "letting-come of existence" (81). We step into meeting existence by meeting the breath that allows us "to live otherwise" (Irigaray 2002, 6)—an issue that chapter 5 focuses on—rather than being enclosed in a system of signification and a "crisis of sense" (Nancy 1997a). Kwong (2010) describes the aliveness Zen masters bring to everyday life as follows:

> True Zen masters live *through and through*. You can see it in the way they pour tea, place their shoes together outside the meditation hall, walk down the road. You can feel the presence of their intimacy with all things in their undivided engagement in any activity their lives may bring. There is a vitality in their manner of speaking and in their gestures, no matter how small, that makes it seem that the whole of life has just entered the room. And it has. (18)

Living "through and through" in complete intimacy with all things, this "letting" oneself simply exist, is a continuous practice of surrendering the self to experience. Buddhist teachings, Zen koans and stories serve as pointers to realize this existential rootedness. It is in this sense of being fully present to and with things of the world that the practice of signlessness cultivates

1. Aesthetic attentiveness that was discussed as part of Gadamer's (2004) discussions on aesthetic experience and participation (*methexis*).
2. The oscillating dynamic between presence- and meaning-based relations with the world (Gumbrecht 2004).
3. Aesthetic orientation and experience as part of everyday life (Dewey 1958).

In the introduction to the book, I offered Gadamer's (2007) discussion of participation as *methexis* that involves a belonging-together and giving oneself to the point of forgetting the self in attending to someone or something. This resonates with the example of the Zen master in the quote above by Kwong (2010) that highlights "the presence of their intimacy with all things in their undivided engagement in any activity their lives may bring" (18), whether it is pouring tea, speaking, or putting one's shoes together. Yet this intimacy is not an absorption that leads to the loss of differentiation due to the fusing of the self with the other. As Davey (2013) explains, Gadamer's (2004) discussion of "aesthetic attention" (80) involves a "doubled form of attentiveness" (80) that is both fully present and distant. Letting go of signs including the signs of self, human being, living being, and life span as Hanh (2008) highlights facilitates an expansion of one's "horizon" (Gadamer 2004) beyond a dualistic sense of existence and subjective preferences, making space for letting ourselves "simply exist" (Nancy 1997a, 82).

Furthermore, the practice of signlessness allows for engaging the world through the senses and being fully present to whatever arises in one's experience—in their *suchness* as Hanh (1999) puts it. In this sense, it resists the forgetting of "presence–based relations" with the world as Gumbrecht (2004) fears as part of the conditions of contemporary life that tend to highlight meaning effects over presence effects. And, finally, signlessness facilitates "that delightful perception which is esthetic experience" (Dewey 1958, 19) due to the present-moment orientation to the extraordinariness of ordinary everyday moments, things, or activities. Just like the discussion earlier on the practice of breathing that most people usually ignore, our attentiveness to what we categorize as ordinary allows us to see beyond the already established and taken-for-granted perspectives, transforming what has become dull to "moments of intensity" (Gumbrecht 2004) in the midst of everyday life. Thus, through the practice of rooting ourselves in existence, we come to taste and realize the delightfulness and intensity of "simply existing."

REFERENCES

Davey, Nicholas. 2013. *Unfinished Worlds: Hermeneutics, Aesthetics and Gadamer*. Edinburgh: Edinburgh University Press.

Dewey, John. 1958. *The Art of Experience*. New York: Capricorn Books.

Francis, Pope. 2015. "Laudato Si: On Care for Our Common Home." *Our Sunday Visitor*.

Gadamer, Hans Georg. 2004. *Truth and Method*, 2nd rev. ed. London: Continuum. First published in 1975.

———. 2007. "The Universality of the Hermeneutical Problem." In *The Gadamer Reader*, edited by R. E. Palmer, 72–88. Evanston, IL: Northwestern University Press.

Geertz, Clifford. 1968. *Islam Observed*. New Haven: Yale University Press.

Gumbrecht, Hans Ulricht. 2004. *Production of Presence: What Meaning Cannot Convey*. Stanford, CA: Stanford University Press.

Hanh, Thich Nhat. 1992. *Peace Is Every Step: The Path of Mindfulness in Everyday Life*. New York: Bantam Books.

———. 1999. *The Heart of the Buddha's Teaching: Transforming Suffering into Peace, Joy & Liberation: The Four Noble Truths, the Noble Eightfold Path, and Other Basic Buddhist Teachings*. New York: Harmony Books.

———. 2006a. "Dharma Talk: Throwing Away." *The Mindfulness Bell* 43. http://www.mindfulnessbell.org/archive/2015/03/dharma-talk-throwing-away-2.

———. 2006b. *Transformation and Healing: Sutra on the Four Establishments of Mindfulness*. Berkeley, CA: Parallax Press. Kindle Edition.

———. 2008. *Cultivating the Mind of Love*. Berkley, CA: Parallax Press.

———. 2009. *The Heart of Understanding: Commentaries on the Prajnaparamita Heart Sutra*. Berkley, CA: Parallax Press.

———. 2011. *Awakening of the Heart: Essential Buddhist Sutras*. Berkley, CA: Parallax Press.

———. 2012. "Dharma Talk: Free from Notions." *The Mindfulness Bell* 59. https://www.mindfulnessbell.org/archive/2016/03/dharma-talk-free-from-notions.

Irigaray, Luce. 2002. *Between East and West: From Singularity to Community*. Translated by Stephen Pluhacek. New York: Columbia University Press.

Kotoh, Tetsuaki. 1987. "Language and Silence: Self-Inquiry in Heidegger and Zen." In *Heidegger and Asian Thought*, edited by Graham Parkes. Honolulu: University of Hawaii Press.

Kwong, Jakusho, 2010. *No Beginning, No End: The Intimate Heart of Zen*. Edited by Peter Levitt; with foreword by Thich Nhat Hanh. Boston: Shambhala Publications.

Laycock, Steven William. 2001. *Nothingness and Emptiness: A Buddhist Engagement with the Ontology of Jean-Paul Sartre*. Albany, NY: SUNY Press.

Loori, John, Daido, 1988. *Mountain Record of Zen Talks*. Edited by Bonnie Myotai Treace; with foreword by Hakuyu Taizan Maezumi. Boston: Shambhala Publications.

———. 1999. *Teachings of the Insentient: Zen and the Environment*. Mt. Tremper, NY: Dharma Communications.

Macy, Joanna, Rogers. 1979. "Dependent Co-arising: The Distinctiveness of Buddhist Ethics." *The Journal of Religious Ethics* 7(1): 38–52.

Nancy, Jean-Luc. 1997a. *The Gravity of Thought*. London: Humanities Press.

Watts, Allen. 1995. *Buddhism: The Religion of No-Religion*. Boston: Tuttle Publishing.

Chapter Four

Learning to Be (in Con/Tact)

This chapter expands the discussion on existential rootedness to include the experience of the body in illness where there is a significant change in one's bodily appearance. We rely on our bodily existence to be in contact with the world and with others, yet the body is impermanent. Learning to inhabit one's constantly changing body is a fundamental aspect of our lives through growing up, aging, illness, and even in the final stages of our existence. This chapter highlights one's contact with and through her impermanent body as the foundation for existential rootedness and shows that coming to terms with and learning to inhabit one's changing, or radically changed, body is possible through becoming what Merleau-Ponty (1968) refers to as a "participation" in the family of visible things beyond dualistic thought. This chapter is an exploration of this concept and process of becoming a "participation" (Merleau-Ponty 1968) through contact. I first examine this theme in the context of seeing and visibility, and next in the context of mindfulness as a practice of being, or "dropping into being." Overall, I show that it is through contact with one's bodily presence in the world and engaging the sensible, with all of its struggles and challenges, that one cultivates a "presence-based relation" (Gumbrecht 2004, xv) and an aesthetic orientation to the world.

In *The Experience of Communication: Body, Flesh, and Relationship*, Macke (2015) states, "To see one's Self is to make meaningful and substantial contact with the ecstasy and tragedy of one's fleshy being" (65). This quote stands out for this chapter due to its framing of seeing as making contact, which resists the dominance of the eye over the other senses. Macke's emphasis on seeing one's self as making *meaningful* contact with *the ecstasy and tragedy* of one's bodily being initiates significant discussion on our connection with our visible reflection beyond reducing it to a mere image. As Macke (2015) highlights, the embodied connection with one's mirrored reflection allows the ongoing facilitation of a sense of self and constitutes a meaningful post-Cartesian intellectual discourse.

Making contact with the body, however, can be a challenging experience especially when one's body goes through various degrees of transformation such as the bodily changes in teenage years, during pregnancy, or in a more radical sense, when one's body is altered due to a major accident or a significant illness such as breast cancer. This chapter expands Macke's (2015) discussion on contact to the challenges of learning to inhabit one's altered body as a result of cancer treatment (chemotherapy and/or surgery). Utilizing Merleau-Ponty's (1968) discussion of visibility, and specifically "coupling" and "intertwining," I first examine various self-narratives, including a small sample of self-reports of breast cancer survivors, on encountering one's visual reflection to discuss the process of seeing as contact. Secondly, in the next half of the chapter, I examine mindfulness-based discourses (conversations, self-reported narratives, and written texts) to explore the language and practice of mindfulness in enabling a sense of being in con/tact with things as they are (i.e., with the body as it is in its changed, or changing, form). I use con/tact to refer to the mindful, tactful ways in which we recognize the reciprocal coexistence (a belonging together) of the self and the other, subject and the object, in inhabiting present experience.

Overall, this chapter shows that existential rootedness is facilitated by *contact*, a dwelling in one's present bodily experience—including the experience of one's bodily appearance rather than a quick consumption of one's visual reflection as something that she likes/wants or not. Finally, I make connections of the discussion on con/tact to the aesthetic ecology of communication ethics based on Merleau-Ponty's (1968) discussion of "participation" and Gumbrecht's (2004) framework of presence-based relations to the things of the world.

CON/TACT WITH (THE VISIBLE REFLECTION OF) ONE'S CHANGING BODY

Macke (2015) highlights the following sentence from Merleau-Ponty's (1964) "Eye and Mind" essay as he explores the question of the self in the mirror, "A Cartesian does not see *himself* in the mirror; he sees a dummy, an 'outside,' which, he has every reason to believe, other people see in the very same way but which, no more for himself than for others, is not a body in the flesh" (as qtd. in Macke 2015, 53). This quote not only points to the problem of mind/body dualism but, as Macke explains, it also shows Descartes's failure to see the communicative event of one's visual encounter with her body and its transformative effects.

For the Cartesian, the mirror image is a mechanical technicality that is not perceived and processed as an extension of one's lived body; it does not belong to him (Merleau-Ponty 1964). "If he recognizes himself in it, if he thinks it 'looks' like him, it is his thought that weaves this connection" (Merleau-Ponty 1964, 170). In contrast, following Merleau-Ponty's critique of Descartes, Macke (2015) highlights that "to see one's Self is to make meaningful and substantial contact with the ecstasy and tragedy of one's fleshy being" (65). The Stephanie Project, a visual-verbal chronicle of Stephanie Byram who was diagnosed with breast cancer in her early thirties, is illustrative. Stephanie worked with her photographer Charlee Brodsky taking photos of Stephanie's transformed body (after her double mastectomy) that facilitated contact with the image of her body in an aesthetic way (attending to the light and shadows, lines and curves, and various metaphors and analogies that emerged in the process of looking together). This process was crucial in going beyond the medical diagnostic discourse (including the visual) that separates the body from the self, focusing only on what is wrong with the body, which leads to a diminished sense of self (Üçok 2005). Stephanie's experience in turning toward and making contact with the images of her transformed body—that she initially only perceived as disfigured—illustrates Macke's (2015) discussion of seeing "*something* meaningful of oneself when one looks at the reflection of one's body" (64). In dialogue with Charlee, her photographer, Stephanie was able to see and relate to the images of her changed body otherwise.

In a much different and lighter context than the Stephanie Project, Macke (2015) writes about his memory of his own experience of seeing his image as a teenager where he took a considerable amount of time attending to the blemishes in his face, longing for a face that he could take for granted due to its predictability; a face he "did not have to notice" (62), a face that he "*could not see*" when looking at the mirror. When he turned thirty years old and his body image became more stable, however, his actual contact with his body became more removed. Macke (2015) states that he did not look at the mirror to take note of any subtle changes on his face or to see a Self anymore; rather, he began to "treat myself like my automobile" (64), attending to dings and spots if noticeable as part of routine maintenance. He did not really *see* himself; did not make contact with himself and his changing sense of self when he looked at his mirrored reflection. What Macke deeply longed for as a teenager when he wanted to take his face for granted in terms of its predictability actually came true in his thirties, but he no longer maintained the contact he had with his body/self. He saw himself as an image, as a vehicle, as an "outside." In the comfort of his habituated image and self, Macke connected with his visible reflection just as an image.

One might be tempted to question the problematic being raised here. What is wrong, one might wonder, in habituating one's visual reflection and connecting with it at a superficial level without necessarily making *contact* with it? As discussed above, one consequence is the reduction of the reflected vision to a mere sign and loss of wonderment about this vision as part of one's bodily existence. Furthermore, Macke (2015) claims that caring about one's mirrored reflection as an aspect of his or her body, and "imagining what others see when we look at ourselves in the mirror" (66), serves as a foundation for contact with the other. It allows one to imagine what others see in the mirrored image and to "find possibilities of being through aspects of my body that have come to life in the perceptions of others" (67). The mirrored reflection as a source of meaning that is mutually constituted with the other facilitates inquiry and "the experience of depth" (Macke 2015, 68) beyond a flat image regarding our ever-changing bodily existence.

I now turn to a discussion of the following excerpts from three breast cancer survivors that illustrate the challenges of making contact with one's altered bodily appearance as a result of treatment.

"Not Me": Mirrored Reflection of a Changed Body

Shirley, a breast cancer survivor who reflected on her experience of seeing herself in the mirror and who was thrilled to have newly growing hair after having lost all her hair due to chemotherapy, reported that there was a problem for her: her hair grew back curly and she looked very different from her previous appearance. This created an experience of "This wasn't me. It didn't look like me." She further said, "And I saw myself a certain way and this wasn't me, no matter how adorable it might be, it wasn't me and that took quiet a long time. . . . I think what made it less acceptable, even though it was my hair, was that it wasn't the me I was used to and once I decided 'okay this is the me I'm going to be,' it became more acceptable to me" (Shirley, March 1, 2002).

This excerpt connects to the Merleau-Ponty quote cited earlier on the Cartesian seeing himself in the mirror: "If he recognizes himself in it, if he thinks it 'looks' like him, it is his thought that weaves this connection" (Merleau-Ponty 1964, 170). In Shirley's case above, she did not recognize herself in her mirrored reflection; she did not *think* it "looks" like her, for a long time. The changed mirrored image disrupted the thought process that facilitated a quick, surface-level connection between the visible (image) and the seer and created an unsettling experience for Shirley who no longer could take her visible reflection for granted. Although Shirley acknowledged that the newly growing hair was her own hair, her prior identification with and attachment to a particular physical appearance (having straight hair) as her "self" prevented her from embodying her changed image as part of a self-in-process. In a way, Shirley did not want to "see"—be in touch with—herself as this new, changed image that emerged beyond her control. Her initial, intimate contact with her bodily appearance was interrupted and she needed to reorganize, to reconnect with the "fleshy being" she has become. It is when Shirley intentionally decided to release the fixed self-concept ("this is me") organized around a specific physical appearance that she was able to open to and *start* accepting the new body/self that she is becoming.

The "phatic function" of communication, the element of contact, highlights the experiential meaning of the communicative event that is *"outside* the realm of cognition and of thought" (Macke 2015, 78). Just as "one cannot think one's way out of a depression" (78) and "one cannot think one's way into an intimate contact with others" (78), one cannot think one's way into the emerging self one is becoming in relation to a changed bodily appearance. As in Shirley's case, one can start turning toward the new image through which she experiences herself and others. It is the "thickness of the body" (Merleau-Ponty 1968, 135) through which "I have to go unto the heart of things." Shirley had to struggle through this transformative process, to allow herself to experience her changed image, which, after a while, she did.

Merleau-Ponty (1968) writes about the "participations" that are part of a visible (color or a thing, and in this case a mirrored reflection) that is immersed in its surroundings. A red color, for instance, or a red dress is what it is in connection to the other reds and other colors that bring it about rather than being a fixed structure.

> If we took all these participations into account, we would recognize that a naked color, and in general a visible, is not a chunk of absolutely hard, indivisible being, offered all naked to a vision which could be only total or null, but is rather a sort of straits between exterior horizons and interior horizons ever gaping open, something that comes to touch lightly and makes diverse regions of the colored or visible world resound at the distances, a certain differentiation, an ephemeral modulation of this world. (132)

Visibility, as Merleau-Ponty highlights above, is relational and transient, and emerges in the opening and meeting of the internal and external horizons. In Shirley's case discussed earlier, it is when she was able to release the fixed image of her visibility (internal horizon) that she firmly held onto and to allow the changed reflected image to be a "participation" in the family of visible things (external horizon) that she started contacting and accepting it.

Merleau-Ponty (1968) explains that the body that sees is at the same time a seen, "a sensible for itself" (135) and a sentient, a visible thing among the things that it sees. The body as a visible belongs to the things that it sees and touches; "it uses its own being as a means to participate in theirs" (137). It is by this participation in the world of the visible, "and not as the bearer of a knowing subject" (136), that the body brings us to the things themselves and unveils them. One can say that moving from "this is not me" to "this is the me that I'm going to be" in Shirley's experience of seeing her changed visible reflection is a move from being the distanced seer only to becoming a participant in the world of the seen at the same time with being a seer.

It is this "double belongingness to the order of the 'object' and to the order of the 'subject'" (137) that is at the heart of Merleau-Ponty's discussion of the "flesh of the world." "We have to reject the age-old assumptions that put the body in the world and the seer in the body, or, conversely, the world and the body in the seer as in a box. Where are we to put the limit between the body and the world, since the world is flesh" (138). Merleau-Ponty (1968) problematizes the dualistic views of the body/world, as well as the seer/body, and the conventional boundaries that establish limits between them. Questioning these dualisms, Merleau-Ponty highlights the emergence of visibility in the "coupling" (139) of a part (a particular visible, a body) and the whole of the visible (the world), and in the reciprocal coexistence of the visible (the seen) and the seer; the "intertwining of one in the other" (138). When the seer belongs to (participates in) the seen just as the seen belongs to the seer, the world of each opens up to each other and they inhabit a vision—the flesh of the world—which neither belongs to the seer nor the seen. Flesh is a principle of "intercorporeity" (141) between the seen (the visible) and the seer, a "pact" between the things themselves and me "according to which I lend them my body in order that they inscribe upon it and give me their resemblance, this fold, this central cavity of the visible which is my vision" (146). Repeatedly, Merleau-Ponty (1968) highlights that vision emerges not as a dominating activity of a knowing subject, the seer, who imposes her projections on the seen but as a reversible relational system in which the visible and the seer are in contact with each other, where the seeing body becomes a visible at the same time as being a seer. When this reciprocal coexistence of the seen and the seer is not acknowledged and their "intertwining" (138) not realized, it creates disorientation and alienation from one's bodily existence.

Sandy, who also survived breast cancer, puts it very articulately:

> I mean, you're used to your hair and you're used to your, you know, eyes and eyebrows and all of a sudden they're not there. . . . It's just mentally, you can't get used to this new body that's looking at you in the mirror, okay? So it's almost like a stranger looking at you. . . . You come from work and you take that

wig off and you say "who is this, *it's not me*," because we've grown up with our body image as we are. (Sandy, March 25, 2002; emphasis added)

In the final line of this excerpt Sandy states the reason for not being able to recognize her changed body as her self; people identify with their body images as who they are. Yet the self that is defined through one's bodily appearance is not effortlessly changed along with a change in the visible presence of the body. The seer, the Cartesian looking at the mirror and not being able to *think* that the visible reflection looks like her, struggles to connect with it. It is the *memory* of the physical features of her body such as her hair, eyes, and eyebrows that Sandy describes, and it is her attachment to the familiarity of these features that is disrupted. Sandy explicitly states that it is the "mental" connection to her mirrored reflection that she could not restore. The seen, rather than being a "part" of a transformed and newly emerging visibility, is a "stranger" that looks back in the mirror. It is apart from—not a part of—the seer. In short, no "intertwining" (Merleau-Ponty 1968, 138).

Most often this tension and alienation leads to a struggle to restore the prior sense of self constructed around the prior, familiar bodily appearance to feel whole and at home again, as in Lily's case whose hair grew back with lots of gray after chemotherapy:

After probably a year I decided to go back and bleach my hair because I just felt lost. That wasn't me. I'd look in the mirror and I'd say "who is that person" so I did go back and start coloring my hair again as I do today. But that's who I am. I've been blonde since I can ever remember. (Lily, March 8, 2002)

The fixed idea of a self, "that's who I am," along with its habituated visual appearance, "I've been blonde since I can ever remember," is so strong that Lilly experienced her changed bodily appearance as "not me" even after a year. The interaction between Lily and her mirrored appearance brings to mind the knowing subject, the seer, who imposes her projections on the seen rather than participating in the world of the seen. Lily felt lost when she could not see the familiar reflection of her appearance in the mirror.

Along these lines, Macke (2015) writes about one's comfort level in his or her body as a "function of desire," which is "a ratio of reflected presence to reflected vision" (63) where "we take note that we are not *where* we want to be, that we have a vision of ourselves some place else, at some other time, in a different body state and with a different body-image" (63). Our desire for a vision of our mirrored reflection that does not correspond to reflected presence leads to an "oppositional assessment" (63) of one's body image where the reflected presence is in contest with reflected vision that is framed as "not self." In an "*a*ppositional assessment," on the other hand, one anticipates and accommodates potential changes in one's body image that is grounded in one's embodied presence and is able to make meaningful contact with one's reflected presence. In Lily's case above, she adapted her reflected presence to match the reflected vision to mediate the tension between the two; however, one questions whether this image management technique allows for making "meaningful and substantial contact with the ecstasy and tragedy of one's fleshy being" (65) as well as "the experience of depth" (68) beyond a flat image regarding our ever-changing bodily existence. Does the choice of reconstructing one's prior appearance offer a possibility beyond the re-creation of a prior, habituated self and self-image toward learning to be and to be in touch with a changed self/body? Finally, what if the restoration of one's prior self-image and self-concept is neither easy nor possible as in the case of putting a wig on (which might not be as convenient or comfortable as it might sound) or coloring your hair? There are cases of leaking prosthetic breasts that require repeated surgeries or cases of disfigurement that can only be restored up to a degree (such as loss of body parts or having burn marks or other permanent bodily changes). Macke (2015) writes:

> My body—*any* body—is not a fully established empirical fact. It is always in composition and decomposition. My envelope, my skin, is a sign of me and the complex sign-system that I embody. My vision of this sign is both index and icon, signal and symbol. I bear the relationship of my "I think" as the live event of "I *am*" and *re-member* the body of my assembled world. (65)

The last line in Macke's quote above is crucial toward creating a "meaningful post-Cartesian intellectual discourse" that links thinking to the present lived experience where the interplay of "I think" and "I am" make space for the emergence of a changing connection with one's body and the world she experiences through it. The thinking/knowing subject in touch with the being/experiencing subject is no longer positioned as the distanced seer/knower but becomes a participant in the world, and it is through this nondualistic coexistence that vision or knowing emerges. The challenge, however, especially in the Western world is the cultivation of this nondualistic thinking/being subject given the cultural emphasis on the mind and the disembodied knower.

Building on the discussion above, the rest of the chapter examines various discourses and practices of mindfulness that highlights purposeful, nonjudgmental paying of attention to the unfolding of experience that grounds the thinking subject in the present moment lived experience. It is through this rootedness that one is able to be in touch with one's self and the other and make sense in a way that is in tune with things as they are.

"DROPPING INTO BEING": EXISTENTIAL CONTACT

It is worth repeating Macke's (2015) quote on seeing one's mirrored reflection: "To see one's Self is to *make meaningful and substantial contact with the ecstasy and tragedy of one's fleshy being*" (65; emphasis added). This section and the rest of the chapter focus on making such contact in a specific context (mindfulness) and as a specific practice. The mindfulness discourses I examine below include two audio recordings from a "Mindfulness-Based Stress Reduction (MBSR) in Mind-Body Medicine" professional training I attended in the summer of 2005; two narratives based on real-life experiences of a breast cancer survivor and a traumatic brain injury survivor; and a dialogue between an MBSR teacher and a participant in an MBSR class. They all point to and invite this crucial, existential contact "with the ecstasy and tragedy of one's fleshy being" in the present, lived experience.

In the brochure prepared by the Center for Mindfulness in Medicine, Health Care, and Society that offers information on the Stress Reduction Program at the University of Massachusetts Medical School, mindfulness is described as "a basic human quality, a way of learning to pay wise attention to whatever is happening in your life that allows you a greater sense of connection to your life inwardly and outwardly. Mindfulness is also a *practice*, a systematic method aimed at cultivating clarity, insight, and understanding" (Stress Reduction Program brochure, www.umassmed.edu/cfm/stress-reduction).

As a basic human quality and a practice, mindfulness can be understood as attentiveness to the inner and the outer experience that leads to insight. Without intellectualizing it further at this point, I offer the opening words of Jon, one of the two leading teachers at the "Mindfulness-Based Stress Reduction in Mind-Body Medicine" professional training I attended in the summer of 2005:

1. So let's take a few moments (3.0) before the next moment (1.0)
2. And be in this one (3.0)
3. Dropping in on ourselves and on (6.0) simply being here (8.0)
4. So settling into arriving (9.0)
5. And how this is in the body in this very moment (12.0)
6. In the vast array of the sensescapes (1.0)
7. including this bathing in the sounds (7.0)
8. And the air (12.0)
9. And now it is in the mind and in the heart
10. In this moment (8.0)

[The numbers in parentheses indicate seconds of silence according to the transcription system developed by Gail Jefferson (2004).]

The teacher starts the retreat with an invitation to slow down and attend to the experience of the present moment. The large crowd of participants is seated on cushions on the floor in a cross-legged position mostly or on chairs on the sides and at the back of the room. Jon speaks slowly with pauses in between his words in a quiet tone. He then continues with some "strange" instructions such as "dropping in on ourselves" (line 3) and "settling into arriving" (line 4). The teacher continues to give details on his instruction on "arriving" by inviting attention to the body and exploring the bodily experience in the present moment (line 5). Then after a longer silence, he goes on to provide further instructions on attending to various sensory experiences (which he poetically refers as "sensescapes" on line 6) such as the sounds being received ("bathing in the sounds," line 7) and the air touching the body (line 8) as he slowly moves on to attending the mind (thoughts, line 9) and the heart (feelings that are present). From this brief excerpt, we learn that "arriving" includes attentiveness to the sensations of bodily experience including hearing and touch (of the air on the skin), as well as to thoughts (mind) and emotions (heart). Some other mindfulness practices also include attending to eating/tasting as examined in the final excerpt in this chapter, as well as the body as a whole (sitting or walking or lying down).

This practice of slowing down and attending to our presence in this way is not a common practice in contemporary Western cultures, especially in the United States where drive-in fast food restaurants, pharmacies, coffee shops, and gas stations such as On the Run are common parts of a fast-paced life. For most people, this is unfamiliar and unexplored territory, but ironically the words above refer to our embodied everyday presence. A quote from a short story by James Joyce that was highlighted in this retreat comes to mind: "Mr. Duffy . . . lived at a little distance from his body." The language and practice of mindfulness invites us to enter and explore this unexplored, thus, unknown domain of our lives. Mindfulness is a practice of "coming home to ourselves," "learning to live inside" and "*opening* to accepting things inwardly and outwardly in this moment, just as they are" (Meili and Kabat-Zinn 2004, 10; emphasis added).

Mindfulness

> lies at the heart of this learning to live inside. It lies at the heart of discovering our limits, and working with them at our growing edges; and the adventure of being alive and continually *coming home to ourselves* and seeing what is possible, and honoring both the possibilities and the actuality of this moment, even if it feels somewhat limited. Just *opening* to accepting things inwardly and outwardly in this moment, just as they are. (Meili and Kabat-Zinn, 2004, 10; emphasis added)

As this quote indicates, mindfulness involves opening to the experience and to actually be present in one's body, to "come home to ourselves." And what does it mean to open to the experience of being alive, to "come home to ourselves," to actually be present in one's body? Where and how does one start? Furthermore, this paragraph points to a way of being and a practice of being: living inside (a sense of bodily dwelling in the world acknowledging limitations and possibilities inwardly and outwardly), coming home to ourselves, and opening to experience as it is. It is important to note that "living inside" does not mean a disconnection from the external world but rather it involves acknowledging the inner landscape along with the outer, something that gets undermined despite its significant ethical implications in our lives that I discuss later in this chapter.

The excerpt below from Santorelli's (2000) poetically written, deeply insightful and informative book, sharing his personal and professional experiences at the Stress Reduction Clinic at the University of Massachusetts Medical Center, provides us with a specific illustration of "coming home to ourselves." The following is Santorelli's introduction of Marie, a participant of the eight-week stress reduction program who has been a high-powered businesswoman for a long time. Marie came to the program feeling much anxiety and experiencing episodes of panic attacks; she carries a big bag with her all the time, like a survival kit, filled with water bottles, address books, keys, and so on. Santorelli writes:

> She begins her introduction with a disclaimer, telling us that the person before us isn't who she really is. Her words attest to just how much we live our lives as disclaimers—when I become, if only I were like her, when I was young, before this happened—and how we easily disown or become separated from ourselves and the actuality of our lives. . . . I am struck most powerfully by her final testament: "I want to take back my life." There is some silence between us, and then we have a brief conversation. (2000, 28–29)

Santorelli points to the human tendency of living our lives as "disclaimers," providing Marie's self-introduction in his class as an example, where she introduced herself by disowning herself in that moment. He gives various examples from our everyday language where people either identify with a self that belongs to the past ("when I was young," "before this happened") or future ("when I become"), or with someone that they are not ("if only I were like her"), and disown their present experience. Santorelli then introduces the final part of Marie's introduction, where he was most influenced by her statement: "I want to take back my life." The conversation that follows (Santorelli 2000, 28–29, *line numbers added*) starts with a silence following Marie's comment on "taking back my life," continuing with Santorelli's question on line 1:

Excerpt #1
S: Saki
M: Marie

   1. S: Can you say something about what you mean by "taking back my
   2. life?"
   3. M: I want to be the way I was before all of this happened. I want to get
   4. back to being who I used to be.
   5. S: Do you think that you can ever go back to who you were? I'm not
   6. sure that's possible. I'm not sure that you would want to, even if
   7. you could.
   8. M: But I used to be so strong, so energetic, so able to handle all kinds
   9. of situations, and now look at me. I'm a mess. I've got to have this
10. bag. I didn't drive here, someone drove me. I'm in therapy. I cry a
11. lot—my eyes are always red. I want to get better.
12. S: When I said I'm not sure if you can ever go back to who you were,
13. I didn't mean that you can't, as you say, "get better" or grow, just
14. that you have changed. You just told us that you've gone through
15. something that has altered you. There's no telling how you will be,
16. but if you place a memory of how you were over what you are
17. becoming, you might close out all sorts of possibilities. Can you
18. sense what I mean?
19. M: I think so.

Santorelli's (S) inquiry about Mary's (M) utterance on her desire to take her life back highlights it as a significant utterance for mutual attention and further exploration. Similar to the excerpts I shared from the breast cancer survivors, Marie's statement shows a desire to restore a prior self-concept (and to reclaim her past identity and life). Upon Saki's questioning of Marie's desire and his doubt about her actualization of her desire even if it were possible, Marie provides a favorable assessment of her past self (line 8), emphasizing her independency (describing her past self as strong, energetic, and able), which she follows by a negative assessment of her present self (lines 9–11), describing herself as a "mess" who is dependent on her bag as well as others (she didn't drive to the class, she is in therapy) and unable to control her emotions (she cries a lot and her eyes are always red). M's display of a contrast between her past self and present self serves as an account in response to S's doubt and a justification for her wish to "take her life back" and to "get better" (line 11), implying her preference for her past self. Saki then clarifies his prior statement on lines 5–6 as he aligns with M on her desire to "get better" and expands M's use of the term "get better" to include "growing" (line 13). Bringing up the term "grow," S then brings attention to the change M has experienced (lines 13–15) and explains that holding on to the memory of a past self to "get better" might close the possibility of "growing" into the self that she is becoming, suggesting growth as a way of "getting better" (lines 16–17). S's remarks on lines 16–17 brings an alternative to M's polarized display of her transformation where she characterized herself as either a "mess" (that she rejects) or as on top of everything (which belongs to the past) and points to "all sorts of possibilities" (line 17) that are present in her *process of "becoming."* As he mentions the present possibilities, Saki states a condition ("if" on line 16) that might lead to a potential loss of the possibilities: placing a memory of her past self ("take back my life" on lines 1–2) over who she is becoming in the present. It is important to note that Saki introduces the verb "to become" in the present tense ("what you are becoming" lines 16–17) and not in the future (as in "what you will become"), which he already indicated the uncertain status of (line 15: "there is no telling what you will be"). *Thus, by framing the future as uncertain and the past as potentially limiting, Saki grounds M's transformational process in the present, suggesting exploration of and inhabiting the present experience (contact), as he introduces "becoming" as an alternative to "taking back life."* This attending to and grounding in (and the implied invitation to inhabit and explore) one's present experience illustrates *"learning to live inside," a significant aspect of existential contact*: "coming home to ourselves and seeing what is possible, and honoring both the possibilities and the actuality of this moment, even if it feels somewhat limited. Just opening to accepting things inwardly and outwardly in this moment, just as they are" (Meili and Kabat-Zinn 2004, 10). Although this quote does not refer to the concept of contact directly, the act of coming home to oneself and accepting things as they are resonates with Macke's (2015) statement on making "meaningful and substantial contact with the ecstasy and tragedy of one's fleshy being" (65) that I shared earlier. What we learn from the dialogue between S and M above is the emphasis on turning toward and meeting existence on its own terms rather than turning away from making contact because what we see or experience is not likable, preferable, or is vulnerable. At the end of this conversation, Saki asks for feedback from M where she responds with an answer that shows openness with some degree of hesitation, "I think so," indicating processing of the interaction that just took place. The two narratives I share below illustrate the practice of mindfulness as making contact and learning to inhabit one's life on its own terms that I connect to existential rootedness.

Two Narratives on "Learning to Live Inside"

In the following I present parts of Elana Rosenbaum's experience of surviving cancer (non-Hodgkin's lymphoma) that illustrates the process and implications of "living inside," opening and being present to one's experience in the face of life-threatening illness. Elena states, "Staying present and paying attention *without judgment* was vital if I didn't want to get lost and swallowed up by self-pity or despair. It became imperative that I focus on what I did have control over—my attitude—in order to maintain a sense of well-being" (Rosenbaum 2005, 14). She further states:

> I'd like to be free of cancer, but that's not within my control. The way I approach this time is within my control. It's important to me to free myself from that which binds and perpetuates suffering. I hope to be free to see clearly, to experience happiness and well-being and to face what arises with courage and faith. The present moment is my home. The more I can be HERE with acceptance, the happier I can be. (Rosenbaum 2005, 73)

Elana emphasizes focusing on that which is under her control rather than worrying about what she cannot control, and on being present to her experiences with acceptance to maintain a sense of well-being. She describes her attitude about freeing herself from suffering and to meet her experiences with courage and faith. This includes acknowledging thoughts and emotions as well as physical limitations whether one likes them or not:

> I am committed to being wherever I am as fully and as honestly as possible. I do not like acknowledging limitations or facing my vulnerability. I do not like choosing rest over activity. Yet, I have learned that to maintain my equilibrium, I must be ruthlessly honest with myself and admit when I have to "stop." This is new to me and confronts any shred of omnipotence I might once have held. . . . To be fully in the moment, here, not lost in the thought of a wish or a "should," is my challenge, and I find it necessary to be a warrior through the jungle of myself. . . . And as I open to these thoughts, these fears, these illusions of control, these wishes to be different, I also open to a deep sense of peace and appreciation of life itself. I receive succor from nature. I have celebrated snowfall and rain. I feel the wind on my cheek and appreciate my warm coat, the solace of my home, and my husband, friends, and colleagues. I feel more deeply connected not only to myself but to others and the universe around. (Kabat-Zinn et al. 2002, 293).

Elana writes about listening to the actuality of one's experience and accepting whatever is present beyond expectations or thoughts of wishing to be different. She refers to this process as a challenge and uses metaphors like "being a warrior" and "the jungle of my self" to express the struggle to meet one's experiences. Struggling in this way has its rewards as well, as Elana explains: opening to meet challenging thoughts and emotions also brings a "deep sense of peace and appreciation of life" for her. She states that she feels deeply connected to herself, others, and the universe as well. For Elana, learning to live inside meant opening to and acknowledging thoughts, emotions, physical limitations, and being connected to whatever is present in her experience rather than rejecting or resisting them. Furthermore, and importantly, this connection with her self extends to include others and nature as well, resulting in a peaceful state of being and an appreciation for life.

Kabat-Zinn et al. (2002) state that "mindfulness encourages a willingness to look deeply into any and all emotional states and life circumstances, even negative or scary ones, simply because they are already present and a part of your experience. If pain and suffering suddenly become part of your life, they thus become appropriate to embrace with mindful awareness" (291). Furthermore, they emphasize the difference between *pain* and *suffering*, which are often used as interchangeable terms. They state that pain refers to "basic sensory input, whether physical or emotional, that is perceived as hurtful" (292), whereas suffering "describes an emotional interpretation of that input." Applied to the context of women with breast cancer, the authors state that mindfulness practice can provide insight into coping with one's situation and complement the use of medication when needed for the control of pain.

> Meditation calls on you to look deeply and nonjudgmentally into the experience of pain as bare sensation, even if it is only for a few moments at a time at first.... When you are in pain, this might mean directing your attention to a particular region of the body and coupling it with a sense of the breath moving in and out of that region, observing any changes in sensations from moment to moment.... In this way, you might find that thoughts and feelings about pain, such as "this is killing me" or "I don't know if I can stand this" are in fact different from the actual hurtful sensations, like burning, shooting, squeezing, tearing and aching. And if you ask yourself, "Is this killing me right now, in this very moment?" the answer is almost always no. It is thinking about the duration, meaning, or intensity of the pain that produces most of the suffering. This one realization can reduce both emotional distress and suffering from physical pain. (Kabat-Zinn et al. 2002, 292)

Trisha Meili's experience illustrates the above paragraph clearly. Ms. Meili experienced traumatic brain injury after being attacked, raped, and beaten in Central Park until she was unconscious. In a presentation at Spaulding Rehabilitation Hospital in Boston with Dr. Jon Kabat-Zinn (founder of the Center for Mindfulness in Medicine, Healthcare and Society at the University of Massachusetts) she revealed her identity as the "Central Park Jogger" and talked about her recovery process. Ms. Meili explained that when she was going through her recovery, her "body instinctively took over in a mindful way," which she thinks was essential to her healing (Meili and Kabat-Zinn 2004, 7). She says that although she did not consciously make the decision to mindfully relate to her situation, she later realized that she began to "live inside" naturally, living in the present and accepting/meeting her reality. She explains:

> I wasn't thinking, "Why did I go out running that night?" A friend of mine had called me earlier in the afternoon, about 5 o'clock to go to dinner, and that phone call was the last thing I remember. I had said to my friend, "You know what, I can't go. I've got some work to do." In the hospital, I didn't think, "Why didn't I go to dinner?" or "Why didn't I go to run 10 minutes earlier or 20 minutes later so that this wouldn't have happened?" I didn't think such things, and was told by several nurses that early on I never said anything like, "Why did this happen to me, why didn't I do something different?" What I did seem to be thinking without knowing is, "Here it is—this is my situation." I'll try to make the most of this reality that's mine, and "I've got a lot of work to do." (Meili and Kabat-Zinn 2004, 11–12)

Rather than being lost in and carried away by doubtful thoughts about her experience and questioning and resisting her present situation, Ms. Meili explains that she was focused on what she could do in the moment to heal, and the first step toward it was accepting her reality. She did not create and feed suffering by useless thoughts and emotional interpretations of her situation but acknowledged her current situation to be part of her life and intended to live it fully. She adds that she "somehow wasn't terribly worried about what I was going to do in six months, where I was going to be. I just had this feeling that I was going to be okay. I wasn't quite sure what that meant. But I just had this calmness, this sense that it's going to be all right" (12). Thus, in addition to her focus on the present, Ms. Meili highlights trusting an inner knowing and not worrying about the future as part of her healing process. Step by step, she attended to the needs of her life and her bodily existence as it is, meeting the challenges by listening and discerning.

The narratives of Elana and Trisha both highlight the importance of attending to the actuality of one's experience beyond judgment and meeting whatever is present beyond thoughts of wishing to be different and resisting the current situation in their processes of healing. In this way, they could focus on the healing process itself rather than spending their time and energy with unnecessary thoughts and questioning. Both Trisha and Elana attended to their bodily experience moment by moment, step by step, which illustrate learning to "live inside" as they deeply listened to discern what is needed beyond the impositions of willful thinking.

By meeting the challenges and needs in this attentive way, it seems that Trisha and Elana worked to cultivate what Gumbrecht (2004) refers to as a "presence-based relation" (xv) to the world and to their bodily existence. They resisted the presence effects (Gumbrecht 2004, 108) to be hijacked by meaning effects by staying close to their bodily, sense-based experience, and by observing their own thoughts and meaning-making processes. By doing so, they could discern what distracted their attentive orientation to the present and made a choice to come back to meeting existence.

AN INQUIRY ON SENSE-MAKING AND THE SELF

The excerpt below from a participant (Sandy) in the MBSR (mindfulness-based stress reduction) training followed by a dialogue between her and the teachers complement the narratives above as well as the first excerpt I presented. It adds a significant layer to our exploration of mindfulness in underlining the awareness and discernment of the sensible and the conceptual as part of our human experience and contact with the world as well as ourselves.

Following a "mindful eating" practice where the teachers led the participants in the group in eating two raisins mindfully (very slow, attentive eating practice engaging all five senses), Sandy takes her turn to talk about her experience of this eating meditation. Sandy starts with a personal account of her experience:

> I've done this exercise a lot with clients as well. I teach mindfulness based nutrition and mindfulness eating and I hate raisins, and so I began to feel the pattern of anxiousness when I saw the bowls coming down the aisle like "oh no I have to eat a raisin." And this is one of the first times that I actually stayed with the experience of chewing and feeling the spurt of the raisin juice in my mouth and I actually liked the raisin (laughter) the first time in my life. It was a really powerful experience to— to feel that for the first time and to stay with it. My anxiety about eating the raisin subsided really quickly when I just stayed with each moment of feeling it on my tongue and chewing it and just stayed with each moment I— I felt much better about the process. (Sandy, June 4, 2005)

After reporting her experience with eating raisins mindfully as a part of her profession, Sandy states that she hates raisins. She also tells us (or rather, confesses) that for the first time of all these experiences she actually attended to the eating experience, that is, she did not distance herself from it but she was present and attentive to the chewing and feeling the taste and the whole process and found out that she actually liked it. Sandy characterized this experience as "powerful" and indicated that when she was present to each moment in the eating experience her anxiety dissolved. Upon hearing this account, Saki (S) asked Sandy about her experience.

> Excerpt #2
> S: Saki (teacher)
> P: Participant (Sandy)
> J: Jon (teacher)
>
> 1. Saki: So you actually—what's your name
> 2. P: Sandy
> 3. S: You discovered something about the difference
> 4. between thinking and sensing
> 5. P: °Yeah°
> 6. S: Caus' you said it very strongly ↑I don't like raisins
> 7. I hate raisins actually
> 8. ((audience laughter))
> 9. S: Well (.) who is the I that enjoyed it
> 10. ((hmm from audience))
> 11. S: And then where is the I that hates them
> 12. (0.7)

[The transcript symbols used were developed by Gail Jefferson (2004): bubbles indicate quieter speech, upward arrows indicate marked rising shifts in intonation, and a dot in parenthesis indicates a micro pause, less than 0.2 seconds.]

On lines 3 and 4, Saki frames P's report as a "discovery" and identifies what the discovery is by distinguishing two processes: "thinking" and "sensing." Sandy confirms Saki's framing and identification in a quiet tone. Saki then continues with an account on lines 6–7 and repeats Sandy's verbalization of her relation to raisins. On lines 9 and 11, Saki inquiries about the personal pronouns that Sandy used in reporting her contradictory experiences regarding her relation to the raisin. Bringing attention to Sandy's paradoxical reports of her relation to raisins, one that is based on generalization and thinking ("I hate raisins") and the other based on sensing (tasting and liking the raisin), allows Saki to question the way Sandy makes sense of the world and draws fixed conclusions leading to generalizations. At that point, the other teacher joins in the inquiry process of making sense through fixed concepts and ideas:

> 13. J: And maybe that's just a concept (.) you know that
> => 14. You know— you (.) may (.) never have tasted a raisin
> => 15. Maybe you're just tasting your concept
> 16. ((quiet audience laughter))

Jon's remark on line 13 highlights Saki's questioning of the use of personal pronouns and concepts in making sense of one's experiences. Jon brings up the possibility that Sandy's expression of her relation to the raisin is based on an idea ("that's just a concept") and expands the possibility further to include that she might not have "never" really tasted a raisin (experientially, beyond the idea) on line 14. Thus, he points to the possibility of making sense in abstraction rather than based on the actual tasting by being in the experience (line 15). The conversation ends by Sandy's acknowledgment that she was chewing on her concept: "I think I was chewing on my concept and it was—it was really powerful for me to chew that huh huh." Sandy's response shows that she indeed "discovered something," as Saki suggested at the beginning of the conversation (line 3,) as she is now reflecting on as a "powerful" experience. Through her acknowledgment and self-reflective response, she displays her recognition of her conceptual sense-making.

"There is all the difference between thinking and knowing that thought is happening," writes Larry Rosenberg (2004, 15) in his book *Breath by Breath*. And he goes on: "Thinking is a marvelous human activity . . . , but thinking often comes between us and our experience. In as much as it does, we are not intimate with that moment. We are not mindful" (Rosenberg 2004, 16). It seems like this is what the teachers in the above excerpt are pointing to and demonstrating through their inquiry; the sense-making through thinking, in abstraction, and bringing attention to this abstract sense-making process ("who is the I that hates it and then where is the I that enjoyed them," "May be that's just a concept," "Maybe you're just tasting your concept," "chewing on them all day long have you noticed"). From all the discourses analyzed in this paper, it seems like this discernment process is essential to mindfulness discourses: distinguishing thoughts as thoughts, not to be confused with the actual, moment by moment unfolding of the present experience (such as being in touch with the tasting of a raisin).

Rosenberg (2004, 66–67) articulately illustrates the process of sensing and attending to sensations versus jumping into abstractions and separating ourselves from the present experience in the following:

> As I write, there is a small knot at the top of my stomach. I focus on the feeling: a slight pressure, a full feeling, at the top of the stomach. Perhaps there is some vivid feeling in your body that you can focus on as you read this. That feeling of pressure becomes the object of my attention. I don't pull back from it; I come in close and touch it. There is the feeling in my stomach, which is unpleasant; there is mindfulness, which is able to turn to it; and there is conscious breathing, which nourishes the mindfulness and keeps it on course. *Part of the way it does is to cut down unnecessary thinking.* . . . Everything is focused on that sensation. We're not trying to add to it, subtract from it, make it feel better, change it in

any way. We try to experience it with *no separation whatsoever*. Even being a self-conscious observer is separation. We have spent years being ego-centric and divided. It feels as if there's me and there's a pain in my stomach, as if the pain is an alien thing, attacking me. There's a struggle going on; *I* want to get rid of it. (Rosenberg 2004, 66–67; emphasis added)

Rosenberg describes his experience of stomach pain and his relation to it in a specific and mindful way as he explains and illustrates the practice of mindfulness. Similar to the narratives and excerpts analyzed before as in "*I* want to take back my life," and "*I* hate raisins," Rosenberg expresses the struggle he observes, "*I* want to get rid of it," and makes a point about the tendency to separate himself from the experience. He then describes mindfulness as the act of turning toward the present experience and attending to it without trying to change it in any way. He goes on to say that

"I" is just a notion. This sense of "I" serves to distance and separate us from the unwanted.... We don't *become* one with the object [object of attention such as the breath, pain, or sounds]. We already are *one* with it.... I am at this moment the pain in my stomach and the breathing and the sound of a machine thudding in the distance and the squawking of a bird outside my window and my pen moving across the page; you are your eyes taking in these words and whatever else is going on for you. (Rosenberg 2004, 67)

The sense of self that Rosenberg discusses above merges the doer and the experience; where there is no separate "I" having an experience as it is commonly assumed and experienced. Thus, rather than a self that is experienced as separate from the bodily experiences and its surroundings, Rosenberg is pointing to an expansive "self" that is inclusive of all that is going on inside and outside. The boundaries of a conventional self is under exploration here and questions like "who is the I that hates it [the raisin]" or "who is the I that enjoyed it" serve as pointers to pay attention to how experience actually unfolds beyond the conceptual and conventional boundaries.

IMPLICATIONS FOR AESTHETIC ECOLOGY OF COMMUNICATION ETHICS: BEING A "PARTICIPATION" IN THE WORLD OF THINGS

At the beginning of this chapter, I highlighted Merleau-Ponty's (1968) framework of the reciprocal coexistence of the seen and the seer, being a "participation" (Merleau-Ponty, 1968) in the world of visible things and "intertwining" as part of the discussion on contact with one's visible reflection. For Merleau-Ponty (1968), it is through becoming a part of the visible things that the mystery and the possibility of the visible can be unveiled—though never completely—rather than the enveloping of the things with the gaze that "imposes my vision upon me as a continuation of its own sovereign existence" (131). It is this attitude of imposition versus a receptive-interactive-inquiry of becoming that this chapter explores through a variety of narratives and dialogues.

The mindfulness-based discourses I examined, including Elena and Trisha's self-narratives, the dialogue between Saki and the participant in the MBSR class, the dialogue on eating a raisin, and the quotes from Rosenberg above lead to a major common theme: nondual existence; regrounding (rooting) the separate "I" in experience. In Merleau-Ponty's (1968) terms: being a "participation." In the *Phenomenology of Perception,* Merleau-Ponty (2002) compares the relation of the sentient and the sensible to the sleeper and his slumber:

> Sleep comes when a certain voluntary attitude suddenly receives from outside the confirmation for which it was waiting. I am breathing deeply and slowly in order to summon sleep, and suddenly it is as if my mouth were connected to some great lung outside myself which alternately calls forth and forces back my breath. A certain rhythm of respiration, which a moment ago I voluntarily maintained, now becomes my very being, and sleep, until now aimed at as a significance, suddenly becomes a situation. In the same way I give ear, or look, in the expectation of a sensation, and suddenly the sensible takes possession of my ear or my gaze, and I surrender a part of my body, even my whole body, to this particular manner of vibrating and filling space known as blue or red. (245–46)

It is this surrendering of the sentient to the sensible, the seer to the seen, that gives way to the "great lung" that, with its own rhythm, takes possession of the subject and takes it beyond signification to the situation, to the vibrations of experience. Merleau-Ponty (2002) highlights this reciprocal relation in the process of perception between the sensible and the body, the intertwining that is the "great lung outside myself," which he earlier (in *The Visible and the Invisible*) refers to as the flesh of the world to which the seer and the seen belongs. Similar to Rosenberg's (2004) discussion of the "I" that resists surrendering to experience and struggles—who can't fall asleep either—Merleau-Ponty points to the merging of a part with the larger whole that already is a part of, a rerooting of the sentient in the sensible, an "intertwining."

The mindfulness discourses analyzed in this chapter all point to the common human tendency of separating ourselves from the present experience through our unique capacity of making sense in abstraction (facilitated through language). They also highlight attending to one's experience moment by moment and remind us about our capacity to make sense by actually sensing, by inhabiting and embodying the present experience rather than separating ourselves from it (in other words, becoming a "participation"). Distancing ourselves from the actuality of our present experience through identification with fixed concepts about self, others, and other aspects of life create a sense of dividedness and suffering as in the narratives of breast cancer survivors presented in the introduction (identification with a fixed past self-image: "Who is this? This isn't me") or, in excerpt 1: "I want to take back my life" (identification with a fixed sense/idea of "life" or position in life). The narratives of Elana and Trisha show that coming to terms with and learning to inhabit one's changing or radically changed body is possible when we turn toward the present experience and attend to it through becoming a "participation" (Merleau-Ponty 1968) beyond dualistic thought.

I heard many stories in my interviews with breast cancer survivors and elsewhere about the initial reaction of "why me?" upon learning about a diagnosis of a life-threatening illness and how this questioning/resisting and disclaiming process can be lengthy, consuming much energy and long periods of time that one could use toward healing. Trisha offers a different alternative when she says "I wasn't thinking, 'Why did I go out running that night' . . . or 'Why didn't I go to run 10 minutes earlier or 20 minutes later so that this wouldn't have happened?'" Rather than worrying about the past that she could not change, she acknowledged and focused on the present situation: "Here it is—this is my situation. I'll try to make the most of this reality that's mine, and "I've got a lot of work to do" (Meili and Kabat-Zinn 2004, 11–12). Elana also emphasizes focusing on that which is under her control rather than worrying about what she cannot control and on being present to her experiences with acceptance to maintain a sense of well-being. What we learn from these narratives is that the discursive choices we make construct the way we make sense of and relate to illness, as well as who we are. As Elana and Trisha's narratives illustrate, focusing on what one can control and not worrying about what one cannot control alleviates unnecessary suffering and helps save energy toward working on what one can do to heal.

Along these lines, the mindfulness-based excerpts and texts I analyzed in this chapter point to and remind us of our "presence-based relation" (Gumbrecht 2004, xv) to the world along with the "meaning effects" that usually dominate. It seems that by guiding our habits of attention that ordinarily skip the present moment experience toward inhabiting it, the practice of mindfulness facilitates an aesthetic orientation in the midst of the struggles of everyday life that Dewey (1958) highlights in *The Art of Experience*. As discussed in the introduction, for Dewey (1958) being part of the immediate environment, valuing and integrating one's present experience to the continuum of the past and the future, is an important source of aesthetic experience. The discussions in this chapter up to this point show that being in contact with one's bodily presence in the world in its various stages and changes, including the visible reflection of one's bodily appearance, facilitates a way of being that is rooted in existence as well as an aesthetic orientation that engages the sensible and cultivates participation in the present.

Acknowledging and cultivating a "presence-based relation" (Gumbrecht 2004, xv) to the world, and an aesthetic orientation that is attentive to one's present experience and the sensible along with the conceptual, is connected to a "situated communication ethic" that Arnett (2012, 166) writes about. Arnett (2012) explains that a situated communication ethic begins with responsiveness—not willful imposition—to existence itself without assuming that we are in control of the world. Such attentiveness to existence invites us to walk in "the mud of everyday life" (as qtd. in Arnett 2012, 164) and to engage the messy, the strange, and the uncertain. A "situated communication ethic" is connected to the discussion of "embedded identity" (Arnett, 2011) that "assumes that we are derivative creatures. We are not self-made persons who pull ourselves by our own bootstraps" (241). Embeddedness highlights that our identity is a product of situations, relationships, stories, and culture that constitute the ground for life. We do not exist independent of these sources of our life. In contrast to embedded identity, Arnett (2011) refers to individualism in "disembedding the human being from a situated existence" (243) and as a willfulness that "takes the ground that situates us from under our feet." The discussions on con/tact throughout this chapter underlining the inhabiting of one's life and one's changing bodily existence reflect an "embedded identity" (Arnett 2011) as opposed to a willful, autonomous agent that disregards our situated existence. Learning to be in con/tact and becoming a "participation" (Merleau-Ponty 1968) in the world facilitates the possibility of a way of being (or moments of being, at least) that is rooted in existence, alleviating suffering even in the midst of a life-threatening illness.

REFERENCES

Arnett, Ron C. 2011. "Embeddedness/Embedded Identity." In *Encyclopedia of Identity*. Edited by Ronald L. Jackson, 241–43. Thousand Oaks, CA: Sage.

———. 2012. "Communication Ethics as Janus at the Gates: Responding to Postmodernity and the Normativity of Crisis." In *Communication Ethics and Crisis: Negotiating Differences in Public and Private Spheres*. Edited by S. Alyssa Groom and Janie M. H. Fritz. Lanham, MD: The Fairleigh Dickinson University Press.

Gumbrecht, Hans Ulricht. 2004. *Production of Presence: What Meaning Cannot Convey*. Stanford, CA: Stanford University Press.

Jefferson, Gail. 2004. "Glossary of Transcript Symbols with an Introduction." In *Conversation Analysis: Studies from the First Generation*, 13–32. Philadelphia, PA: John Benjamins Publishing Co.

Joyce, James. 1914. *Dubliners*. New York: Oxford University Press.

Kabat-Zinn, John, Ann Ohm Massion, James R. Hèbert, and Elana, Rosenbaum. 2002. "Meditation." In *Breast Cancer: Beyond Convention*, edited by Tagliaferri, Mary., Isaac Cohen, and Debu Tripathy, 284-214. New York, NY: Atria Books.

Macke, Frank. 2015. *The Experience of Human Communication: Body, Flesh, and Relationship*. Lanham, MD: Fairleigh Dickinson University Press.

Meili, Trisha, and Jon Kabat-Zinn. 2004. "The Power of the Human Heart: A Story of Trauma and Recovery and Its Implications for Rehabilitation and Healing." *Advances in Mind-Body Medicine* 20(1).

Merleau-Ponty, Maurice. 1964. "Eye and Mind." In *The Primacy of Perception: And Other Essays on Phenomenological Psychology, the Philosophy of Art, History, and Politics*. Evanston, IL: Northwestern University Press.

———. 1968. *The Visible and the Invisible*. Translated by Alphonso Lingis. Edited by Claude Lefort. Evanston, IL: Northwestern University Press.

———. 2002. *Phenomenology of Perception*. Translated by Colin Smith. New York: Routledge Classics.

Nancy, Jean-Luc. 2000. *Being Singular Plural*. Stanford: Stanford University Press.

Rosenbaum, Elana. 2005. *Here for Now: Living Well with Cancer through Mindfulness*. Hardwick, MA: Satya House Publications.

Rosenberg, Larry. 2004. *Breath by Breath: The Liberating Practice of Insight Meditation*. Boston: Shambhala Publications.

Santorelli, Saki. 2000. *Heal Thy Self: Lessons on Mindfulness in Medicine*. New York: Bell Tower.

Üçok, Özüm. 2005. "From Diagnostic to Aesthetic: Moving Beyond Diagnosis." *Language Power and Social Process* 16: 65.

Chapter Five

Attending to the Breath (of The Other)

This chapter is an exploration of a subtle yet transformative perspective regarding communication ethics, in calling for attentiveness to the breath, and the breath of the other beyond a "visual or an audio-ethic" (Arnett 2017). I explore the breath as a phenomenological element of human experience that facilitates a way of being in direct contact with one's bodily participation in the world. Cultivating the breath calls for being in touch with the sensation, texture, and rhythm of one's breath as well as learning to yield to the life of the breath, receiving its life-giving power and extending this gift to the other. Thus, it might be considered as an ethics of in-touch-ness and conceived as a form of tactile ethic that invites us to be anchored in existence through this most existential yet invisible element. As Rilke (1995) puts:

> We, who are still the breathed-upon,
> today still the breathed upon, count
> this slow breathing of earth,
> whose hurry we are.

This chapter shows that attending to and cultivating the breath facilitates *methexis* (Gadamer, 2007), a sense of belonging together and presence. Being in touch with one's breath and the breath of the other invites an aesthetic sensibility that engages the senses, enabling a present-moment orientation that is receptive, responsive, and in Dewey's (1958) terms, aesthetic. I then conclude this chapter with a discussion on *aesthetic ethic of speaking* that emerges in connecting the breath with speech, making space for the coming together of the "will to speak" (Bachelard 2002, 243) and the "poetic will" (244). I argue that speech that is immersed in the silence of the breath, and awakened by the breath, is not self-focused but responsive to the breath of the other.

In *Breath of Proximity: Intersubjectivity, Ethics and Peace*, Škof (2015a) writes about "the Western condition of being oblivious to the breath" (7) and questions our tendency to "still . . . forget the breath in philosophy" (7). "Why do we avoid this original phenomenon, maybe the only phenomenon that can lead us to the proximity of creation as ethical beings, that can guide us towards new forms of reciprocity, perhaps towards a new ethico-political non-violent conversation which could be part of this creation" (Škof, 2015a, 7). Škof argues for an ethics of breath(ing) that would serve to cultivate an ethical (inter)subjectivity, as well as a possible nonviolent, ethical-political conversation. In framing an "ethics of radical (inter)subjectivity," Škof (2015a, p. 8) highlights a task that needs to be undertaken that is a *"spiritual transformation of humanity."* This task involves not only to learn "how to ethically respond to the call of another human being or of a non-human species" but also "their *breathing*, since breathing means staying alive and sensing everything and everyone that is alive around us" (Škof, 2015a, 8). The (inter)subjectivity that Škof (2015a) proposes is "radical" in its emphasis on becoming more "receptive to the breath and the life of the other" (8).

Before diving into a discussion of an ethics of breath(ing), I first offer some historical and intercultural context on the principle of air as the first principle of nature (based on Anaximenes's theory of air, one of the first pre-Socratic philosophers of the sixth century) and on the understanding and importance of air/breath as *prana* (universal life energy) in Indian thought. Following this discussion, I explore Luce Irigaray's (1999, 2002, 2010) philosophy of breath in connection to communication ethics. Finally, Gaston Bachelard's (2002) work on the life-giving role of the breath in relation to words—and poetry specifically—conclude the chapter.

THE PRINCIPLE OF AIR

In *Philosophy Before Socrates,* McKirahan (1994) writes that the work of Greek philosophers including Socrates (born in 469 BCE) have been strongly influenced by the philosopher-scientists known as "pre-Socratics." However, given that the work of these early pioneers has not been preserved (printing was invented in the fifteenth century CE), we only have partial access to their writings (quotations, paraphrases, summaries, etc.). McKirahan's (1994) work in gathering together precious fragments from early Greek philosophy, along with other evidence on their thought, has served as a significant source for the first part of this chapter in facilitating a historical connection to the discussion of a philosophy and ethics of breath. McKirahan (1994) quotes Hippolytus on Anaximenes of Miletus who theorized about air as the basic principle:

> Anaximenes . . . said that the principle is unlimited [apeiron] air, out of which come to be things that are coming to be, things that have come to be, and things that will be, and gods and divine things. The rest come to be out of the products of this. The form of air is the following: when it is most even, it is invisible, but it is revealed by the cold and the hot and the wet, and movement. It is always moving, for all the things that undergo change would not change unless it was moving. For when it is dissolved into what is finer, it comes to be fire, and on the other hand air comes to be winds when it becomes condensed. Cloud results from air through felting, and water when this happens to a greater degree. When condensed still more it becomes earth and when it reaches the absolutely densest stage it becomes stones. (Hippolytus, *Refutation*, 1.7.1–3 = DK 13A7, as qtd. in McKirahan 1994, 48–49)

Anaximenes highlights that everything has properties of air, including fire, wind, clouds, water, earth, as well as stones. Anaximenes refers to the form of air as invisible yet it becomes perceptible in connection to the surrounding conditions such as the heat and the cold, movement, or processes such as condensation or rarefaction. Anaximenes's teacher Anaximander theorized about the ultimate source of all things as *apeiron*, which is "eternal, ageless, and in motion, and that a plurality of heavens and worlds arise or are born out of it and are surrounded by it" (McKirahan 1994, 34); however, he left the discussion on *apeiron* indeterminate. It was Anaximenes who declared the underlying principle as air, which takes on different properties (such as fire, wind, water, earth) depending on the conditions. At the end of the first sentence in the quote above, Anaximenes states that air is the source of the gods and divine things ("air, out of which come to be . . . gods and divine things"). Along these lines, McKirahan (1994), cites Cicero on Anaximenes: "Anaximenes determined that air is a god and that it comes to be and is without measure, infinite, and always in motion" (Cicero, *On the Nature of Gods* 1.10.26 = DK 13A10, as qtd. in McKirahan, 52). Cicero's account of Anaximenes's theory of air differs from Hippolytus's (in the block quote earlier) in that Cicero states that for Anaximenes "air is a god" rather than air being the source of gods.

Whether air is a god for Anaximenes or is the source of divine qualities is not a central concern for the purposes of this essay; however, the connection of air to the breath that Anaximenes described needs to be highlighted. McKirahan (1994) directly quotes Anaximenes on another role of air: "Just as our soul, being air, holds us together and controls us, so do breath and air surround the whole KOSMOS" (Anaximenes, DK 13B2). Anaximenes compares and connects the function of breath and air to the function of the soul, which is to "hold us together." As the soul gives life to humans, air and breath surround the universe and hold it together. Air is the life-giving principle, and Anaximenes identifies the soul with air. In this short quote Anaximenes connects air, breath, and the soul, and according to McKirahan (1994) offers a microcosm-macrocosm analogy, "the view that humans and the universe are constructed or function similarly" (54). (In a footnote, McKirahan (1994) explained that he translated *SUNKRATEIN* as "hold together and control" in the above quote, which he states could be an overtranslation, and the Greek might mean "hold together" only. Therefore, I did not include the control-related discussion here.)

In a chapter titled "The Wind" in his poetic and influential book *Air and Dreams: An Essay on the Imagination of Movement*, Bachelard (2002) writes about the dynamism of air and the vitality of the blowing wind and touches on the relationship between the wind and the breath. Bachelard (2002) highlights the importance of breathing exercises that have a major importance in Indian thought, which "are actual rites that put man in contact with the universe," and which "take on a moral value in this system" (236–37).

Although "breath(ing) is undoubtedly the most forgotten and neglected aspect of all cosmological and bodily phenomenon" (Škof 2015a, 11), prana—"breath, respiration, life, vitality, energy or strength" (Iyengar 2008, 13) or "vital breaths or currents of energy" (13)—and pranayama has a significant place in ancient and contemporary yoga philosophy. Yogacharya B. K. S. Iyengar, a leading Indian international yoga master, writes, "According to the Upanishads, prana is the principle of life and consciousness. . . . Prana is the breath of life of all beings in the universe. They are born through and live by it, and when they die their individual breath dissolves into the cosmic breath (Iyengar 2008, 12). Iyengar highlights the connection between the individual breath and the cosmic breath through the discussion of prana, the principle of life. It is this connection of the breath as a bodily phenomenon with the cosmological sphere, the microcosm-macrocosm connection between humans and the universe through the life-giving breath that is at the center of an ethics of being in Indian philosophy that the next section explores.

PRANA: THE UNIVERSAL BREATH

In "Ethics of Breath: Towards New Ethical Spaces of Intersubjectivity," Škof (2015b) writes about the "breath as an intercultural phenomenon" and states that

> Different macrocosmic and microcosmic designations for wind/breath (or wind/spirit) in the history of religions and philosophies (mana, orenda, ka, ruah, prana, atman, aer, psyche, pneuma, anima, spiritus, ik', ki/qi, etc.) point to a common physico-anthropological phenomenon of life and, more importantly,

to our common physiological roots, which are not conceived as a substance of *human nature* but as a primal phenomenon prior to any philosophical or metaphysical theory. (Škof 2015b, 200)

Breath as a primal phenomenon that is common to our human existence across cultures precedes all philosophical or metaphysical reflection. (For instance, as written in the Bible, "And the LORD God formed man *of* the dust of the ground, and breathed into his nostrils the breath of life; and man became a living soul" [Genesis 2:7, KJV]). Whatever cultural or religious designation it might have, pneuma, prana, ki/qi, or else, breath is at the heart of our "human, common *and* communal relatedness" (Škof 2015b, 200).

As stated earlier, breath (along with mind and speech) has a significant place in Indian thought. Škof (2015b) writes about the Indian Vedic collections (Samhitas) that have references to cosmic wind/breath, including the Indian concept of *prana*, and highlights the "Wind-Breath teaching" (Wind-Atem-Lehre), which elaborates the macrocosmic Wind (*vayu*) and microcosmic Breath. Below, I quote directly from the 1896 translation of *Jaiminiya Upanishad Brahmana* (JUB), which establishes the wind as the "entire deity" since all the other "half-deities" return to it and the wind is never exhausted as the other half-deities are.

> III. 1. 1. One entire deity there is; the others are half-deities. [It is] this one namely who cleanses here (the wind). 2. He [represents] the seizers of all the gods. 3. He, indeed, is "setting" by the name. "Setting" they call here the seizers in the west. 4. In that the sun has gone to setting, it has gone to the seizers. Therefore it is not whole. It goes unto that [god]. 5. The moon sets. Therefore it is not whole. It goes unto that [god]. 6. The asterisms set. Therefore they are not whole. They go unto that [god]. 7. The fire goes out. Therefore it is not whole. It goes unto that [god]. 8. Day goes; night goes. Therefore they are not whole. They go unto that [god] . . . 12. So, as this all goes unto wind, therefore is wind the *saman*. 13. He is *saman*-knowing, he [knows] the entire *saman*, who knows thus. (Oertel 1896, 158–59)

The wind endures, it does not go to "setting," yet it is the "setting" that the rest of the elements and deities return to, which makes the wind whole—and a whole deity—according to the text above. The wind is the deity that is "saman-knowing," that is, it knows all the other deities. Thus, the wind is established as the source that all return to and the all-knowing. At the microcosmic level, the level of the human/self, the same text (JUB) refers to the breath as the source and the *saman* (deity) to which all the other senses as well as the speech return:

> III. 1. 14. Now with regard to the self. One who sleeps speaks not with the voice. That same [voice] goes unto breath. 15. He thinks not with the mind. That same [mind] goes unto breath. 16. He sees not with sight. That same [sight] goes unto breath. 17. He hears not with hearing. That same [hearing] goes unto breath. 18. So, as this all goes together unto breath, therefore is breath the *saman*. 19. He is *saman*-knowing, he [knows] the entire *saman*, who knows thus. 20. Now when they say: "Lo! It doth not blow to-day," it is then resting within man; he sits full, sweating. (Oertel 1896, 158–59)

The macrocosmic Wind (vayu) at the human level becomes the microcosmic breath. Since all the senses as well as speech return to the breath during sleep and it is only the breath that remains during sleep—although it could be disputed—breath is elevated to be the complete saman. Furthermore, when the wind is not blowing, it is stated that it rests within man.

The connection of the microcosmic and macrocosmic energies is examined in detail in *Light on Pranayama: The Yogic Art of Breathing*, where Yogacharya Iyengar (2008) writes about the discipline of pranayama, the art and science of breathing:

> Pranayama is a conscious prolongation of inhalation, retention and exhalation. Inhalation is the act of receiving the primeval energy in the form of breath, and retention is when the breath is held in order to savour the energy. In exhalation all thoughts and emotions are emptied with breath: then, while the lungs are empty, one surrenders the individual energy "I," to the primeval energy, the Atma. (Iyengar 2008, 10)

The connection between the breath and the primal, vital energy is attained through the acts of inhalation, retention, and exhalation. It is clear that the breath serves a significant function of not only connecting the individual energy ("I") with the universal, but it also facilitates the surrendering of the "I" to the Atma, the universal Self.

Although it is difficult to explain prana, Iyengar's (2008) pointers are helpful: "Prana is the energy permeating the universe at all levels. It is physical, mental, intellectual, sexual, spiritual and cosmic energy. All vibrating energies are prana. All physical energies such as heat, light, gravity, magnetism and electricity are also prana" (66). Iyengar (2008) further explains that prana is one of the five kinds of vital energy (prana-vayus) or vital breaths/currents that performs functions of the body: prana (thoracic region, controls breathing), apana (lower abdomen, controls elimination), samana (abdominal organs, aids digestion), udana (throat, controls the vocal cords, intake of air and food), and vyana (pervades the entire body; distributes energy from food and breath through the arteries, veins, and nerves). Inward breath activates the prana-vayu and the outward breath activates the apana-vayu.

The discipline of pranayama frames a connection of the body to the larger universal energies that work through the body rather than an understanding of these functions as bodily functions only. Our bodily existence, according to the yoga philosophy and Indian thought in general, is rooted in an exterior universal system with which it is constantly in touch with rather than being rooted in itself as an isolated entity. The practice of pranayama focuses on regulating "the prana throughout the body" (Iyengar 2008,14), which also regulates the "thoughts, desires and actions" and "gives poise and tremendous will-power needed to become a master of oneself" toward the surrendering of the self. Pranayama is not automatic, habitual breathing; it involves specific breathing techniques (ujjayi, viloma, etc.) that regulate the intake and outflow of breath that help concentrate the mind, stimulate the body, and cleanse the various systems (respiratory, circulatory, etc.) and organs of the body through which energy flows.

Iyengar (2008) compares the training required for pranayama to becoming a master musician as he provides instructions for a specific technique called "digital" or "manual" pranayama where the yoga practitioner uses the thumb and two fingers to regulate the flow of breath through the nose (there are forty-three detailed instructions for this practice). Just as a good musician studies the construction, shape, and various characteristics of his or her instrument, the yogi studies "the shape and construction of his nostrils, the texture of their outer skin, the peculiar characteristics of his own nose, such as the width of the nasal passages" (Iyengar 2008, 158). The yogi practices the adjustment of his fingers on the nostrils and the movements of the wrist until he refines them, and he attentively listens to the sound of the breath to adjust its flow, rhythm, and resonance, just like the musician constantly practicing with his or her fingers and ears to be in tune with the sounds, the tone, and the resonance of the music. Pranayama is a deep and challenging practice that requires deliberate, determined training until the breathing is soft and fine. "A beginner in pranayama (adhama) uses physical strength and lacks rhythm and poise. His body and brain are rigid, while his breath is forceful, jerky, and superficial" (Iyengar 2008, 112). With disciplined practice, the yoga student learns "the art of sitting" and maintaining a steady posture, as "his breath is rhythmic, soft and subtle, while his body, mind and intellect are poised" (Iyengar 2008, 112). This soft, subtle, and rhythmic breathing is key to the practice of pranayama since the breath is directly linked to the condition of the body and the mind. Forceful breathing that lacks poise and a balanced rhythm leads to rigidity in the body and mind and cultivates the ego. "Forceful in and out breathing fosters the ego. If the flow is smooth and almost inaudible to the sadhaka, he will be filled with humility. This is the beginning of self-culture" (Iyengar 2008, 174). Iyengar expresses a direct connection between breathing and the self, where the way of breathing leads to a way of being. Cultivation of soft and subtle breathing leads to humility, and forceful breathing promotes the ego.

The next section expands on the discussion on breathing and being, and further connects it to speaking and communication ethics through the work of two influential French philosophers, Luce Irigaray and Gaston Bachelard.

BREATHING, BEING, AND SPEAKING

Luce Irigaray (1999, 2002, 2010) is one of the rare Western philosophers who wrote about the breath in connection to human existence, communication, and ethics. In "The Way of Breath" in *Between East and West,* Irigaray (2002) highlights breathing as the "first autonomous gesture of the living human being" (73), and conscious breathing as "equivalent to taking charge of one's life, to accepting solitude through cutting the umbilical cord, to respecting and cultivating life, for oneself and for others" (74). Irigaray's (2002) discussion of conscious breathing underlines a communication ethic that is essential to acquiring a life that one inhabits intentionally rather than habitually. According to Irigaray (2002), it is through the *practice* of conscious breathing that one gives birth to herself—a second birth. Remaining passive at the level of breathing results in "bathing in a social-cultural placenta that passes on to us an already exhaled, already used, not truly pure air" (Irigaray 2002, 74). Inhaling the already used air without a conscious practice of breathing, we are unable to be connected to the "divine breath" that gives life and remain confused. When we cultivate conscious breathing, we are slowly able to transform our elemental vital breath into "a more subtle breath in the service of the heart, of thought, of speech and not only in the service of physiological survival" (Irigaray 2002, 76). Irigaray (2002) connects the conscious *practice* of breathing to a way of being that serves the heart, thought, and speech beyond just survival. Cultivating the divine breath leads to an ethical being, and the compassionate nourishment of self and others.

> Breathing and speaking use breath in an almost inverse manner, in any case for the majority of the people. From this point of view it is interesting to note that people who do not breathe, or who breathe poorly, cannot stop speaking. It is their way of breathing, and notably of exhaling in order to draw another breath. Frequently, they also paralyze the breathing of whoever takes corporeal and spiritual care of his or her breath, of the breath of others. (Irigaray 2002, 51)

The connection between breathing and speaking that Irigaray (2002) makes is radical such that when speech is disconnected from the life-giving breath and takes over breathing to the degree that it becomes a way of breathing, it takes away from the well-being of self and other, and gets out of control. The inability to stop talking when speech is disconnected from breathing illustrates the balancing, grounding, supporting functions of the breath both for the self and relational engagement with another. Breathing in makes space for speech and as one exhales, he or she speaks from that space that allows receptivity and attunement with the other. When one is breathing and dwelling in that breath even for a short amount of time, she observes, receives, and listens. And when speech arises out of that space, it is attentive to the other rather than absorbing the other or "paralyzing" the breath of the other. Irigaray (2002) ends the paragraph above as such: "To remain silently attentive to the breath comes down to respecting that which, or who, exists and maintaining for oneself the possibility to be born and to create" (51). I would further add that "to remain silently attentive to the breath" is crucial in attending to the other and allowing the possibility for the other to exist beyond appropriation. Thus, one can state that conscious breathing as a *practice* constitutes a ground for an ethic of being, relating, and knowing that guards against reification and sameness.

Irigaray (2002) claims that spiritual and religious practices that are centered on speech and ignore breathing and the silence that accompanies it risk "supporting a nonrespect for life" (51). They become authoritarian and dogmatic as they lack the gift and nourishment of life that comes from the breath. The links between breath and words "allow reciprocally conserving, regenerating, and enriching life and speech" (51). Disconnected from the breath, speech is uprooted from its relation to the body and the surrounding world (Irigaray 2002). Maintaining the life-giving connection of breath and speech, and rooting speech in the breath, is crucial in cultivating an ethic of communication that highlights respect for the self and the other, for difference, and for a creative construction of our relational lives. Befriending the practice of conscious breathing as part of the practice of speaking allows us to be in touch with others and ourselves in ways that facilitate tactful communication. Yet the breath is forgotten; it escapes our attention unless there is a problem with it. It is so close to us that it is not noticed, yet it is the life force that sustains us that makes possible anything else we do.

In "Air Hunger: The Sublime in Nursing Practice," Goble and Cameron (2014) write about attending to the breath of the other and share the existentially revelatory insights that emerged in two instances of nursing practice. In the first instance, the patient (Gwen) experiences severe breathlessness and is very close to respiratory arrest. The young student nurse who is observing Gwen's nurse waits, ready to invoke the code for arrest as the main nurse closely works with Gwen, coaching her to breathe. The young nurse narrates:

> The nurse bends over to Gwen. She seeks eye contact. She speaks softly bur firmly and tells Gwen how to breathe with simple directions. As she speaks she places her hand over Gwen's diaphragm to give emphasis to her words. Her other hand supports Gwen on her back and upper shoulders, gently pushes her forward to a more upright position. She alternately supports and strokes her spine. . . . "Breathe down here, Gwen, push my hand out, that's it, that's really good, now another one." I stand across the bed from the nurse. I look for signs of muscle flaccidity and fatigue to indicate a worsening condition. I see them. The arrest is near yet Gwen's nurse continues. I stand in readiness to invoke the code. The soothing tones of the nurse's voice, her stroking, and her utter calmness envelopes the nurse and the patient. They are only two in this universe. Yet as, and even before, Gwen's breathing slowly returns to slightly approximating normal, I feel a calmness envelope me too. There will not be a respiratory arrest here. Gwen breathes. (Goble and Cameron 2014, 379)

I share this lengthy quote to highlight some of the details of how the experienced nurse worked closely with the patient in attending to her breath. Tactile communication along with gentle yet firm verbal instructions guide the patient as she struggles through the experience of breathlessness. The patient and the nurse work together on the limit—in any moment there can be respiratory arrest and yet the nurse continues to attend to the patient and to her breath rather than invoke the code. The young student nurse states that a less experienced nurse would have acted by the protocol and called an arrest, which requires the patient to be intubated. When she later asked the main nurse what made her hesitate to call the arrest and act in this way, the nurse explained:

> If she had progressed to respiratory arrest and I know she was at that point, the fine moment where it could go either way, I would have acted then as per the protocol for respiratory arrests. *But to worry about that before it happened would have taken me away from the actual moment.* Getting her through it was my foremost thought not treating what might happen. I didn't want her "tubed" (intubated) with everything else that is going on for her. (Goble and Cameron 2014, 379; emphasis added)

The nurse was attentive to her patient *breath by breath* through this experience and she practiced to stay with the actual experience rather than prematurely invoking the protocol. In other words, this nurse practiced presence, she was attuned to the experience itself first rather than theory, concepts, or the protocol. Goble and Cameron (2014) connect this discussion to Nancy's (1993) writing on aesthetics and sensible presentation as a question of presence. The authors ask, "How is it that rather than attending to the experience of what is happening before our eyes, we in nursing would rather embrace a discourse that valorizes a represented discourse of preplanned concepts and theories to apply?" (Goble and Cameron 2014, 380). For Nancy, the covering of experience by representation is nonsensible. Invoking the protocol is safe, yet not fully responsive to the specific moments of experience. Sustained attentiveness to what presents itself in the moment along with the breath of the other (and one's own breath as well) makes space for possibilities to emerge that would have been prematurely closed off otherwise. Goble and Cameron (2014) conclude that "breath and breathing can serve as a meditative focus in nursing practice. They can draw us back to the nursing moment that the routine of our work may cause us to forget" (383). Breath brings us to meet the aliveness of a moment and our existence, breaking the habitual.

The instance from the nursing practice above alerts us to this great capacity we have as human beings that gets forgotten or undermined due to an emphasis on knowing in abstraction, routine/protocol, and/or risk-avoidance. This is not to claim that one should ignore protocol but rather to highlight the creative, essential human capacity that we can cultivate and utilize along with a focus on protocol. It is to connect with our aliveness and to maintain and act out of this connection whether in nursing practice, any other professional contexts (imagine politicians for instance!), and in other aspects of everyday life. Along these lines, Škof (2015a) states that the task waiting to be completed by human beings as part of their spiritual transformation is "to learn to respond to the call of another human being or of a non-human species and their *breathing*, since breathing means staying alive and sensing everything and everyone that is alive around us" (8). Responding to the breathing of the other is to be in tune with the aliveness of the other and to respect the life of the other. It is an awakening to life, "a new sensibility of breath and life" (Škof 2015a, 8). Yet, as Goble and Cameron (2014) state, although we *know* that we are alive in the most ordinary instances of our lives, such as going to the store, talking to our colleagues, or tucking our children into bed, we rarely attend to this most essential, miraculous, and mysterious aspect of our existence that make all the rest of what we consider to be "life" possible. In instances when the body/breath is threatened, injured, or broken we might come to realize that "it is a living, breathing body, pulling in and expelling out the air of this world, her world, our world . . . this breathing body seems to call to ours. Its aliveness calls for our response. . . . As we see this body living, somehow we know—recognizing with our own body—the mystery that we share with this body" (Goble and Cameron 2014, 385–86).

The question is why wait until the body/breath is broken to attend and to inhabit it? What does it take to cultivate "a new sensibility of breath and life" as Škof (2015a, 8) suggests, and a "radical subjectivity that is more receptive to the breath and the life of the other" (6)? I argue that this is an urgent task especially in the scientifically and technologically advanced twenty-first century we live in that is yet to awaken in this ethical sense. The historic moment of global violence we live in does not seem to come to an end with further technological or scientific progress but with a radical shift in our sensibility as human beings to be attuned to the life/breath of the self/other.

A class activity we did in the Exploring Intercultural Communication course this semester is illustrative of this new sensibility. As a way to practice the "familiar and the strange," to learn to expand one's comfort zone in different intercultural environments, and to cultivate space for culturally different practices and others, students sat across from a teammate in silence. Their gazes were lowered so they did not engage in direct eye contact with each other, and the purpose of the exercise for approximately three minutes was to "sit with the other, in silence, and attend to your breathing." I guided the students to breathe mindfully—highlighting that they should not try to control or change their breathing—and to be aware of breathing with the other. For most of my American students, this was a very "strange" practice; however, based on their journal entries it was also very insightful. For instance, some students wrote that sharing the air with someone else helped them to realize that the person sitting across from them is "a breathing, living human being as well." Thus, they connected at a very basic human level, cobreathing and coexisting. Some were surprised to find out that they could "connect with another person without saying any words." Some felt "vulnerable and yet in control" in a way that they were not familiar with. One student wrote that she learned that "the other individual in this exercise is just as important as myself." As we wrapped up the semester, several students offered connections between the breathing exercise they participated in and "cultural empathy" (Calloway-Thomas 2010, 11) that we discussed as part of class. Škof (2015a) writes:

> While we are all aware of the needs of others (including those of the non-human species, including nature), even acknowledging that they exist through breath in every single moment of their lives, we still remain caught up in our worlds—in the hands of primal fear that we would lose control. We keep protecting ourselves while piling up more things around us that we actually need (things we take from others, from nature), causing others to suffocate, as they do not get enough of the elemental ingredients of life—*breath* and peace. (5–6)

Škof's quote highlights our being caught up in our worlds despite being aware of the needs of others. He states that we are afraid of losing control and keep protecting ourselves by accumulating things that take away from others, causing them to suffocate. One wonders whether those who are caught up in this way are also suffocating since they do not seem to be getting enough of breath and peace although they might be "acknowledging that they exist through breath." Some of my students' reflections above following the cobreathing exercise—the feeling of "vulnerable and yet in control" in a way they were not familiar with—finely articulates an attunement with the life of the breath even briefly. This attunement is not just an intellectual acknowledgment but an embodied knowing of our shared vulnerability and a yielding to that which gives life that brings a deep humility. Joined in the life of the breath, one knows that no matter how much one might keep protecting himself by piling things up and taking away from others, it only leads to more suffocation of the self and the other. Thus, one learns to let go, and to share the breath.

IMPLICATIONS FOR AESTHETIC ECOLOGY OF COMMUNICATION ETHICS: BREATHING INTO WORDS

In the chapter titled "Silent Speech" from *Air and Dreams: An Essay on the Imagination of Movement*, Bachelard (2002) writes about poetry as "the outward expression of the joy of breathing" (239). Bachelard (2002) brings attention to "living the word" by breathing it such that the word and the breath are synchronized, "the word takes on its proper sound value only when we have completed the breath" (240). He offers an example through the vocalization of the word *âme* (soul)—the contraction of the Latin word *anima*—such that as we pronounce the word we infuse our breath into it and the word ends as our breath ends. Bachelard (2002) refers to this practice as an exercise in "aerial imagination" (241) where one completely submits to the life of the breath, falls silent, and imagines the word form as she breathes. As the breath leaves, one listens to the breath say "âme." Thus, it is the breath that speaks, "the voice that is totally aerial" (241). In this "aerial imagination," where one is attentive to silence and in touch with the breath, the voice falls silent and words are spoken through the breath beyond the *"will to speak"* (243). This is not a denial or absenting of the power or significance of the will to speak, but to infuse it with the "poetic will" (244) that revitalizes speech by immersing it in aerial substance and silence. Will that desires to speak, Bachelard (2002) states, "is hard to hide, disguise, or hold back" (244). The will to speak needs to be seized and "re-willed" (245), that is, joined with the poetic will to reveal the "splendid phenomena of a will that is specifically human, one that could be termed the *will to logos*" (245). The will to logos dominated by the dialectics of reason and speech (reflection and expression) without joining reflective reason with attentive silence can degenerate. The will to speak that emerges out of the silence of being brings to life the potential of speech. "Before any act, we need to say to ourselves, in the silence of our own being, what it is that we *will* to become; we need to *convince ourselves* of our own becoming and to *exalt* it for ourselves. This is the function that poetry plays in questions of will. The *poetry of will must* then be put in touch with the tenacity and courage of a silent being" (Bachelard 2002, 245; original emphasis).

It is in silence that breath flows into speech and awakens the imagination, reviving the will to speak. The human aesthetic will that emerges from the depths of the emptiness of being that is attuned to the breath rewills and reveals the potential to becoming human. Bachelard (2002) highlights the significance and necessity of silence, and speech that is in touch with silence, toward revitalizing the life of words. The silence Bachelard (2002) refers to is one that is awakened by the breath. It is "a silence that breathes" (242), which in turn gives life to words. Yet, over and over again, most of us forget about silence and the breath and get caught up in words, despite knowing that we have squeezed the life out of them.

Irigaray (2002) wrote about attending to the breath as the "first and last gesture" (5), stating that to cultivate conscious breathing is "equivalent to taking charge of our life, to cutting the umbilical cord in order to respect and cultivate life for ourselves and others" (Irigaray 2008, 4). Attending to the breath as a means of taking charge of our life and the ways in which we breathe life into words, and cultivating the breath to preserve the interior space to tactfully attend to and welcome the other as other in his subjectivity then constitutes the basis for a communication ethic that aims to remember its rootedness in the breath. Bachelard (2002) ends his book by stating that "a philosophy concerned with human destiny must . . . be an openly living language" (266). An openly living language maintains its life through its connection to the breath, silence, and poetic will. Thomas P. Pickett's (2014) "Psalm of Days" is illustrative:

> I   some primordial
>
> I see it clearly now   the clichéd man,
> coat-hangered together.
> Give room; let him breathe.
> That figure on the floor—
> call it a shadow; it grows,
> full of itself, no matter;
> even as it rises   it falls,
> and each surrounding shape, or shadow,
> or collection of bones   clatters around.
> Give room;   breathe him;
> it takes time   a gestation of time,
> and then it rises like some primordial—
> what shall we call it?

Not only the empty spaces within and the rhythm of this poem, but also the image of the clichéd man who is "coat-hangered together" stand out. The poet asks of us to make space for this man, to be hospitable, and reminds us of his breath: "let him breathe." In the earlier pages, I wrote about responding to the breath of the other as being in tune with the aliveness of the other and to respect the life of the other. This responsiveness awakens a new sensibility as Škof (2015a) tells us. We are reminded of this man's breath that was invisible before, and now we are called to be attentive, to make space, to let him be and to breathe, despite him and his shadow being full of itself. As we examine the shape and shadow of this man, the poet calls again, asking more of us: "breathe him." To not only make space in the exterior but also in the interior, to not only let him breathe but to breathe him. Not breathe with him or for him, but to breathe him. Breathing in the coat-hangered man, breathing out the coat-hangered man, one cannot do violence to the coat-hangered man.

The poem not only speaks of this man, but breathes him as the poet calls the reader to breathe him as well. When I first read this poem I wrote to the poet with joy and excitement, saying his poem breathes. This was before reading Bachelard. The poem now comes back to meet Bachelard, Škof, and Irigaray. In the *Breath of Proximity*, Škof (2015a) writes about a "new culture of nonviolence and ethics" (2) and "an ethics of breathing as a newly restored field of intersubjectivity" (2). May this chapter and this poem be one small step toward this new culture that is desperately needed as we move toward the end of another year that has been full of global violence and suffering in our technologically and scientifically advanced but not yet fully human world.

Based on the discussion in this chapter, one might state that attending to and cultivating the breath facilitates *methexis* (Gadamer 2007), a sense of belonging together and presence, "devoting one's full attention to the matter at hand" (122). Being in touch with one's breath and the breath of the other invites an aesthetic sensibility that engages the senses and pulls us to meet the particular needs of the moment. Breathing consciously allows us to maintain a focused attentiveness in the present moment, enabling a present-moment orientation that is receptive, responsive (as illustrated by the nursing-related examples in the chapter, for instance), and in Dewey's (1958) terms, aesthetic.

Secondly, as we have seen in the final section in the chapter, connecting the breath with speech gives life to words, making space for the coming together of the "will to speak" (Bachelard 2002, 243) and the "poetic will" (244) that allows for the potential of speech to emerge. One might refer to this as an *aesthetic ethic of speaking* that is beyond the will to speak which is self-focused: speaking that is immersed in the silence of the breath and awakened by the breath that is not driven by the "originative I" (Arnett 2017, 1), but a "derivative I" (Arnett 2017, 2) that is responsive to the breath of the other.

REFERENCES

Arnett, Ron. 2017. *Levinas's Rhetorical Demand: The Unending Obligation of Communication Ethics.* Southern Illinois University Press.
Bachelard, Gaston. 2002. *Air and Dreams: Essays on the Imagination of Movement, 2nd Ed.* Translated by Robert S. Dupree. Dallas, TX: Dallas Institute Publications. First published in 1988. Second Edition.
Calloway-Thomas, Carolyn. 2010. *Empathy in the Global World: An Intercultural Perspective.* Thousand Oaks, CA: Sage Publications.
Dewey, John. 1958. *The Art of Experience.* New York: Capricorn Books.
Gadamer, Hans Georg. 2007. "The Universality of the Hermeneutical Problem." In *The Gadamer Reader*, edited by R. E. Palmer, 72–88. Evanston, IL: Northwestern University Press.
Goble, Erika, and Brenda L. Cameron. 2014. "Air Hunger: The Sublime in Nursing Practice." Academia.edu—Share Research. https://www.academia.edu/10055199/Air_Hunger_The_Sublime_in_Nursing_Practice.
Irigaray, Luce. 1999. *The Forgetting of Air in Martin Heidegger.* Austin: University of Texas Press.
———. 2002. *Between East and West: From Singularity to Community.* New York: Columbia University Press.
———. 2008. *Sharing the World.* London: Bloomsbury Academic.
Irigaray, Luce, and Michael Marder. 2010. "Ethical Gestures Towards the Other." *Poligrafi* 57(15): 253–71.
Iyengar, Belur Krishnamacharya Sundaraja. 2008. *Light on Pranayama: The Yogic Art of Breathing.* New York: Crossroad Publishing Company.
McKirahan, Richard D. 1994. *Philosophy Before Socrates: An Introduction with Texts and Commentary.* Indianapolis, IN: Hackett Publishing.
Oertel, Hans. 1896. "The Jaiminiya or Talavakara Upanisad Brahmana. *Journal of the American Oriental Society* 16: 79–260. PDF e-book.
Pickett, Thomas P. 2014. "Psalm of Days." *Listening: Journal of Communication Ethics, Religion, and Culture* 65 (Winter).
Rilke, Rainer Maria. 1995. "O Lacrimosa." *Ahead of All Parting: The Selected Poetry and Prose of Rainer Maria Rilke.* Translated by Stephen Mitchell. Modern Library. Kindle Edition.
Škof, Lenart. 2015a. *Breath of Proximity: Intersubjectivity, Ethics and Peace.* Dordrecht, Netherlands: Springer.
———. 2015b. "Ethics of Breath: Towards New Ethical Spaces of Intersubjectivity." *Poligrafi* 17: 199–208.

Chapter Six

Silence, Solitude, Reverence

The minimalism and straightforwardness of Merton's (1967) words in the following from his short essay "Day of a Stranger" capture the gist of his practice as a hermit who made solitude the center of his life to "get at the root of existence" (Merton 1979, 21):

> What I wear is pants.
> What I do is live.
> How I pray is breathe.
>
> (Merton 1967, 213)

This chapter inquires about Merton's discussion of being at the root of existence and its communicative implications. "It would be better simply to say that in solitude one is at the root" (Merton 1979, 21). From Merton's contemplative communicative perspective, embracing one's solitude one learns to be with others; practicing silence one learns to speak. Based on Merton's writings, I focus on four themes including solitude, creative silence, inhabiting space, and reverence. For Merton, it is through the practice of silence and solitude that one cultivates reverence for life. This reverential attitude facilitates the cultivation of an aesthetic orientation to life through attending to "presence effects" (Gumbrecht 2004, xv) along with "meaning effects" (108). In the second half of the chapter, I discuss Merton's ontological perspective to education and explore the pedagogical implications of Merton's work in the classroom, focusing specifically on "inhabiting space" and "reverence."

SOLITUDE

In his writings, Merton (1967) repeatedly distinguishes solitude from isolation and escape as well as solipsism. "Solitude is not withdrawal from ordinary life. It is not apart from, above, 'better than' ordinary life; on the contrary, solitude is the very ground of ordinary life." As the "ground of ordinary life," solitude supports everyday life rather than abandons it. Merton states that for most people, this ground is unfamiliar and unknown though it is always available. In "Rain and the Rhinoceros," Merton (*Raids on the Unspeakable*, 1964) writes about listening to the sound of the rain in his hut in the forest at night in silence. He sits alone listening to "this wonderful, unintelligible, perfectly innocent speech, the most comforting speech in the world" (10) and becomes part of the night. Merton feels that he is a part of this natural world—the trees, the rain, the night—which is not fabricated like the city. In the city, Merton (1964) writes, people have "constructed a world outside the world, against the world" (11) and prefer to live in a "fabricated dream" without a care to be part of the night or the rain. This disconnect of the modern man from the larger external reality, and their absorption in a reality of their own construction/fabrication, is concerning to Merton. The urban man does not take account of the "festival of rain" but plunges through it

> slightly more vulnerable than before, but still only barely aware of external realities. They do not see that the streets shine beautifully, that they themselves are walking on stars and water, that they are running in skies to catch a bus or a taxi, to shelter somewhere in the press of irritated humans. . . . But they must know that there is wetness abroad. Perhaps they even *feel* it. I cannot say. Their complaints are mechanical and without spirit. (Merton 1964, 11)

Absorbed in their everyday tasks and struggles, Merton states that city people miss the aesthetic qualities of life that take place right in front of them such as the shiny streets after the rain that they are walking on and the reflection of the stars and the skies on the streets. This lack of attentiveness and sensitivity makes Merton wonder about the degree of this desensitization; "But they must know that there is wetness abroad. Perhaps they even *feel* it. I cannot say." He is not sure whether "they" have lost the capacity for feeling/sensing or not, but perhaps.

Merton repeatedly refers to the people who are out of touch in this way as "they," starting from the very first line of "Rain and the Rhinoceros." And immediately after the first line, he explains who "they" refers to: those who attach a monetary value to everything, including the rain; those who think that to be appreciated something has to have a price; those who are unable to appreciate the festival of rain without turning it to a utility to be distributed for money. "The time will come when they will sell you even your rain. At the moment it is still free, and I am in it. I celebrate its gratuity and meaninglessness" (Merton 1964, 9). "They" are those who would not hesitate to sell what is given as a gift of nature, those who miss what is to be celebrated as a "festival" of life in their absorption of usefulness. Merton listens to the rain in silence to be reminded over and over again that "the whole world runs by rhythms that I have not yet learned to recognize, rhythms that are not those of the engineer" (Merton 1964, 9). Merton's listening is a practice of opening, and attunement, to the larger external reality that we are part of beyond our own construction. The sound and rhythm of the rain serves as a reminder of this rootedness for Merton that gets ignored or forgotten in the isolated container of city life.

As part of his discussion of silence and solitude, Merton (1964) references Philoxenos, a sixteenth-century Syrian hermit, whom he read in his cabin in the woods. Philoxenos stated that one has to be alone to discover his or her true identity that is not "limited by the laws and illusions of collective existence" (14). This aloneness is not being an "individual," or being lonely, but an awakeness. In solitary life, Merton (1964) writes, one confronts the fear of "being nothing," and awakens to one's vulnerability and death as necessary conditions to realize one's true identity. This awakening is not one of despair but a learning to accept "emptiness" and "uselessness" that the collective mind condemns (18). In awakening to one's vulnerability and death, one comes to see the fabricated nature of a self whose experience of feeling real is based on a system designed to create and fulfill its needs by suppressing one's awareness of contingency, and by promises of fun and satisfaction. The solitary man who dares to be alone comes to see the illusory nature of this fabricated self and the suffering associated with it as well as the collective efforts to protect and affirm it.

Moreover, the awakening of the solitary man is not for the sake of personal liberation but "the contemplative must assume the universal anguish and the inescapable condition of mortal man. The solitary, far from enclosing himself in himself, becomes every man. He dwells in the solitude, the poverty, the indigence of every man" (Merton 1964, 18). Thus, the solitary person is not an isolated individual who has escaped from the crowds, but rather in facing his own mortality, vulnerability, aloneness, and fears of uselessness and nothingness, she comes to empathize with the larger humanity. The spiritual identity of the solitary man is shaped in response to the suffering of others, emerging as a "derivative self" (Arnett 2003) in contrast to originative agency that is based on the autonomous human agent.

For Merton (1964), the solitary person acts as a reminder of humankind's capacity for liberation, maturity, and peace. Having renounced the routine concerns, demands, and attachments of everyday life, the solitary person focuses on exploring a "freer response to the basic existential challenge that summons us to make sense out of our life. Not just to accept someone else's answers, but to discover by *personal experience* and to verify existentially the meaning and values of human life" (Merton, as qtd. in Arcilla 1987, 96). Solitude then is necessary to realize the "existential fullness of the human person" (96), yet "people avoid solitude and try to fill their loneliness with artificial substitutes because they are averse to this basic and inevitable fact of life" (98).

In an essay titled "Solitude Is Not Separation," Merton (*New Seeds of Contemplation*, 1972) acknowledges the challenges of solitude and its complexity, yet he goes on to state that the solitude of the man who is lost in the crowd is the most dangerous. "He does not face the risks of true solitude or its responsibilities. . . . He is burdened by the diffuse, anonymous anxiety, the nameless fears, the petty itching lusts and the all-pervading hostilities which fill mass society the way water fills the ocean" (54). The man lost in the crowd is swallowed in a collectivity filled with common noise and general distraction, isolated yet not in touch with his solitude. Immersed in a world of noise whether by machinery, loud speakers, or meaningless talk he is enveloped by "thick layers of insensibility" (55) and "he doesn't hear, he doesn't think. He does not act, he is pushed. He does not talk, he produces conventional sounds when stimulated by the appropriate noises" (55). This man that Merton describes does not know of true solitude, of meeting one's aloneness, vulnerability, emptiness, limitations, and fears along with the preciousness, sacredness, and joy of life. She lives an atomized existence and has not become a "person" who has discovered her place in relation to others in a community. Merton explains repeatedly that without exploring one's own solitary existence and the depths of her true being, one cannot find true peace, love, freedom, or create a common life with others that is not a mere crowd.

In the next section, I will explore an essential aspect of solitude for Merton, silence, which allows for the encounter with the deeper aspects and layers of the self, and the questions that accompany it regarding our existence. It is out of this deep engagement and exploration of one's being in silence that one grows roots into her life and learns to inhabit it with a sense of reverence.

CREATIVE SILENCE

In an essay titled "Creative Silence," Merton (*Loving and Living*, 1979) distinguishes positive (creative) silence from negative silence and states that negative silence can be an escape; it might blur and confuse our identity and "we lapse into daydreams or diffuse anxieties" (39). Positive silence on the other hand leads to self-discovery, presence, and awareness: It "pulls us together and makes us realize who we are, who we might be, and the distance between these two. Hence, positive silence implies a disciplined choice, and what Paul Tillich called the 'courage to *be*'" (39). Positive, or creative silence, is an intentional choice to stop the constant movement, business, and action and to be still, to just *be*. It is a space one creates to meet one's self fully beyond the "social self" that one performs in everyday life. It is a practice of wondering and exploring who else one is and one might be. The choice and practice of silence requires courage as Tillich states in Merton's quote above, since it is the coming face to face with the unknown and with the "stranger" that is not yet welcomed.

> When we are quiet, not just for a few minutes, but for an hour or several hours, we may become uneasily aware of the presence within us of a disturbing stranger, the self that is both "I" and someone else. The self that is not entirely welcome in his own house because he is so different from the everyday character that we have constructed out of our own dealings with others—and our infidelities in our selves. (Merton 1979, 39)

Being silent is a practice of meeting and learning to welcome a part of ourselves that is the "stranger," the part that we have ignored in the constant movement and noise of our lives. It is a practice of learning to be at home in our selves, growing roots into our lives rather than living a distracted life "floating along in the general noise" (Merton 1979, 39). Writing about Merton's discussion on the discipline of silence, Arcilla (1987) connects the disorientation in the life of contemporary man to the lack or fear of silence. Absorbed by the messages of mass media and advertisements in a consumerist society, and not disciplined in the practice of silence, contemporary man has "effectively lost control of his life, surrendered the power to decide for himself" (109). Silence allows for taking time to connect with one's own voice, and to think, discern, and make decisions beyond the noise of the external world. In silence one learns to inhabit and take ownership of her life. One needs to move away from "floating along in the general noise . . . in a state of constant semi-attention . . . not fully present and not entirely absent" (Merton 1979, 39) to take ownership of his or her life. Yet, as Senachal (2014) explains, constant engagement in social activity through digital technology has resulted in a "weakened capacity for being alone" where most have "become anxious about walking away from crowds, even for brief intervals" (5). Senechal states, "As soon as the noise stops, we often lose our footing" (5). An interaction with a couple of my students is illustrative.

Two of my students a few years ago approached me after class inquiring about a mindfulness meditation class I offered on campus, which is basically about learning to inhabit one's life by cultivating attention and taking some time to be quiet together. One said that they wanted to go to this class but were afraid. "Afraid of what?" I inquired. They giggled and paused. Upon my repeated and curious inquiry, they both said "afraid of not being able to do it." When I explained to them—with relief—that "this class is not about doing. We just sit in silence attending to what is present in the mind and the body, so it is about a way of being rather than doing," there was a brief silence. A few moments later, one of them cried out, "What if I can't 'be'?" and her words pierced through my heart. I now better realize the truth in her expression. How would she know how to "be"? What would be the source to learn it from since all that we are surrounded by is focused on an incessant doing over being and getting through the to-do list every day? Where and how does one learn about cultivating a sense of being from which doing emerges in an age characterized by distraction, consumption, speed, entertainment, and constant action? Merton (1979) describes the lack of attentiveness to the inner, silent self in American culture:

> Now let us frankly face the fact that our culture is one which is geared in many ways to help us evade any need to face this inner, silent self. We live in a state of constant semi-attention to the sound of voices, music, traffic, or the generalized noise of what goes on around us all the time. This keeps us immersed in a flood of racket and words, a diffuse medium in which our consciousness is half diluted: we are not quite "thinking," not entirely responding, but we are more or less there. We are not fully present and not entirely absent; not fully withdrawn, yet not completely available. (Merton 1979, 39)

This diffused way of being, divided and pulled in many directions, never fully present yet not fully absent, has significant consequences for communication. Caught in a cycle of noise and activity, one is pulled away from oneself and others. In a life habituated by being in the crowd and always in search for some outside stimulation, distraction, or busyness, one becomes forgetful about the value and meaning of one's existence and commitments in life. Living in a state of semi-attention, we semi-listen, semi-respond, and semi-exist.

Senechal (2014) explains that without time to be quiet and alone, one has minimal opportunity to form independent thoughts. Rather, grabbing someone else's thoughts to have something to say becomes easier because of rush, convenience, or insecurity. Merton (1979) highlights how silence allows us to understand our selves and our lives better. It helps reveal the deeper needs of our being. It is in silence that we start to discern and draw together our fragmented existence, learning to inhabit our own life.

In *Thoughts in Solitude*, Merton (1958) writes about silence in relation to solitude. In solitary life, one delivers oneself to silence, and to the silence of the woods, the sea, the mountains, or the desert: "To sit still while the sun comes up over that land and fills its silences with light" (101). In this stillness and silence, one greets the first lights of the day. Working, praying, resting, laboring throughout the day, and then "to sit still again in meditation in the evening when night falls upon that land and when the silence fills itself with darkness and with stars" (101). In this silent presence, one is attuned to the time of the day, to the surroundings, to the light, land, and the stars. Merton writes about becoming fully in touch with the sacredness of life as the silence deepens and one is "willing to belong completely to such silence" (101), which is when the living of life itself becomes a prayer. "When I am liberated by silence, when I am no longer involved in the measurement of life, but in the living of it, I can discover a form of prayer in which there is effectively no distraction. My whole life becomes a prayer. My whole silence is full of prayer. The world of silence in which I am immersed contributes to my prayer" (Merton 1958, 93). In silence, one starts to be fully immersed in the living of life without distractions, including the analyzing or calculating of it. Silence has a liberating function in this sense, as Merton puts it above; it liberates one from the measuring and evaluating of life into immersion in the experiencing in silence, which becomes a prayer. Living life as a prayer can be understood as living life with gratefulness, kindness, and in unity. Merton (1958) states that silence supports and contributes to his living life as a prayer. In the continuation of the above quote, Merton (1958) explains that silence is receiving without expecting; it is a way of emptying oneself from desires and possessions, including the seeking of any special spiritual experiences. One needs to be "poor" and empty to be immersed fully in silence without any distractions. That is when life turns into prayer. "Let me seek, then, the gift of silence, and poverty, and solitude, where everything I touch is turned into prayer: where the sky is my prayer, the birds are my prayer, the wind in the trees is my prayer" (94).

Merton refers to words as getting in the way of meeting and knowing the world in silence. Rather than a rejection of words and language, however, Merton's discussion of silence highlights a respect and reverence for things and making sense of reality with an awareness of language rather than a habitual reliance on it to reveal reality. Merton (1958) explains that words organize, categorize, and control the way we make of reality; in silence we learn to receive and know beyond the "smoke-screen" of words.

> The solitary life, being silent, clears away the smoke-screen of words that man has laid down between his mind and things. In solitude we remain face to face with the naked being of things. . . . The world our words have attempted to clas-

sify, to control and even to despise (because they could not contain it) comes close to us, for silence teaches us to know reality by respecting it where words have defiled it. (Merton 1958, 85–86)

Silence, as Merton discusses it, makes space for a way of knowing that is not limited to the structure imposed by words. It allows us to respectfully meet the world beyond the screen of words. Words get in the way of our being fully immersed in things as they are, the "naked being of things." Silence is a practice of keeping awake to receive the world beyond the distraction of words and to attend by deep listening to let the world reveal itself as one suspends the imposition of words on it.

From the above quotes and discussion, it is clear that Merton's silence is not passive or disengaged but it is a practice of cultivating a contemplative sense of being in the world. In the *New Seeds of Contemplation*, Merton (1972) writes that every moment and event in one's life on earth "plants something in his soul" (14), just like the wind carrying seeds. Yet most of these seeds perish and get lost since people are not ready to receive them. Habituated in the conventional ideas and desires of the "external self" (7), most people identify with the reality of an "I" that is not attuned with its own existential depths and mystery. It is through the awareness and cultivation of the deep self in contemplation that one becomes fully alive, awakening "to the Real within all that is real" (Merton, 1972, 3). In this opening beyond the confines of the first person singular, the superficial "I," one receives the gift of the seeds of life that the wind blows her way.

Merton (2008, 78) writes about contemplation as a "listening in silence" without prior expectations to receive a particular message. It is a kind of listening where one remains empty; empty of desires, including any anticipation for transformation. In this silent listening, one surrenders the "I," the ego-identity that defines and maintains itself through identification with the exterior and contingent things that keep her busy, preoccupied, and distant from existential contact. Assuming a sacred and humble attitude toward life in the silence of deep listening, one does not escape from her own inner emptiness but meets it with a sense of reverence and with the awareness of mystery. In this sense, contemplation is a turning toward meeting one's own experience of life, which requires courage and faith. "The sacred attitude is, then, one of deep and fundamental respect for the real in whatever new form it may present itself" (Merton 2008, 143). Not attached to prior ideas, distractions, or things, one listens silently to the unknown in active contemplation.

The contemplative listening practice discussed above resonates with what Lipari (2014) articulates superbly in *Listening, Thinking, Being* where she writes about listening as a "constitutive communicative action" (3) that "brings humans into being" (2). Something happens in the attentive presencing of deep listening that transforms us, and our "world." Lipari (2014) highlights a process of listening that makes space for *not* understanding such that rather than capturing and finalizing an evolving movement of meaning, she suggests an approach to understanding that can be seen as a "momentary pause in an ongoing movement of unfolding, like a rest in a musical score, or a pause in a story, or a swirling eddy in an exorable, ongoing river of meaning" (139). The pause, or the rest, echoes the "sacred attitude" that Merton (2008) highlights in contemplative listening: a sacred attitude that allows for possibilities of meaning and being to be revealed rather than a premature closing of the "living moment of understanding" (Lipari 2014, 138) due to our inability to tolerate ambiguity and not understanding. The perspective Lipari offers highlights "understanding as mystery, uncertainty, ambiguity, rather than as facticity, certainty, or precision" (139), which at the same time acknowledges the ongoing movement and interplay of "holding on and letting go—both understanding and not understanding at one and the same time" (139). This view on the process of listening and understanding aims to maintain openness to possibilities of meaning, learning, and being, that makes space "to simply stay with some something, be it a poem or a painting, music or someone's words—and just be with it, experience it, appreciate it, without having to fit it into some tiny box of 'understanding'" (136).

This "sacred attitude" to life and listening presents a major challenge, however, to the "external self" that "fears and recoils from what is beyond it and above it. It dreads the seeming emptiness and darkness of the interior self" (Merton 2008, 137). Due to the fear of the unknown, the external self distracts itself through keeping busy, or through addictions, entertainment, and so forth. Merton states that this "diversion" (137) is a tragedy since "it is a flight from life and from experience—an attempt to put a veil of objects between the mind and experience itself" (140). In active contemplation, one learns to notice, and relax (let go of) the tensions, demands, and cravings of the external self, and to be at home in her immediate experience of life whether that involves joy, excitement, delight, or emptiness, indefiniteness, darkness, or else. "The sacred attitude is then one of reverence, awe and silence before the mystery that begins to take place within us when we become aware of our inmost self" (143). With the sacred attitude in active contemplation, one "abandons himself . . . to the stream of reality and of life itself" with a sense of faithfulness, wonder, humility, and respect for "the real in whatever new form it may present itself" (143). Merton's discussion of contemplation, then, is a way of opening (letting ourselves) to the direct experiencing of life in silence rather than distracting ourselves through various means in an effort to protect a fabricated self in a system that is disconnected from the existential rhythms of a larger world. It is a challenging practice of learning to let go of the demands and desires of the external self to receive the world with its offerings with a humble attitude. In the following, I share some examples from Merton's own experience highlighted in *When the Trees Say Nothing: Writings on Nature*:

> Yesterday I was sitting in the woodshed reading and a little Carolina wren suddenly hopped on to my shoulder and then on to the corner of the book I was reading and paused a second to take a look at me before flying away.... (Same wren just came back and is singing and investigating busily in the blocks of the wall over there.) There is something you cannot know about a wren by cutting it up in a laboratory and which you can only know it if it remains fully and completely a wren, itself, and hops on your shoulder if it feels like it. (Merton 2003, 44)

Examining, observing, and scientifically investigating a Carolina wren or any other living or nonliving thing offers us one kind of knowledge, which is a product of the way we set up the investigation in the first place (experiment in the lab, or measurement scales, the conditions in which we operate, etc.). That is, when we manipulate things to know about them, we know *about* them in the ways we have manipulated them, rather than have a sense of them as they really are. When the wren hops on Merton's shoulder, it makes itself available through a living contact where one can *meet* the wren in that brief, spontaneous encounter. Merton (2003) distinguishes between knowing about and *knowing* living things, where to know something is simple and "poor" (45) and beyond one's ideas. Once again, the simplicity and the "poorness" Merton (2003) refers to is a spiritual emptiness that is receptive, attentive, and contemplative. Just as he listens to the rain in his hut in silence, and he participates in the night through this deep listening, or he walks in the woods in silence to know the woods, Merton's knowing of the wren is through his receptive participation in their encounter, in silence and attentive to the wholeness of the wren.

This contemplative way of being with things and inhabiting one's life resonates with Dewey's (1958) discussion of aesthetic experience as an attentive orientation to the present as well as the value of the present as part of the ongoing continuum of one's life. It is through this participatory orientation to the present that leads to the "delightful perception which is esthetic experience" (Dewey 1958, 19). Whereas one could easily ignore the wren, or the rain, or the beauty of the woods in a habitual, result-oriented, self-centered way, Merton's participation in them facilitates a sense of richness and intensity, an aesthetic quality to life.

Merton's (2003) contemplative knowing of the Carolina wren, the forest, or the rain also resonates with Heidegger's (1959/1966) discussion of *Gelas-*

senheit or "releasement toward things" (54) that is accompanied by "openness to the mystery" (55). "Releasement toward things" is a practice of dwelling in the world grounded in "meditative thinking" (46). As an alternative to "calculative thinking" (46) that plans, computes, collects, and organizes information to serve specific purposes, meditative thinking "contemplates the meaning which reigns in everything that is" (46). Whereas calculative thinking never stops or collects itself, meditative thinking dwells and ponders, keeping awake for the emergence of insight. Thus, meditative thinking is revelatory. It allows for the hidden, withdrawn aspects of things to show themselves through its passively active engagement of the world. Heidegger (1959/1966) underlines with urgency that in the dawning of atomic age during the time when he wrote, "the approaching tide of technological revolution in the atomic age could so captivate, bewitch, dazzle, and beguile man that calculative thinking may someday come to be accepted and practiced *as the only* way of thinking" (56). The danger of forgetting of meditative thinking would be, as Heidegger puts it, "total thoughtlessness" and the throwing away of men's special nature that "he is a meditative being" (56). Thus, Heidegger (1959/1966) concluded his *Discourse on Thinking* by highlighting that a major issue of that time was to keep meditative thinking alive, which he warned does not happen by itself. "Releasement toward things" (54) and "openness to the mystery" (55) flourish through "persistent, courageous thinking" (56). Merton's deep commitment and practice throughout his life, as discussed above, finely illustrates this thinking, which is desperately needed in the nuclear age that we live in.

The next and final section of this chapter explores Merton's (1979) discussion of inhabiting space with specific connections to the classroom and offers pedagogical implications and applications.

INHABITING SPACE, INHABITING ONE'S LIFE: PEDAGOGICAL APPLICATIONS

In his 1979 essay titled "The Street Is for Celebration" in *Love and Living*, Merton writes about the city and the street as spaces that we occupy or inhabit. Distinguishing between occupying versus inhabiting a space, Merton (1979) focuses on the city as a space that can be "filled or lived in" (46) where occupying/filling in by itself does not lead to inhabiting/living in. He states that the quality and the character of a city depends on whether its streets, buildings, and rooms are inhabited or just occupied (filled in). As an exercise in class, we replace the terms *city* and *street* with *classroom.*, and I instruct my students to read selected parts of Merton's (1979) essay, inviting them to share what stands out to them in the text. The following is a section that attracts most students' attention (remember to replace city/street with classroom as you read):

> Suppose the street is a tunnel, a kind of nowhere, something to go through. Something to get out of. Or a nightmare space where you run without getting away. Then the street cannot be an inhabited space (unless something happens to it). When a street is like a tunnel, a passage, a tube from someplace to someplace else, the people who "live" on it do not really live on it. The street is not where they live but where they have been dumped. When a street is not inhabited it is a dump. A street may be a dump for thousands of people who aren't there. They have been dumped there, but their presence is so provisional they might as well be absent. They occupy space by being displaced in it. They are out of place in the space allotted to them by society. (Merton 1979, 49)

Students comment on the classroom as a space that can be seen as a tunnel or a passage where one comes and goes without really being present in it, without participating, engaging in discussion or the activities, and just occupying space. One student recently said that the classroom could be a dump, as described in the above paragraph, if its members do not inhabit it. He seemed to be familiar with the experience, and the body language and facial expressions of the others confirmed their familiarity as well, including myself. Another student commented on this section from the same text: "An alienated space, an uninhabited space, is a space where you submit. You stay where you are put, even though this cannot really be called 'living'" (Merton, 1979, 50). She highlighted the part on "living." And we discussed how we can actually live in the classroom space and bring it to life! How? How can we inhabit the classroom and bring it to life? Some students commented on engaging in discussion, coming prepared, asking questions, and participating in class. Another student pointed to the following section: "The street can be inhabited if the people on it begin to make their life credible by changing their environment. Living is more than submission: it is creation" (Merton 1979, 51). In class, we talked about the ways in which we can affect and change the environment through our input, through the questions, examples, stories we bring and share. One student commented on owning the classroom, making it your classroom so that it is not "somebody else's classroom" or "a kind of nowhere" (Merton 1979, 49).

Following this discussion on the first day of class, one could feel the shift in the energy of the students, they looked motivated, curious, hopeful. More important, they felt responsible for inhabiting the classroom space and creating the class. Some got started right away in bringing materials to share in the next class. Some slowly got into the habit. Overall, we started to establish a classroom culture toward inhabiting and creating it rather than just occupying. Engaging Thomas Merton's writings in class guides us in realizing the potential of our classroom space, and of ourselves, in bringing it to life. This is only a discussion of one selected piece from Merton's writings that illustrates how and why Merton is an essential resource for the classroom, and specifically the communication classroom, offering a "greater sense of what a college education should mean" (King 2009, 70). I agree with King that Merton "can and should be taught as other American contemplatives are taught" and that he should be included and invited to the classroom (2009, 70). So we continue to ask along with Merton (1979, 48), replacing "street" with "classroom" for pedagogical purposes:

> Can a street be an inhabited space?
> This question begins to take shape.
> We begin to guess the answer.

Merton states that to inhabit a space, it needs to be engaged and transformed. And to do that "the people who are merely provisionally present, half-absent non-persons must now become really present on the street as themselves. They must be recognizable as people. Hence, they must recognize each other as people" (1979, 48). Merton highlights that to inhabit a space, people need to become present and move away from "floating along in the general noise" (1979, 39) and take ownership of their lives by recognizing their presence along with others. In other words, they need to "begin to make their life credible" (1979, 49) and not just passively submit to it. Making one's life credible, according to Merton, does not take place by being a "half-absent non-person" but by fully inhabiting and engaging one's life, transforming and creating it.

In "Education and Being: A Reflection of Thomas Merton's Life," Del Prete (1992, 460) writes about the significance of Merton's life and work for education in offering an ontological perspective for education that takes into account "not simply what we can or cannot do" but also "what it means to *be*." Highlighting Merton's own journey and struggle in finding his vocation in life in terms of writing—as participation in the world—and leading a silent, contemplative life, Del Prete (462) writes that Merton gradually recognized that "it was not *doing* itself that he called into question but whether the doing emerged from his own *being.*" As Merton engaged in writing as an activity that emerged from the deeper ground of his being, he realized that he could surrender and serve (God) through writing. Merton's struggle and realization offers major insight for education. Del Prete writes:

> The focus of education tends to be almost exclusively on doing, on activity, on results; and the results are often defined in self-serving or socially competitive rather than deeply personal or communal terms. Such education is disembodied; what we do is essentially disconnected from who we are. Educational discourse is depersonalized, focused on "what" or "how much" rather than on "who." Merton's example suggests an education aimed at cultivating a sense of being, what Merton might call an education grounded in life. In this ontological perspective, activity and learning become an expression or an enlivening of one's deeper life—not simply an assumed measure of it, as we are so often prone to make it. (1992, 462)

The disembodied education model that Del Prete writes about above does not guide students in exploring and discovering what is most meaningful and important to them. It fills students with information with a focus on doing, disconnected from a sense of being, but does not fill the heart, mind, and the spirit as a whole. Accordingly, a significant number of students come to class having long lost faith in the education system, and this is observable from the first day of class from their attitudes, approaches, and engagement (or lack thereof.) This observation led me to start inquiring and initiating discussion with my students on the first day of class by asking them what comes to mind when they hear the terms "education," "teacher," "classroom," "student." A common and honest response I receive is "boring." It takes the first half of the semester to regain their trust that learning can be enjoyable (despite the struggle). Arthur Zajonc (2006) states that several of his students have disclosed to him "they had given up on education, becoming cynical about it in high school. They learned to perform whatever was asked, even if it failed to connect to their lives, their deepest questions, and most intense longings. Big jobs with big salaries were the material carrots for high performance" (37). Can education be life giving in such conditions? What we learn from Merton points to the college classroom as one space to cultivate being—and the doing that emerges out of being—that complements the empirical-rational-critical ways of knowing.

Merton's writings on silence, solitude, inhabiting space, and education among many others serve as an antidote to the distracted, fast, and noisy lives most people lead who are "not fully present and not entirely absent," "more or less there" for their own lives (Merton 1979, 39).

In the final section of this chapter, I connect Merton's writings on the themes stated above to reverence in the classroom space, in connection to Bertrand Russell's (1916) critique of education, and offer a few examples that illustrate Merton's (2008) discussion of "sacred attitude" (143) in the classroom.

IMPLICATIONS FOR AESTHETIC ECOLOGY OF COMMUNICATION ETHICS: RECOVERING "REVERENCE" IN THE CLASSROOM

In his 1916 book, *Principles of Social Reconstruction,* Bertrand Russell writes that education is "the strongest force on the side of what exists and against fundamental change" (144). Rather than cultivating the ability to think independently, education as a political institution functions to "form habits and to circumscribe knowledge in such a way as to make one set of options inevitable" (145). Given this background, Russell refers to "the great responsibility which rests upon teachers" (145), which is to balance authority with a spirit of reverence toward students. "A man who is to educate really well, and is to make the young grow and develop into their full stature, must be filled through and through with the spirit of reverence." The teacher *without* reverence assumes the duty of "moulding" the student as the potter molds the clay. On the contrary, the teacher who has reverence, rather than assuming a duty to "mould" the young, "feels in all that lives, but especially in human beings, and most of all in children, something sacred, indefinable, unlimited, something individual and strangely precious, the growing principle of life, an embodied fragment of the dumb striving of the world" (Russell 1916, 147). There are three more characteristics of the teacher with reverence that Russell highlights that are important to mention here: humility, responsibility of a trust, and longing.

Russell states that humility of the teacher with reverence is not easy to account for rationally, "yet somehow nearer to wisdom than the easy self-confidence of many parents and teachers" (147). The teacher feels humbled in encountering the sacred growing principle of life that is precious and unique to each student. The student's dependency and vulnerability in being shaped creates a responsibility of trust in the teacher with reverence and a longing to guide the child toward "the ends which the child's own spirit is obscurely seeking" (148) rather than the outcomes proposed by some external authority.

Russell states that the education system does not function with such a spirit of reverence for the student (unfortunately, this is also true the other way around for most students in the United States). Rather, the focus is on the maintenance of the existing order and worldly success—making money or achieving social status. He argues that "almost all education has a political motive: it aims at strengthening some group, national or religious or even social, in the competition with other groups" (148). Russell explains that mainly this political motive determines the kind of knowledge offered to and withheld from students, as well as the mental habits cultivated where the "inward growth of the mind and spirit" (148) are ignored. According to Russell, the more educated one is, the more "atrophied" they are in their mental and spiritual life.

This is where Merton's writings offer significant insight and resources for educators, not only through his views on an ontological perspective in education but also through the contemplative themes discussed throughout this chapter on silence, solitude, and the "sacred attitude" toward life that resist the atrophying of one's mental and spiritual life that Russell (1916) wrote about. For the growing field on contemplative education, Merton's work is a rich yet undermined resource that could initiate academic discussions and pedagogical practices that aim to cultivate the heart and the spirit along with the intellect. Merton's (2008) discussion of contemplative listening with a "sacred attitude" (143) that I discussed earlier in the chapter is one example to illustrate my point. Merton (2008) highlights listening in silence with a humble openness that acknowledges the mystery of the other as part of this sacred attitude, a practice of abandoning oneself with a sense of wonder and reverence, to be in living contact with the rain, with the Carolina wren, and I expand this to our students. Acknowledging the "mystery" of the student, that he or she is always more than what I can know, *is* the sacredness of the student that as a teacher one could deeply respect and feel responsible to protect. This orientation reflects a deep reverence for the "absolute otherness" (Levinas 1969) of the student who always exceeds my knowing. The example I offered in the introduction chapter with the student reading Harry Potter at the back of the class illustrates this orientation. Though I did not approve or like his choice since it was not appropriate for our purposes, at the back of my mind I held the intention to go beyond an immediate reaction and to find a response that would maintain a sense of reverence that acknowledges the sacredness of the student even though it was not immediately recognizable. This gesture offered its fruits later in the semester as the student became an engaged listener and participant in the classroom, as well as an inspiration for the aesthetic framework for this book!

Another example of reverence based on my experiences in the classroom comes from the Exploring Intercultural Communication course I teach. Last year, we discussed *Precarious Life* by Judith Butler (2014) in this class. In one of the classes, five students acted as panelists and discussed the main points that stood out for them from the first two chapters of the book. The first student who spoke had been attentively observing the course from her seat at one corner of the classroom since the beginning of the semester, participating quietly here and there. As a panelist, she spoke with such clarity and enthusiasm, summarizing the chapters in a highly articulate way, and then connecting the contents with her lived experience as a child who grew up in an orphanage in Russia where the kids did not have any belongings that they owned; no toys or room of their own and no special care that they could personally own. She expressed that when she starts to accumulate belongings now, she starts to feel very uncomfortable. She connected her life to the book in such a powerful way that the whole class was touched by her presentation as the deep listening followed by a moment of pure silence showed when she was done—which was followed by applause and cheers. Who could know? And who else could interpret the course material in this way except for this student who speaks from the sacredness of her life? How can one not feel humbled listening to her? Each of us are rooted in the sacredness of our own lives by being part of *this* human experience and the "growing principle of life" (Russell 1916, 147). When we are able to connect to it, and speak from that connection, it is transformative.

When I enter the classroom and encounter the group of young adults in front of me, I feel awake to the sacredness of life we share through being human and our responsibility in preserving, cultivating, and contributing to it. As I reflect further on the sacredness of life, and the classroom as a "sacred space," I come to realize that our work in the classroom is closely linked to two fundamentals we experience as human beings: life and death. I would go so far to claim that education is a matter of life and death, which is another reason I would claim it to be sacred. The life-giving—and life-saving—aspects of education are more common to acknowledge in the sense of "lift[ing] lives up through learning" (Doughterty 2010) by expanding the mind, teaching new skills, preparing for a career, transforming ways of being, thinking, and relating. Education that is attentive to the whole person offers ground on which one can build a life, not just a career. There is a risk involved, however, for both the teacher and the student, who are to engage education in this deeper, existential way. As one of the Spiritan Fathers expressed powerfully in a recent Spiritan Pedagogy meeting on campus, teaching and learning involves risking yourself, "a giving yourself to the other." One must be willing to be transformed and to let go of previous thoughts, ideas, and habits that have shaped a life for education to come to life. As teachers and students, we have the capacity to breathe life into the texts and materials that we are to learn from by bringing our full presence to them and sharing how we connect with them (please see discussion of "knowledge by presence" in Hart 2007 as well as in Üçok-Sayrak 2014). In this process, however, one needs to be able to let go—even momentarily—of her attachment to what she might be holding on to so tightly, what she might have so firmly believed in, to be able to receive the new. Both the teacher and the student are transformed in the teaching/learning process if they can make space for the other in the process. When this is experienced, it is powerful; it shakes you at the core of your being, turns you upside down sometimes, as new life emerges within you. It takes even a brief moment of dying to the ego-self, the known, the familiar, the comfortable to step into this transformative space in between the self and the other. Defining the "sacred" as "that which is worthy of respect," Palmer (1999, 21) states that

> The university is a place where we grant respect only to a few things—to the text, to the expert, to those who win in competition. But we do not grant respect to students, to stumbling and failing. We do not grant respect to tentative and heartfelt ways of being in the world where the person can't think of the right word to say, or can't think of any word at all. We do not grant respect to voices outside our tight circle, let alone the voiceless things in the world. We do not grant respect to silence and wonder.

Palmer connects the reason to the loss of the sacred in education. According to Palmer, when we know the sacred, we are not afraid of the "*precious otherness* of the things of the world" (23). When we know the sacred, we respect radical otherness rather than attempt to reduce it to our known categories. Furthermore, we respect the "precious *inwardness* of the things of the world" (Palmer 1999, 24), that is, their inner dynamics as well as their integrity and intelligence that is different from one's own. Palmer (1999, 29) explains that recovering our sense of the sacred would allow us to recover humility that allows for knowing reality in its own terms. Rather than acting as the knower independent of that which we are to know, humility awakens us to the reality that we are participants in cocreating knowledge with the other (and others, which includes our students and what they bring to the table, the textbook, our backgrounds, histories, cultures. etc.). Thus, recovering sacredness and reverence in the classroom involves a "giving one's self over to the material, and to the other," as the Spiritan Father mentioned earlier stated.

As a learning community, as we engage in teaching and learning with humility, openness, and reverence for the sacredness of the self and the other, we make room for the "precious *inwardness* of the things of the world" (Palmer 1999, 24) to reveal themselves. This is the "driving force," the "charism" (Koren 1990, 15) of the classroom with reverence. It is through this reverential attitude that we cultivate an aesthetic orientation, attending to "presence effects" (Gumbrecht 2004, xv) such as our bodily coexistence in the classroom space (or any other space), the ways in which we affect each other, as well as how we inhabit the classroom together, and create the climate of the classroom along with "meaning effects" (2004, 108).

REFERENCES

Arcilla, Jose, S. 1987. "Through Silence to the Self According to Merton." *Landas: Journal of Loyola School of Theology* 1(1): 91–111.

Arnett, Ronald, C. 2003. "The Responsive 'I': Levinas' Derivative Argument." *Argumentation and Advocacy* 40(1): 39–50.

Butler, Judith. 2014. *Precarious Life: The Powers of Mourning and Violence.* New York: Verso.

Del Prete, Thomas. 1992. "Education and Being: A reflection of Thomas Merton's Life," *Religious Education* 87(3): 459–70.
Dewey, John. 1958. *The Art of Experience.* New York: Capricorn Books.
Dougherty, Charles. 2010. "Duquesne University of the Holy Spirit." *Spiritan Horizons* 5.
Gumbrecht, Hans Ulrich. 2004. *Production of Presence: What Meaning Cannot Convey.* Stanford, CA: Stanford University Press.
Hart, Tobin. 2007. "Reciprocal Revelation: Toward a Pedagogy of Interiority." *Journal of Cognitive Affective Learning* 3(2): 1–10.
Heidegger, Martin. 1966. *Discourse on Thinking.* Translated by John M. Anderson and Hans Freund. New York: Harper and Row. First published 1959.
King, David. 2009. "Fine and Dangerous": Teaching Merton. *CrossCurrents* 59(1), 69-87.
Koren, Henri. 1990. *Essays on the Spiritan Charism and on Spiritan History.* Bethel Park, PA: Spiritus Press.
Levinas, Emmanuel. 1969. *Totality and Infinity: An Essay on Exteriority.* Translated by Alphonso Lingis. Pittsburgh, PA: Duquesne University Press.
Lipari, Lisbeth. 2014. *Listening, Thinking, Being.* University Park: Pennsylvania State University Press.
Merton, Thomas. 1958. *Thoughts in Solitude.* New York: Farrar, Straus and Giroux.
———. 1964. *Raids on the Unspeakable.* New York: New Directions Publishing Corporation.
———. 1967. "Day of a Stranger." *The Hudson Review* 20(2): 211–18.
———. 1972. *New Seeds of Contemplation.* New York: New Directions, Penguin Books.
———. 1979. *Love and Living.* Edited by Naomi Burton Stone and Brother Patrick Hart. New York: Farrar Straus Giroux.
———. 2003. *When the Trees Say Nothing: Writings on Nature.* Notre Dame, IN: Sorin Books.
———. 2008. *Choosing to Love the World.* Boulder, CO: Sounds True Inc.
Palmer, Parker. 1999. "The Grace of Great Things: Reclaiming the Sacred in Knowing, Teaching, and Learning." In *The Heart of Learning: Spirituality in Education*, edited by Steven Glazer, 15–32. New York: Penguin/Putnam.
Russell, Bertrand. 1916. *Principles of Social Reconstruction.* London: George Allen & Unwin, Ltd.
Senechal, Diana. 2014. *Republic of Noise: The Loss of Solitude in Schools and Culture.* Lanham, MD: Rowman & Littlefield.
Üçok-Sayrak, O. 2014. "Knowing with One's 'Whole Self': Contemplation as Embodied Knowing in the Communication Classroom." *Listening: Journal of Communication Ethics, Religion, and Culture* 49(1): 44–64.
Zajonc, Arthur. 2006. "Cognitive-Affective Connections in Teaching and Learning: The Relationship Between Love and Knowledge." *Journal of Cognitive Affective Learning* 3(1): 1–9.

Closing

In his essay "Building Dwelling Thinking," Heidegger (2001, 145) refers to dwelling as "the manner in which human beings *are* on the earth." "To be a human being means to be on the earth as a mortal. It means to dwell" (145). Yet, he continues, "dwelling is never thought of as the basic character of human being" (146). When we speak about dwelling, Heidegger (2001) explains, we speak about it alongside some other activities such as doing business, traveling, or practicing a profession. "We attain to dwelling, so it seems, only by means of building" (143). Building, constructing, working, producing are seen as a means to attain dwelling; however, Heidegger underlines that building *is* dwelling, not just a means toward it. Furthermore, he states, "*only if we are capable of dwelling, only then we can build*" (157) [original italics]. Dwelling, Heidegger explains, is not just constructing but also cultivating, preserving, keeping, remaining (staying with), and letting. And how this remaining/letting is experienced is to explore the nature of dwelling. "Mortals ever search anew for the nature of dwelling, that they *must ever learn to dwell*" (159). Heidegger connects our lack of acknowledgment of this issue, this "*real plight of dwelling*" (159), to man's homelessness (which does not refer to lack of houses, though he acknowledges it as a serious issue). When people think and build out of dwelling, they attend to their homelessness, as mortal beings on the earth.

Despite all the cries and screams that repeatedly demonstrate the homeless, restless, and violent state of modern humans on this earth that I discussed in the introduction—that Heidegger (2001) referred to as "our precarious age" (158)—attending to the "real plight of dwelling" (159) is still not a major concern for most. In *Ethics from the Edge: A Sketch of Precarity from a Philosophy of Communication*, Ramsey (2016) states that we are still in a precarious age due to our flawed ways of understanding ourselves, our precarious nature, and our being-together. Ramsey (2016) connects the lack of understanding of ourselves and being-together to our misunderstanding of communication and language, that is, to the popular belief that communication is "mere information exchange between isolated and self-contained subjects—as if we exhausted all we needed to say whenever we talk of human beings as senders and receivers of messages" (34). Attending to the plight of dwelling is to attend to our understanding of communication and language that shapes the way we understand who we are as human beings and our being-together. What makes human beings uniquely human, as Ramsey (2016) explains through referencing Heidegger's (1998) lecture on traditional and technological language, is our capacity for language use, our faculty of speech. Yet when language is reduced to mere information exchange and becomes dominated by calculation, efficiency, and utility then our humanness is also reduced and our dwelling in the world is threatened. We become homeless, and more precarious, losing our capacity for language toward disclosing the world.

This project has been an exploration of learning to dwell on the earth as human beings, or as Ramsey (2016) puts it, to lead an "accomplished dwelling" that reflects a "fitting understanding of the self" beyond a "collection of isolated message-sending and message-receiving 'I's" (36). My discussion of existential rootedness is a step toward acknowledging, reminding, and turning toward the homeless state of the modern humans, in our globalizing, digital, and distracted age that Heidegger referred to as "our precarious age" (2001, 158). The various elements and themes that are part of the aesthetic ecology discussion in this book support and cultivate dwelling in the sense that "dwelling itself is always a staying with things" (Heidegger 2001, 149). Staying with things involves a sense of belonging together, devoting one's attention, and participating in the world of the other. Participating in the life-promoting ground of the earth that evokes "passions of the soul" (Tymieniecka 1990) such as the passion for grounding (2001); being exposed to the "weight" of meaning; practicing signlessness that manifests the co-appearance of all phenomena; being in con/tact with and through one's impermanent bodily existence; engaging the breath intentionally and giving life to words; and making space for silence/solitude allow us to meet the aliveness of the present moment through an awakened sensibility that is responsive to the other. The chapters in this book explore the concept of existential rootedness in relation to exteriority rather than an understanding of rootedness in being itself that is insular and isolated.

Moreover, what I have offered in this book constitute *an* aesthetic ecology of communication ethics rather than *the*. I have gathered together themes that stand out for me as part of my academic explorations on existential rootedness that are connected to the material, conceptual, and contemplative aspects of the meaning-making process of communication. Yet an exploration of existential rootedness framed as an aesthetic ecology of communication ethics is not limited to the themes I selected in this project: Earth and the "passion for place" (chapter 1); "weight" of meaning (chapter 2); signlessness (chapter 3); con/tact (chapter 4); breathing (chapter 5); silence, solitude, and reverence (chapter 6). All these elements included as part of this aesthetic ecology function to resist the "forgetting of presence" (Gumbrecht 2004, xv) in our relation to the world and the others, and encourage an aesthetic attentiveness (Gadamer 2004) that facilitate the oscillating dynamic between "meaning effects and presence effects" (108) rather than abandoning either of them (please refer to the introduction for a detailed discussion of the aesthetic ecology framework in relation to communication ethics). Further studies that expand this initial framework through additional themes and conceptualizations of aesthetic ecology in relation to communication ethics in particular, and communication studies in general, would facilitate the development and growth of this project.

Finally, one could imagine making sense of the discussions in this book reflected through Leonard Cohen's lyrics in a song titled "A Thousand Kisses Deep":

> You lose your grip and then you slip
> into the masterpiece

We all hold onto some things, and sometimes too tightly, yet in a paradoxical way the tighter we hold onto our individual preferences, desires, and expectations the less we feel rooted in the larger masterpiece. Sometimes, for some people, it takes a radical turn of life such as being diagnosed with a life-threatening illness or losing a loved one to come to one's senses and start to inhabit one's life with a sense of belonging, dwelling, grace, and gratefulness. It takes a losing of our grip to realize the masterpiece we are part of. Existential rootedness can be seen as the acknowledgment and the practice of this loosening of the individual grip to let ourselves fall into the masterpiece and to reemerge with a sense of aliveness and con/tact with the world rather than a habitual continuation of living "life as if it's real" (Cohen 2001). This would be nothing less than letting go of the grip of the autonomous willed agent and taking a step toward exploring what Arnett (2004) asks, "What might a communication ethics look like that does not begin with a sense of will?" (76–77).

REFERENCES

Arnett, Ronald C. 2004. "A Dialogic Ethic 'between' Buber and Levinas: A Responsive Ethical 'I.'" In *In Dialogue: Theorizing Difference in Communication Studies*, 75–90. Thousand Oaks, CA: Sage Publications.

Cohen, Leonard. 2001. *Ten New Songs*. Sony BMG Music Entertainment. CD.
Gadamer, Hans-Georg. 2004. *Truth and Method: Continuum Impacts*. Translated by Donald G. Marshall and Joel Weinsheimer, 2nd ed. London: Continuum. First published in 1975.
Gumbrecht, Hans Ulrich. 2004. *Production of Presence: What Meaning Cannot Convey*. Stanford, CA: Stanford University Press.
Heidegger, Martin. 1998. "Traditional Language, Technological Language," translated by Wanda Torres Gregory, *Journal of Philosophical Research* 23, 129–145.
———. 2001. *Poetry, Language, Thought*. New York: Perennial Classics.
Ramsey, Ramsey Eric. 2016. "Ethics from the Edge: A Sketch of Precarity from a Philosophy of Communication." *Atlantic Journal of Communication* 24(1): 31–39. doi:10.1080/15456870.2016.1113964.
Tymieniecka, Anna-Teresa. 1990. "The Passions of the Soul and the Elements in the Onto-Poiesis of Culture." *The Elemental Passions of the Soul Poetics of the Elements in the Human Condition: Part 3*, 3–141. doi:10.1007/978-94-009-2335-5_1.
———. "The Passions of the Earth." 2001. *Passions of the Earth in Human Existence, Creativity, and Literature*, 1–12. doi:10.1007/978-94-010-0930-0_1.

Index

absolute otherness 148
adiaphorization 9
aerial imagination 129
aesthetic
   atmosphere 45, 47
   attention 12, 19, 89
   attentiveness 3,10, 13, 20, 22, 74, 89, 155
   distance 10, 12
   ecology 3, 7, 10, 17, 19, 21–22, 54, 71, 74, 94, 154, 155
   ecology of 48, 70, 87, 112, 129, 147
   function 44, 47, 49, 50
   orientation 23, 74, 89, 93, 114, 115, 133, 150
   sensationalism 12
   sensibility 24, 131
aesthetics of reading 54, 61, 65, 70
Agamben, Giorgio 21, 29, 34–36
Air 23, 36, 38, 42, 74, 78, 102, 124–125
   Principle of 118, 119
   Theory of 25
   Sharing 128
Anaximenes 25, 118–120
Arnett, Ronald C. 3, 7, 8, 11, 20–21, 23, 34, 40, 48, 50, 115, 117, 131, 135, 155
Attentiveness 1, 7, 12, 13, 16, 17, 23, 48, 87, 90, 101–102, 115

Existential 3, 8–9
Contemplative 11, 14, 19, 117, 131, 134, 138

Bachelard, Gaston 24, 117–118, 120, 124, 129–131
being-to 53–55, 57–58, 67
belonging together 11, 48, 89, 94, 117, 154,
bodily experience 9, 23, 36, 94, 102, 108
bracketing 13, 63–64, 79
breath 23–24, 36–37, 77, 88–89, 119
   and speech 117, 122, 130,
   ethics of 118, 120–121, 123–29
Butler, Judith 20, 148

calculative thinking 4, 35, 143
co-appear 59, 68–69
co-essentiality 58–59
communication ethics 2, 7, 10, 17, 19–20, 23, 48, 50, 70–71, 87–88, 94, 112, 117, 129, 147, 155
communicative engagement 21, 29–30, 31, 35, 42, 48
contact 12, 23, 57, 60, 63, 67–68, 88, 93–94, 95–97, 100–101, 105, 112, 117, 120, 140, 142, 148
contemplation 8, 39, 81, 141,

and solitude 136, 140–141,
contemplative attentiveness (*See* attentiveness)
coupling 94, 08, 107
creative silence 136–37
crisis of sense 54, 73, 89
cultural empathy 18–19, 128

deep ecology 78
Del Prete, Thomas 145–146
dependent co-origination 74
derivative I 131
derivative self 135
desensitization 142
Dewey, John 3, 10, 14–17, 20, 23–24, 48, 74, 89–90, 114, 117, 131, 142
Diamond Sutra 75, 77–79
difficult reading 66, 68
discriminative perception 75
disembodied education model 146
distanced proximity 59, 70
distanciation 19, 35, 40
divine breath 124
dualistic vision 76, 80

embedded identity 115
emptiness 22, 73, 75–76, 81–82, 87, 130, 135–136, 140, 141–142
enframing 35
existential attentiveness (See attentiveness)
existential connection 34, 49
existential ground 45–46
existential homelessness 7–8
existential rootedness 1, 3, 7, 10, 21–23, 29, 36–37, 40, 48–49, 50, 53, 73, 78, 80–81, 88–89, 93–94, 105, 154
existential traction 4

fabricated self 135, 141
felt meaning 33
fragmented existence 138
Frankl, Viktor 21, 29, 32–34, 37–40, 45–49,

Gadamer, Hans Georg 3, 10–13, 17, 19, 22, 24, 48, 74, 89–90, 117, 131, 155
Gelassenheit 2
grounded normativity 2
groundlessness 58
Gumbrecht, Hans Ulrich 3, 10, 12–15, 17, 20, 23–24, 54, 70, 74, 89–90, 93–94, 109, 115, 133, 150, 155

Hanh, Thich Nhat 22, 73–80, 86–88, 90
haptocentric 59
Heidegger, Martin 4–5, 58, 142–143, 153–154
hermeneutical aesthetics 3, 10, 12
heuristic reduction 63
homo creator 40–41, 47
homeless modern 3
horizon 3, 10, 11–12, 17, 19–20, 90, 97
horizonal blindness 10–11
human nest 44–45

identification 97, 110, 114, 140
Imaginatio Creatrix 39, 41
impermanence 22, 73, 88
impermanent body 23, 93
individualism 8–9
inhabiting 3, 23–24, 44, 94, 105, 114–115, 133, 102, 143–146
interbeing 74–80, 84
intercorporeity 98
interdependent co-arising 22, 73–78, 81–88
intersubjectivity 118, 131
intertwining 23, 94, 98–99, 113
Irigaray, Luce 24, 118, 124
isolation 5
Iyengar, B.K.S 120, 122–123

Kabat-Zinn, John 102, 105–108, 114
Koan 22, 74, 83, 85, 87, 89

Laycock, Steven W. 1–2, 10, 80, 81, 84
Lipari, Lisbeth 140–141
lived experience descriptions (LED) 64–65, 70

logos 129
Loori, John Daido 78, 81–87

Macke, Frank 93–97, 99–101, 105
macrocosmic Wind (vayu) 121–122
meaning effects 12–13, 15, 20, 24, 70, 90, 109, 114, 133, 150, 155
meditative thinking 4, 5, 35–36, 143
Merleau-Ponty, Maurice 23, 26, 94–99, 112, 113–115
Merton, Thomas 133, 134–146, 148
methexis 3, 11, 19, 24, 89, 131
microcosmic breath 122
mindfulness 23, 87–88, 93–94, 100–103, 105, 107, 109, 111–114, 138
modalities of meaning 30–31, 48
modernity's amnesia 3, 7, 8–9
moral blindness 2, 7–9, 20
moral vacuum 9
Miner, Myrtilla 29, 31, 32

Nancy, Jean-Luc 3, 22, 53–65, 67–73, 88–90, 126–127
negative capability 35
noise 136–138, 145
non-dualistic ontology 76
non-self (emptiness) 22, 73, 75–76, 81
non-western perspective 22, 73–74, 81
nondiscriminating wisdom 75

ontopoíēsis 39
originative I 131

participation 3, 10–13, 19, 23, 41, 70, 75,
passional promptings 89, 93–94, 97–98, 112, 112–113, 117, 142, 145
phatic function 97
Philoxenos 135
Pickett, Thomas P. 130
plural unity 59
poetic will 24, 117, 129, 130–131
poíēsis 21, 29–32, 34–36, 42, 45, 49
poíētic sense 21, 29–33, 35, 36–41, 48–50

positive silence 136–137 *See also* creative silence
prana 23, 118, 120–123
pranayama 120, 122–123
praxis 35
prereflective experience 62, 64
presence 19–20, 23, 35–36, 39, 48, 56, 100, 102, 115, 126, 131, 137, 139, 144–145, 149
  effects 12–15, 20, 24, 70, 90, 109, 114, 133, 150, 155
  based relation 3, 10, 17, 22–23, 54, 70, 74, 89–90, 93–94, 109, 114, 114–115
pre-Socratics 23, 118
provisional existence 37, 45–47

re-willed 129
reading 22, 54, 61–71, 80
relational existence 2
releasement 35, 143
responsiveness 1, 20, 131
responsibility 1, 22, 31–32, 34, 47, 85–86, 147, 149
reverence 24, 133, 136, 139–141, 146–148, 150, 155
rootedness 1–10, 21–23, 29, 36–37, 40, 42–45, 48–50, 53, 73, 78, 80–81, 88–89, 93–94, 100, 105, 130, 135, 154–155 *See also existential rootedness*
Rosenbaum, Elana 106–107, 108–109, 114
Rosenberg, Larry 111
Russell, Bertrand 146–147

sacred 147, 149, 150
  attitude 140–141, 146, 148
sacredness 136, 139, 148, 149, 150
Santorelli, Saki 103–104, 105, 110–111, 113
Satipatthana Sutra 87
Schrag, Calvin O. 30, 37
self-identification 80
semi-attention 137–138

Senechal, Diana 137–138
sense 53–57, 66–67, 70–71, 110, 113
    of why 8–9
    scapes 102
    of self 112
sense-making 40, 47, 109, 111
shock of meaning 55
signlessness 10, 21, 22, 73–77, 79–83, 86–88 154–155
silence 1, 10, 18, 24, 39, 82, 103, 117, 125, 128–131, 133–142, 146, 148–150 (Also see creative silence)
singular plural 53, 58–60
Škof, Lenart 118, 120–121, 127–128, 131
solipsism 134
solitary life 135–136, 139
solitude 9, 24, 124, 133–136, 139, 146, 148, 154–155
suchness 76, 78–80, 90
suspension 54, 61, 65–69, 80

Tathagata 76, 78–79
theoria-poíēsis-praxis 30, 31, 36, 49
theoria-praxis 30–32, 34, 49

thoughtlessness 11, 143
transformative freedom 43
Tymieniecka, Anna-Teresa 29–30, 39–47, 49–50, 154

Upanishads 120
Upatthana 87
Uprootedness 3, 5
Uselessness 135

van Manen, Max 61–65
visibility 23, 93–94, 97–99

weight 10, 21, 61, 67
    of meaning 22, 53–56, 61, 67, 69–71, 154–155
Weil, Simone 5
will to speak 117, 129–131
willed action 35
wind-breath teaching 121
wondering 2, 40, 55, 137
    attentiveness 62, 63

Zajonc, Arthur 146
Zen 22, 74, 78, 81–82, 84–85, 89

About the Author

Özüm Üçok-Sayrak, PhD, is assistant professor at the Department of Communication & Rhetorical Studies at Duquesne University where she teaches courses on intercultural communication, integrated marketing communication, business and professional communication, and public speaking. She received her doctorate in communication studies from the University of Texas at Austin. Dr. Üçok-Sayrak has published papers on communication ethics, culture, and agency; embodiment and identity; aesthetic communication; and interactive making sense of art. Her research interests include communication ethics, philosophy of communication, ethics and epistemology, contemplative education, and communicative construction of identity. Her work has been published in scholarly journals such as *Review of Communication, Journal of International and Intercultural Communication, Human Studies, Communication and Medicine, Symbolic Interaction,* and in several edited books.

www.ingramcontent.com/pod-product-compliance
Lightning Source LLC
Chambersburg PA
CBHW050908300426
44111CB00010B/1439